pg. 50 — "honor" is based only on perception, not fact

pg. 51 — incredible brutality against women who've been "dishonored"

pg. 49 — women are not necessarily terribly oppressed in Palestine

pg. 53 — Tina even supports this stuff to some extent (?)

pg. 55 — Palestinian looooove Germans. Can you guess why?

pg. 56 — Palestinians' sense of the passage of time

pgs. 61-62 — The correct way to arrange a marriage

pg. 141 — funny comment by police officer on why he keeps getting promoted

pg. 179-181 — the Isas are not at all the typical Palestinian family; they are lower class, vulgar, violent, cruel, u

ALSO BY ELLEN HARRIS

Dying to Get Married

GUARDING THE SECRETS

*Palestinian Terrorism
and a Father's Murder
of His Too-American Daughter*

ELLEN
HARRIS

A LISA DREW BOOK

SCRIBNER
New York London Toronto Sydney Tokyo Singapore

SCRIBNER
Rockefeller Center
1230 Avenue of the Americas
New York, NY 10020

SCRIBNER and colophon are registered trademarks of Macmillan, Inc.

DESIGNED BY ERICH HOBBING

Manufactured in the United States of America

10 9 8 7 6 5 4 3 2 1

Library of Congress Cataloging-in-Publication Data
Harris, Ellen Francis.
Guarding the secrets: Palestinian terrorism and a father's murder
of his too-American daughter/by Ellen Harris.
p. cm.
"A Lisa Drew book."
Includes bibliographical references and index.
1. Isa, Tina, 1972–1989. 2. Filicide—Missouri—Saint Louis.
3. Isa, Zein, 1931– . 4. Isa, Maria, 1943– . 5. Terrorism—United States. I. Title.
HV6534.S19H373   1995
364.1'523'0977866—dc20
94-29681

ISBN 0-02-548335-8

To BYRON LEE KINDER,
Who is wise and loyal and helpful and fun-loving
and who always makes me laugh.

Contents

List of Characters

The Isas: Isa (or Issa, as it is commonly spelled) means "Jesus" in Arabic.
Jesus is the Latin version of the Hebrew Joshua.

Zein Isa (Zane Ee-sah), born 1931
Maria Matias Isa, born 1943
Leilah* (Lay-lah), born 1963
Mona,* born 1965
Soraia (So-roy-ah), born 1967
Palestina (Pah-lah-steen-ah), or "Tina," born 1972

Azziz (Ah-zeez) Hamed, Leilah's husband
Nai'el (Nile) AbdelJabber (Ab-del-jah-bar), Mona's husband
Amjad (Am-jahd) Salem (Sah-lem), Soraia's husband

Foiziya (Foy-ee-zah) Isa, Zein's double first cousin and first wife
Faisal (Fie-zell) Isa,* Zein's son by earlier marriage
Fayrouz (Fay-rooz) Abdeljabber, Zein's daughter from an earlier marriage
Faiza (Fie-zah) Darwish (Dahr-wish), Zein's daughter from an earlier
    marriage
Amir Darwish, Faiza's husband

Clifford Walker, Tina's boyfriend
Helena Mylanos, Tina's best friend

The Nijmehs: Nijmeh means "star"
Sausan (Sows-an, which is the same as Suzanne or Susan) and Ahlam
    (Ah-lahm) Nijmeh, twin nieces of Maria Isa, whose sister Irecema
    married a Nijmeh just after Maria married Zein.
Saif (Safe), or "Steve," Nijmeh, husband and cousin of Ahlam

Loqai (Low-kay), or "Luie," Nijmeh, Saif's brother and the husband and cousin of Sausan

Tawfiq (Taw-fick) Musa (Moo-sah), Zein's cousin; Musa is the Arabic equivalent of Moses.

Abu Nidal leaders formerly in the United States
    Mahmoud Atta (Mow-muhd Ahh-tah)
    Samir Darwish (Sah-meer Dahr-wish)

Ramsey Clark, Atta's defense attorney, the former U.S. attorney general under Lyndon Johnson

PART TWO

Lieutenant Harry Hegger, St. Louis Police Department, later Captain Hegger.
Sergeant Michael Guzy (Guh-zee), St. Louis Homicide
Detective Billy Qualls, St. Louis Homicide, later Sergeant Qualls.
Sergeant Tom Murphy, chief investigator, circuit attorney's office
Mike Tully, investigator, circuit attorney's office

Judge Charles A. Shaw of St. Louis Circuit Court
Charles M. (Charlie) Shaw, Maria's defense attorney
Daniel Reardon, Zein's defense attorney
Dee Joyce-Hayes, assistant circuit attorney, later circuit attorney
Robert (Bob) Craddick, assistant circuit attorney

PART THREE

James Nelson, FBI special agent in charge, St. Louis
Tom Newman,* supervisor, FBI counterintelligence, St. Louis

James Steitz, assistant U.S. attorney, later an administrative law judge
Keith Liberman, Saif Nijmeh's defense attorney
Neil Bruntrager, Luie Nijmeh's defense attorney

Linda Murphy, Tawfiq Musa's defense attorney
Tom Day, Zein's federal public defender

Note: Spellings of Arabic names in this book vary because one is transcribing phonetically from a different alphabet. There is currently no codified English spelling of Arabic, although many well-known Arabic names and places have conventional spellings in English—for example, Cairo, Baghdad, Beirut, Damascus; Nasser, Saddam Hussein, Mubarak, and Assad. However, among the Arab criminal element, spellings and names change as much as the weather during a St. Louis summer week, as one detective remarked.

*Asked that their names be changed.

Righteous women are therefore obedient,
guarding the secret for God's guarding.
And those you fear may be rebellious admonish;
banish them to their couches and beat them.

—The Qur'an (Sura 4, 38),
trans. A. J. Arberry

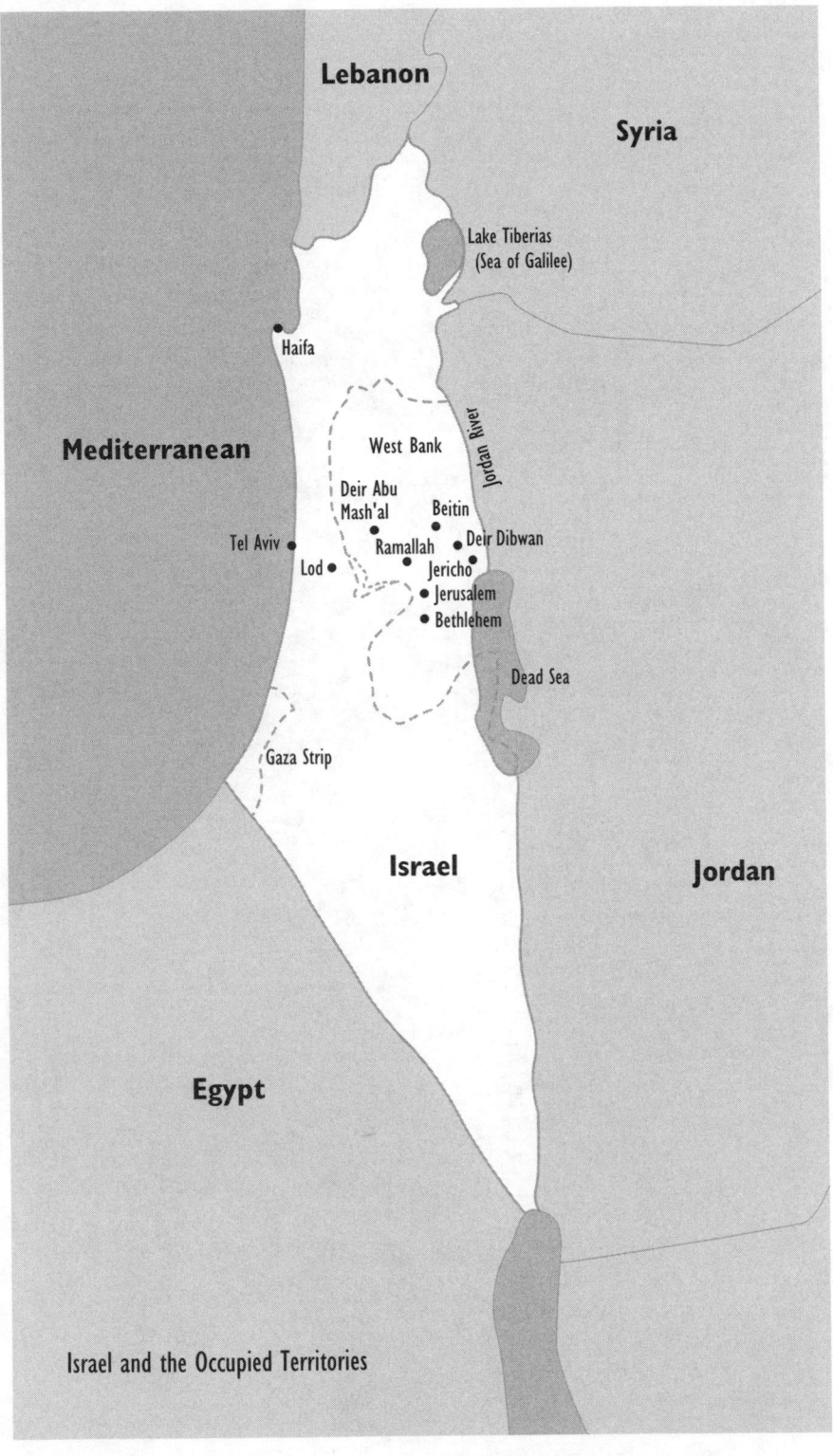

Lebanon

Syria

Lake Tiberias
(Sea of Galilee)

Haifa

Mediterranean

West Bank

Jordan River

Deir Abu
Mash'al

Beitin

Tel Aviv

Ramallah

Deir Dibwan

Lod

Jericho

Jerusalem

Bethlehem

Dead Sea

Gaza Strip

Israel

Jordan

Egypt

Israel and the Occupied Territories

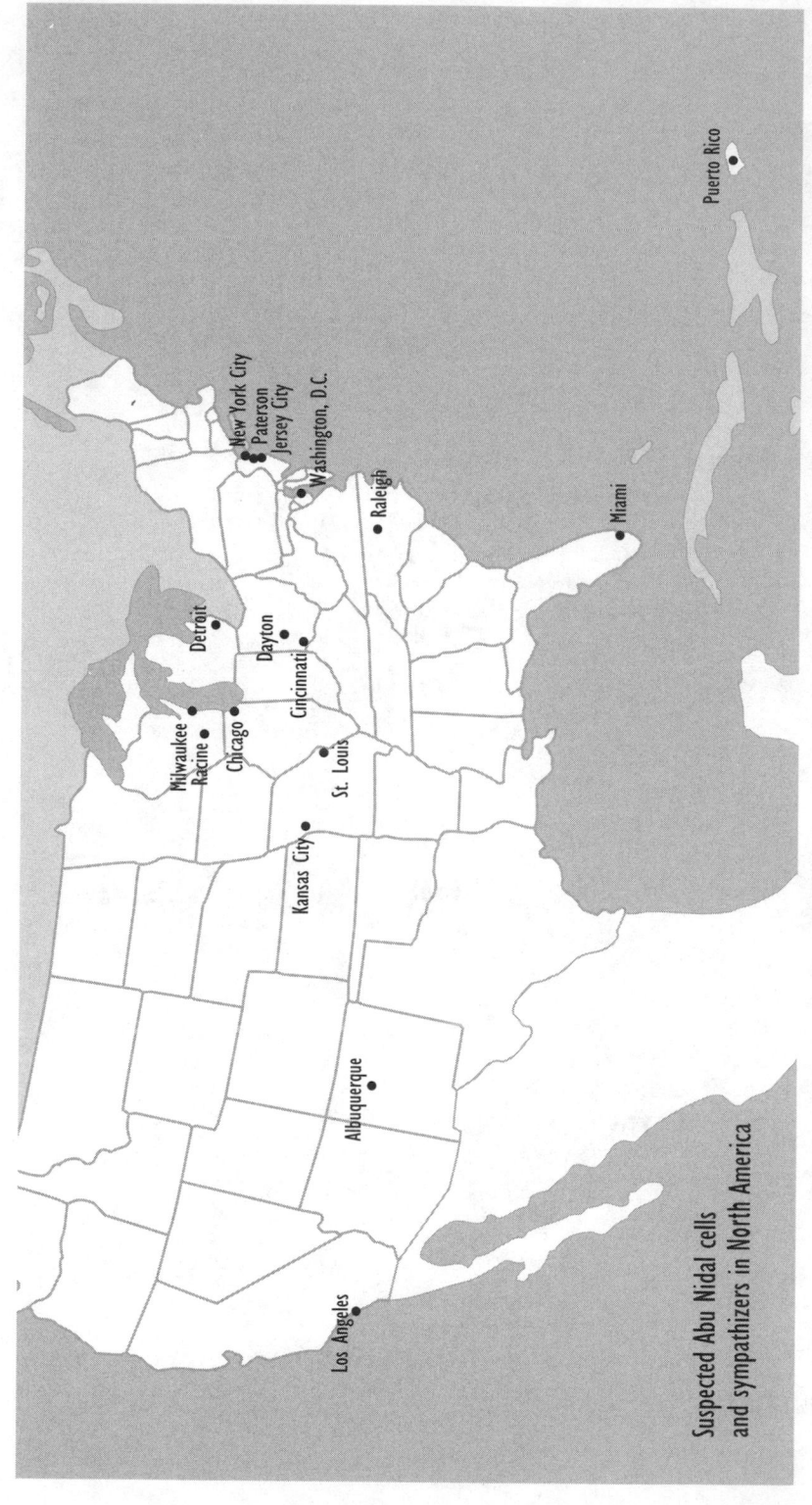

Abu Nidal sympathizers and active collaborators live and work in at least sixteen cities in the United States. Currently, there are active FBI investigations in some of them.

Suspected Abu Nidal cells and sympathizers in North America

Los Angeles
Albuquerque
Kansas City
Milwaukee
Racine
Chicago
St. Louis
Detroit
Dayton
Cincinnati
Raleigh
New York City
Paterson
Jersey City
Washington, D.C.
Miami
Puerto Rico

GUARDING
THE SECRETS

Prologue

DECEMBER 24, 1985 ROME AND VIENNA

The day before Christmas, in two simultaneous attacks, terrorists threw grenades and opened fire on the El Al ticket counters at Rome's Leonardo da Vinci Airport and at Schwechat Airport in Vienna. Eighteen people in the check-in lines were murdered and 101 injured. El Al is Israel's government-owned airline.

The gunmen belonged to the Abu Nidal Organization (ANO). Abu Nidal (Ah-boo Nee-dahl) is the terrorist the U.S. State Department says is the most vicious in the world.

APRIL 12, 1986 DIR ABU MISHAL, WEST BANK

On a spring evening, terrorists threw Molotov cocktails at an Israeli public bus. Despite their wounds, the bus driver and a passenger dramatically rescued the others aboard. The driver, however, died ten days later.

When arrested, two of the Palestinians terrorists said their cousin had planned the murder under orders from Abu Nidal operatives in Europe. That cousin, they told police, had fled to America.

SEPTEMBER 6, 1986 ISTANBUL

One Sabbath morning, a group of Sephardic Jews were praying in the Neve Shalom Synagogue. Two terrorists barred the doors and machine-gunned to death all twenty-one worshipers. The two gunmen then committed suicide. They were members of the Abu Nidal Organization.

19

FALL, 1986   SOMEWHERE IN THE MEDITERRANEAN—
POSSIBLY TRIPOLI, LIBYA, OR ATHENS, GREECE

The spies were fascinated: Who was attending this meeting of Middle
Eastern terrorists? The spooks monitored the secret gathering place
through highly sophisticated electronic surveillance.

They found that the men attending this conference were some of the
most brutal terrorists in the world, the allies of Abu Abbas, who was once
a cohort of Abu Nidal. Abu Abbas's men were responsible for the hijacking of the Italian cruise ship *Achille Lauro* on October 9, 1985, as it sailed
the Mediterranean. The terrorists pushed an elderly crippled Jew from
Philadelphia, Leon Klinghoffer, strapped in his wheelchair, into the sea.

Because Klinghoffer was an American citizen, U.S. intelligence
agencies became involved in the search for his murderers. The FBI had
been restricted to working on U.S. soil. Now, through a special act of
Congress, the FBI could pursue criminal suspects in cases involving
U.S. citizens throughout the world. But the FBI neither infiltrated nor
bugged this convention of high-level terrorists.

Eight years later, the U.S. government would not disclose who monitored that meeting. One official hints the CIA sent agents to stake it
out. Another suggests the National Security Agency (NSA) probably
had installed electronic eavesdropping equipment within the building
or used satellites to copy the conversations, and subsequently pass on
the information to the CIA. Another expert suspects it was a foreign
intelligence operation that gave the membership list to the Americans.

The feds badly needed to know who was there so that counterterrorist agents could tag and follow possible terrorists, as well as confirmed criminals. One unknown man surprised them.

This very ordinary-looking, middle-aged man of average height,
weight, and swarthy coloring limped slowly out of the building. While
the Israelis knew who he was, the Americans did not. To find out, the
CIA sent an agent to tail the Arab; the spy followed him onto a jet
bound for the United States.

When the man landed, the FBI picked up his trail. Agents installed
electronic surveillance in his home and store in St. Louis, and in the
homes and businesses of his family and comrades throughout America.

The man was named Zein al-Abdeen Hassan Isa.

PART ONE

TRIBAL TABOO

CHAPTER ONE

The War Room

FALL, 1986   ST. LOUIS, MISSOURI

"Hegger here," Sergeant Harry Hegger said in a low, throaty voice as he grabbed his phone. It was a counterterrorist expert in the FBI on the line. Hegger, a supervisor in the St. Louis Police Department's Intelligence Division, was so exceptionally bright, so ethical, and so hardworking that federal prosecutors and agents regularly confided in him. Within law enforcement circles in the mid-1980s, the feds acted like Boston Brahmins—speaking only to God and to each other. Hegger was allowed into the sanctum sanctorum because he had a presence that few people, even federal judges, possess.

"We'll have a car pick you up. Come down to the FBI headquarters," the man told Hegger. He did not explain why. Hegger, who looked like the gunslinger Paladin doing a cameo appearance as the Marlboro Man, snuffed out his cigarette and grabbed his jacket. He told the FBI man he would walk.

It was a pleasant fall day, one of the few times St. Louis was relatively cool and not smothered by high humidity. Hegger strolled across Twelfth Street from the police headquarters to Market Street and down to the Federal Building at 1520 Market. There, he was escorted through empty corridors past a large room where a band of FBI agents he knew and a larger group of strangers were gathered. Several of the men were pointing to a spot on a colored wall map of the Middle East and the Mediterranean Sea. Hegger wondered what that had to do with St. Louis and the Midwest.

Through the din of the conversations and the plotting on black-boards, Hegger gathered this was a high-level strategy session of various intelligence agencies—FBI, CIA, and NSA (National Security Agency). It was understood that he was to ignore what was going on. From years of working with the FBI and the U.S. Attorney's Office, as

23

well as the Drug Enforcement Agency and the Bureau of Alcohol, Tobacco, and Firearms, Sergeant Hegger knew when to mind his own business: Don't try to read upside down, don't try to decipher cryptic conversations. When Hegger and the agent came to a small interview room, they closed the door and sat down. Hegger did not ask any questions about what he had seen.

Hegger lit one of what he called his "sissy" low-tar cigarettes. The FBI supervisor began talking about the *Achille Lauro* incident. (Among police and prosecutors, everything from a car crash to a mass murder spree is called an "incident.") The agent explained that the FBI was now involved in this case. Federal intelligence agencies were coordinating forces should there ever be some terrorist act on American soil. They were looking at St. Louis, the man said.

Hegger tried not to smirk. Terrorists along the Mississippi sounded a little far-fetched, a little paranoid. St. Louis had even been immune from the race riots of the sixties while other cities had burned.

"Anything could happen," the FBI was saying. "Which is why we might need several hundred local police officers here in the city at a moment's notice."

Hegger nodded. "So, why are you telling me this?" he asked.

"We need someone who can convince the police chief ASAP to release whole battalions of officers. Hundreds of them. You're well respected in the St. Louis Police Department. The chief would believe you."

The counterterrorist experts never explained to Hegger for what reason, without warning, he would need to summon 400 cops. It would be three years before they gave Hegger a clue. And three years more before the details would be revealed.

Cliff Walker stood on one foot then the other, shivering in the raw November night air. He was waiting to walk Tina Isa home. For almost year now, Cliff had waited for her, escorting her from her classes. Tonight, November 5, 1989, she had started her first job, working at a Wendy's fast-food restaurant on South Grand Avenue.

Tina planned to save her salary so she could afford to leave home and pay her college tuition. An honor student with an upcoming summer scholarship, she wanted to study aeronautical engineering to become an airline pilot. Tina spoke four languages fluently and was ready to travel the globe. Her family already had lived in Puerto Rico, Brazil, and in Israel.

Cliff tried to talk her out of being a pilot. What about all those accidents? he had asked. Why not work on the ground instead? But he admired her ambition.

From the first day they had met four years earlier, when she was twelve and he a year older, Cliff had been attracted to Tina, initially for her beauty. Tina was darkly exotic, with almond, almost Oriental-shaped eyes and dusky olive skin. She was half-Palestinian through her father and one-quarter each Italian and German through her mother, with a drop of South American Indian blood.

What disarmed Cliff was her smile, her laugh. Tina was always laughing. In every picture of her from childhood until the day she died, Tina was ebullient. Introverted and introspective by nature, Cliff grew more expansive around her. Unlike other teenage girls he knew, Tina was never mopey or wistful. She never indulged in self-pity— even when her parents and several of her sisters punched and kicked her for seeing Cliff. She merely reported to him what had happened.

Cliff felt badly for her. He knew Tina's family, especially her father, was very prejudiced against blacks. Zein Isa's animosity was radically different from most St. Louisans', who while somewhat racist, would not throw hot coffee at their daughters for dating an honor student in a special leadership program. If the Isas hated blacks so much, why did they live in a racially mixed neighborhood? Tina's mother, Maria Isa, and her sister Soraia were known for their bigotry as well as their violence. Neighbors reported that they slapped black children, even kicked their mothers and pulled their hair, while they yelled racial epithets.

To get Tina away from "that nigger-slave," as Zein Isa referred to Cliff, he had tried to marry his sixteen-year-old off to several Palestinian men nearly double her age. But Tina had rebelled and refused to see any of them again.

She had told Cliff she did not want to get married until she was well past thirty. But Zein demanded that his youngest child obey him as any traditional Palestinian village girl would. A good girl is obedient above all else, and between the ages of fourteen and eighteen, she marries a man her father has selected. The Isas strenuously disapproved of American values such as free will and individuality. Americans were barbarians, the family said. Satanic, Zein believed.

If they dislike our customs so much, why did they come here? Cliff wondered. Why would Palestinians choose to live in St. Louis?

Tina once confided to him and to her best friend, Helena, that her father was a terrorist. Helena told Cliff that she, Tina, and Maria had dropped Zein off to meet with his terrorist group at some restaurant up in Florissant. Old Zein Isa—the diabetic hobbling around on crutches— a terrorist? Cliff had to laugh.

He checked his watch. It was nearly eleven, about the time Tina had promised to meet him. As he looked up, there she was, bouncing along, waving to him as she left Wendy's. Just before midnight the young couple was heading toward Tina's apartment at 5739 Delor Street. As they stopped in the parking lot for Tina to retie her shoelace, Cliff said, "I'll walk you to the door."

"No." Tina was adamant. "That's all right."

"I'll stay then till you get into the house." Cliff was worried. There were no lights on in the Isa apartment and by this time of night her parents were always home from their corner grocery store.

"Yeah, wait fifteen minutes," Tina said. "If there's any trouble—I'll come back out." She was afraid. She had left a note on the television set in the living room that she had started a job and would be back after eleven. She had not wanted to tell her parents ahead of time about her job. No one in her family ever worked outside the family store.

Whatsamatter, Zein had yelled at her when she mentioned working once before. Don't I give you enough spending money? Can't you work in the family store?

Tina knew her parents would be difficult tonight. Zein, in particular, did not understand her dream of being independent and American. To him, everything should remain as it had been before he had emigrated from his little village in the West Bank back in the early 1950s.

As Tina walked up the steps to the apartment complex, Cliff watched her. His eyes followed her up the stairs to the landing and as she knocked on the door. Her mother opened it, for they had taken away Tina's keys weeks earlier. Turning her head, Tina looked down at Cliff and smiled. He knew she could not wave to him with her mother standing there. If we catch you seeing Cliff again, we'll kill you, her family had screamed at Tina.

Cliff waited. He walked down to the building to make certain Tina had turned on the light in her bedroom and was all right. He sat on the concrete steps a while, but the light never went on.

He walked home. Maybe she's in the kitchen fixing something to eat, he thought. Or they're arguing in the living room. As he walked several miles to the bus stop on Grand Avenue, an ambulance passed him about one A.M.

That stuck in his mind for years.

CHAPTER TWO

"Die, Daughter, Die"

EARLY MORNING, NOVEMBER 6, 1986   ST. LOUIS

It was the top of the hour, time to hear the news. The FBI agent switched radio stations as he drove to work. He wasn't paying much attention to the national and international headlines and had to remind himself not to drive to the FBI office downtown but to a secret location, off-site as they called it, for security reasons, in South St. Louis, about four miles away from Zein Isa's apartment. No one knew there was a Palestinian terrorist ring operating in the United States except the terrorists themselves and the FBI, which had them under surveillance.

The case agent and several translators had been working for several years on this case, which originated in St. Louis but had tentacles reaching across the United States. Each home and store in this terrorist network was under electronic surveillance twenty-four hours a day, every day. The bugs were voice activated; the phone taps were triggered whenever the receivers were lifted. Such eavesdropping was authorized under the Foreign Intelligence Surveillance Act, which meant an agent was not required to listen in at all times. With all these locations in all these cities being wired, tapes were piling up. The FBI was running Arabic translators in and out of St. Louis two to three at a time. Right now, the translators were running about a week behind.

The agent was wondering if they had been missing anything. The Arabists did not translate every word but rather wrote up synopses of each conversation, then compiled those into summaries: eg., 12:03 P.M., Fri., Oct. 13, Zein and Tawfiq discuss politics, with the specifics on what they said about Abu Nidal. Or, 2:30 P.M., Fri., Oct. 13, Zein Isa and his nephew Luie talk about Tina. The details on such personal conversations rarely were noted, the agent recalled.

Just then, he heard Tina's name on KMOX-Radio. The announcer

was saying sixteen-year-old Tina Isa had been murdered at midnight
by her father, who was now in police custody.

"Oh, my God!" screamed the agent as he typed in the computer
access code to the electronic doorknob that would open the secret FBI
office and he tore through the anteroom alerting the translators drinking their coffee.

They all ran into the tape room; one grabbed last night's tapes from
Zein Isa's home. The tapes ran reel-to-reel, which offered higher
sound quality, yet sometimes it was difficult to understand the rural
Palestinian dialect. The agent listened to the end of the phone tap
reel—some man was calling Zein's brother in Milwaukee, something
about Homicide detectives. Whoa! thought the agent.

He quickly punched the fast reverse button. He heard Maria call an
ambulance.

He fast-forwarded the tape. He heard a sergeant call for the medical
examiner. Switching back to the wall bug, he heard a Homicide
sergeant talking with Zein and Maria.

He jabbed the reverse button and listened carefully. Alternating
between the recordings from the microphone in the phone and the one
inside the closet, they heard the family plotting to kill Tina. It was difficult to understand them, they were speaking in Arabic, Portuguese,
and occasionally English, but what was hardest was the conversation
between Tina and her parents.

Listening very very carefully, the agent heard, on the tape, the
sounds of a door being slammed. There was so much arguing back and
forth, mundane stuff about a teenager's curfew. Let's get to the point,
he thought, pushing fast-forward on the wall bug reel. Zein hissing,
"Tonight, you're going to die!"

Listening to those graphic tapes of a child being stabbed through the
heart was harrowing; the FBI agent became distraught. His sympathetic supervisor recommended the agent follow routine Bureau procedure for trauma and seek stress counseling. How could any healer,
medical or theological, exorcise from his heart and soul what the agent
had heard on that tape?

CHAPTER THREE

Ancient Honor

CIRCA 5000–4000 B.C.E.   ANCIENT CANAAN

The forebears of Zein Isa possibly were pagan Canaanites who adopted Judaism when the Israelites conquered the land. With the coming of Christianity, some converted. And some converted again when Islam spread from the Arabian Peninsula. For 6,000 years dozens of Semitic and Mediterranean tribes have settled and intermarried in the land just north of Jerusalem.* Yet, three themes have stayed constant over time there: religious animosity, man's subjugation of woman, and blood vengeance.

One Old Testament tale set in these hills intertwines the three themes. To Zein Isa, the moral of this story is as fresh and true today as it was in the days of the patriarchs. Indeed, to many people in the Holy Land, the past is not dead or even dying. A Palestinian journalist who investigated Tina's slaying saw it as a contemporary version of the ancient story of Dinah—the lost honor of one girl to the foreigner and the tribal revenge for her shame:

Jacob, son of Isaac, went into the land of Canaan, to the city of Shechem (near Nablus, today a large city north of Jerusalem) where he bought land and settled his family. Jacob had a dozen or so sons and one beautiful daughter—Dinah. So exquisite was Dinah that the king's son lusted for her.

The king's son seduced Dinah and "humbled" her. In anger, Dinah's twelve brothers promised to avenge her honor by killing the king. But

---

*While the land around Zein's village has been inhabited for eons, some of his ancestors may have been new arrivals. In the last century there was mass migration throughout the Ottoman Empire into the Holy Land. Regardless what tribes his forefathers belonged to, no ethnic group was indigenous to the area called in biblical times Judea and Samaria.

their father, Jacob, forbade bloodshed. Instead, Jacob went to the king and explained how the prince had besmirched Jacob's honor and shamed their tribe. The king promised a mass intermarriage, free trade, more land—anything to restore favor with Jacob, whom he respected. Dinah, who was not consulted in all this, would be wed to the king's son.

This was not enough for Jacob's sons, who demanded blood vengeance: They proposed that if the king's son and all the men in Shechem would follow Abraham's Covenant with God and be circumcised, then the two tribes could intermarry, including Dinah and the king's son. The king and his son agreed. Thus all the males of Shechem were circumcised. While the men of Shechem were writhing in pain, Jacob's sons attacked the village and killed every man and boy—including the king and his son, "because they had defiled their sister." The women and girls they took as prisoners. Dinah was wrenched from her husband's house.

Grieving, Jacob railed at his sons: Before these pagans, you have shown me to be treacherous and cruel. And his sons justified their savagery with, "Should one deal with our sister as with a harlot?"

Some Arab scholars interpret this carnage as Dinah's fault. What happened to her the Bible does not say. "Apparently, the writers did not think she mattered," remarked a Palestinian journalist.

Zein al-Abdeen Hassan Isa was raised in a place where little had changed since the time of Jacob and Dinah. A land untouched by the Renaissance, the Enlightenment, the Industrial Revolution, even the printing press until late in the nineteenth century. (The Ottoman Empire, which then controlled the Levant, forbade the printing of books.) For many people living in Palestine, biblical tales were more than charming myths explaining human behavior, they were literal truths. Customs and beliefs were fixed for all time. Blood vengeance had continued as a way of resolving conflict.

South of Jacob's Shechem and about ten miles northeast of Jerusalem lies the West Bank village of Beitin (*bait-teen*), aptly named "house of figs" (from *beit*, "house," similiar to the Hebrew *beth*, and *tin*, "fig"). The terraced hills teem with grape vines, olive trees, and fruit trees—oranges, lemons, peaches, almonds, dates, figs. Yet there was little besides subsistence orchard farming amid the limestone outcroppings, and starting around the turn of the twentieth century, men from Beitin began immigrating to the New World for work.

A relative of Zein's sailed for North America before the First World War. He spent the rest of his life as a street peddler in North Carolina, sending nearly all his money home. His brother took his savings and built a large Mediterranean farmhouse of stone blocks with quoining and an orange tile roof. Three extended families, totaling fifty people, once lived in the eight airy rooms with high, pressed tin ceilings and ceramic tile floors set in floral patterns. Now, only a widowed ninety-year-old great-grandmother and her widowed sixty-year-old daughter-in-law inhabit the house.

"Too many men went off to America and not enough came back," the women complain. The older woman's husband immigrated when he was eighteen, leaving behind his fourteen-year-old bride and their newborn boy. He returned for their son's wedding to Zein Isa's sister, then left for another twenty-seven years. Finally he sent for his wife, but he was ill and they had to return to Beitin, where he died. In half a century of wedlock, the older woman spent less than seven years with her husband. She has lived more of her days with her son's widow.

Neither woman learned to read or write, as the village school had been restricted to boys. It was not until Jordan annexed the West Bank after World War II that a school for girls opened, and it was for the lower grades only. The older woman still sports dark blue tatoos on her hands and face made by roaming Gypsies.

The other woman was the daughter of a local farmer, Hassan Isa. When Hassan's third son was born, June 3, 1931, the baby was named Zein al-Abdeen— "the most beautiful of the believers," for Zein means "beauty or beautiful," al is "the," and Abdeen is "the believers"— Hassan Isa. (Isa is Arabic for Jesus, a Romanization of the Hebrew Joshua, and a common surname among Muslims. Palestinian children carry their father's first name as a middle name.) Despite this appellation, Zein was not an observant Muslim. His father called him by a nickname—Abu Faisal*—which became a prophecy.

---

*Abu is an honorific in Arabic, meaning "the father of." In parts of the Arab world, a man is not deemed "whole" until he has sired a male heir. Then he is called by the honorific title of Abu plus the name of his firstborn son. Palestinian political leaders often adapt the allegorical honorific, such as Abu Nidal, the father of Struggle, and Abu Jihad, the father of Holy War. Similarly, Umm, "the mother of," is the name given to women. She is called Umm, plus the name of her eldest son or daughter, if she fails to bear a boy.

During the early days of World War II, Hassan Isa stood in the doorway of his white stone house, built a century or two earlier, calling out to the little girls. "Who wants to marry Faisal when he grows up? He's going to be a doctor."

The girls giggled. The old man had played this game with them before. "Who's Faisal?" one child asked.

"Zein is going to have a son named Faisal and that son will become a doctor. Zein will be called Abu Faisal." Teenage Zein, working the land nearby, laughed. He was not yet married.

During the 1948 war with Israel, Zein and his family remained in their stone house untouched by battle, while Arab refugees relayed horror stories about "the Jews." One family was the Nijmehs, Israeli Arabs from al Qulab, near Lod, who had fled their farmhouse in the middle of the night carrying with them dire warnings: Israeli soldiers in other villages had gripped tiny Arab babies between their knees and slashed their throats before their mothers' eyes. This atrocity probably is not true—there was little wanton killing by soldiers in 1948, and the Jews then wanted the Arabs to stay—but that does not matter: Perception matters more than reality in the Middle East, emotion more than reason. What matters was that the Nijmehs repeated the story to their sons and grandsons. Youssef Nijmeh, now in his fifties, would drive his sons past the old estate and say, "This is your land but for the Jews. Take it back one day."

The Nijmehs went to Beitin where they were taken in by the Musa (Arabic for Moses) family, cousins of the Isas. Together, the three families would sit over coffee and condemn "the Jews."* As is common in these small enclaves, most of the population has intermarried for centuries, and the families have remained close wherever they have lived. Wherever Zein worked in Brazil, Puerto Rico, or continental United States, his neighbors and colleagues were Nijmehs and Musas. They all moved and traveled together, a pattern common among Palestinians

---

*When Arabs verbally attack "the Jews," their argument is territorial and derives from antipathy to Zionism. It is unconnected to Judaism as a religion nor is it remotely related to Christian anti-Semitism. Historically, despite occasional massacres, Muslims treated Jews better than Christians did.

from villages, who prefer the extended family to outsiders. Indeed, some Arab groups consider it acceptable to lie to strangers*.

When in the early 1950s the Brazilian consulate in Lebanon offered visas to entice foreign workers, twenty-three-year-old Zein Isa left for southern Brazil where he wandered in the hinterlands peddling dry goods. Like other Palestinian immigrants, Zein planned to return to his homeland. Home was Beitin. Where he lay his head at night was merely a stopover.

During a business trip to Rondopolis, in southern Brazil, in February, 1963, a friend urged Zein to stop at a particular restaurant. "You've got to see this girl who's a waitress here," he explained. "She's lush-figured and looks like a movie star."

The girl was pretty with dark wavy hair and fresh high coloring. Zein was immediately attracted to her as she poured coffee for the two men. All she would say was "Good morning." She was named Maria Matias. Her father, Irio Gregorio Matias, was of German descent with an Indian grandmother. Maria's mother, Jacomina Magagnin, had been a baby when her Italian parents immigrated to Arapafanga, in southernmost Brazil. Maria was born August 10, 1943, in the state of Santa Catarina and grew up in Mato Grosso, another state nearby.

Maria's parents farmed in the wilderness, with the children clearing the trees. Her parents worked hard, as did the entire family. They had to. Brazil still suffers such poverty that more than half of the population is underfed and malnourished. Maria was taught that if the farm crops fail, go to work in a factory; keep working at all costs or you won't survive. When Maria was fourteen, her parents dispatched her to another city, where she lived with an aunt and sewed wedding dresses for a living. Maria learned to waste nothing. Nearly every crop the Matiases raised, they ate. They needed only to buy salt. Until Maria was five, her mother handstitched all her clothes. Maria, who is placid by nature, believes they had everything they needed.

---

*In a land constantly ruled by conquerors and where there is no free speech, it's been safe to trust only one's relatives. It was unlikely a member of one's tribe would betray one. However, almost all Arab academics and journalists I interviewed spoke with absolute candor on first meeting. Some of the women interviewed took time to open up, but when they did, they were truthful.

Everything but schoolteachers, priests, doctors, and pharmacists. Maria never went beyond first grade, not a startling statistic in Brazil, where even today 70 percent of the population does not finish sixth grade. Not that the Matiases had any choice about education; there were not enough children around to sustain a school. The land was so godforsaken, there was no church, only a priest riding a circuit. Maria became a nominal Catholic, as are many rural Brazilians. She has no idea what a confirmation name is (the saint's name the child chooses when he or she is confirmed into the Church at age seven). The farms in the area were too remote and too few to support any health services. Maria never swallowed any prescription medicine until she was twenty-one years old. Instead, her mother brewed herbal tea from wild plants.

The oldest of seven children, Maria was both grateful and obedient to her parents. Only once did Maria ignore her mother's advice. That was when she met Zein Isa. Zein's friend had proposed to her, but Maria said no. "He was too old for me. I didn't want to marry for money. I marry a person I like."

It was like at first sight with Zein. "The first time I saw him, I liked him. He looked like a hard worker." When Zein sent a man who knew the Matiases, in his behalf, to ask for their daughter's hand in marriage, Maria told her father to accept.

"Maria," Mrs. Matias warned, "he's thirty-two. He's too old for you. There are all these young men around. Take one of them."

"But Mama, I want this one," the teenager argued.

To the poor farm girl, Zein appeared to be the successful worldly older man. In the decade since he had left Beitin, Zein had prospered peddling clothes. He now owned a dry goods shop offering his customers bolts of fabric, ready-made clothes, and shoes. He had mastered Portuguese, the language of Brazil.

Maria accepted Zein's proposal without ever talking with him. A week after she served him coffee in the restaurant, they were married, on February 6, 1963. It was a civil ceremony, the priest refusing to marry a Catholic to a Muslim. Like many young brides, Maria thought she was embarking on a wonderful life with a wonderful man. They spent a month honeymooning in a big-city big hotel.

Three months after her wedding, Maria discovered she had been betrayed.

CHAPTER FOUR

The Second Wife
and the Last Child

Zein was not smiling when he told Maria he had something to tell her, and his bride, still in awe of her older husband, could not believe what he had to say. Afterward, she sat stunned, looking like a slapped puppy, wondering why he had done this to her, why he had lied to her. Three months married and three months pregnant, there was nothing she could do; in Catholic Brazil, divorce was not an option.

"I'm married," Zein had told Maria. "I have a wife back in Beitin and we have three children together—a boy and two girls. I have to tell you now because I've applied for papers to immigrate to the U.S."

According to his standards, Zein was not obligated to mention his first wife to Maria until she needed to know. He was not expected to transform the marital bed into a confessional. He and his life were none of her business. His responsibility was to financially provide for his wives and children. Indeed, the Qur'an is strict about this—men must treat their co-wives equally. The Prophet Mohammed sanctioned polygyny—the practice of having more than one wife at a time—to provide for widows and orphans after wars.

Maria wept for three days. She says she felt trapped. "I couldn't go home to my mama. I picked him," she later told the daughter she had been carrying at the time. "I had to accept the fact he was married with kids." Decades later, Maria explained, "most good people in Brazil won't marry someone with a wife. But most people in Palestine who come to live in Brazil don't tell the truth. If they do, they can't find a good girl."

In Beitin, Zein's first wife, Foiziya, wept. She received the news that her husband had married again with much anguish. Some villagers say her only son, Faisal, who had not seen his father since he was four, was especially distraught and remained so. Some say Faisal and his two sis-

ters resented the second wife and never accepted Maria nor any of her
her children except Tina.

Zein was typical of village men who left for the Americas and begat
another family overseas. The practice is often excused with "It's better
for them to take a 'white' wife and have more kids than to sleep around
or make some woman a mistress," several Palestinian women said.
"More honorable, yes?" ("White" wives carry social status in a land
where fair skin is much prized.) Foiziya may have felt abandoned, but
she was lucky: Zein owned a store in the village which he had put in
her name, and he regularly sent her money. There were many deserted
women in the West Bank whose husbands sailed for South America
and seemingly vanished. Oddly enough, Maria was fortunate. Some
Palestinian men divorce their foreign brides before they return to the
homeland, where, if not already married to Arab women, they take
nice Palestinian girls as brides.

Zein had married his first wife when they were teenagers. They had
long known each other, being double first cousins* (the children of one
pair of siblings who had married another.) Unlike his quick proposal to
Maria, Zein's courtship of Foiziya followed Arab traditions. Most
likely their union had been arranged by their fathers as they sat over
demitasses of thick Turkish coffee.

Marriages between cousins have been common in Palestine for
intramarriage kept property intact and strengthened tribal loyalty.
There are famous Arab proverbs about kinship and marriage: "The
closer you get married, the easier your life will be." A bride, who had
to live with her in-laws, usually would be better treated by a mother-
in-law who was also her aunt. "Your cousin can always bring you
down from the white horse" alluded to the rite of first refusal. A bride
left her father's house on a white horse for her father-in-law's home,
where the marriage ceremony would take place. En route, one of her
father's nephews was entitled to pull her—in all her wedding regalia—
from the nuptial horse and claim her as his bride.

These marriages can be a blessing, argue young educated women in
Beitin today. There was a deaf girl whose cousin so pitied her that he
married her. This may have been more than a noble heart. In the com-

---

*Among traditional Arabs, the best marriages are between the children of two
brothers.

munal Middle East, tribal honor is more important than an individual's feelings. The individual is important in how he strengthens his family.

Others disagree with the custom. Many educated women want to choose their mates. Zein's son, Faisal, a pediatrician with a subspecialty in neonatology, is against consanguineous unions. It causes deafness, low intelligence, and various mental illnesses, he explained. To such a gene pool add the problems of poverty and teenage mothers having too many pregnancies too close together, and the result is an infant mortality rate in the West Bank soaring to more than forty-five per 1,000 births, he said.

When Zein told Maria in the spring of 1963 that he wanted to emigrate to the United States, she fantasized they would live out their lives in America. Instead, they wandered back and forth between Beitin, Brazil, and Puerto Rico, with brief sorties into the U.S. for more than twenty years before finally settling down in St. Louis. Maria never was allowed to put down roots until her late forties, when she was sentenced to life in prison. Maria liked to say, "The day I was born, I knew I'd move too much." Meanwhile Zein's first wife spent all of her life in one place, Beitin.

By fall 1963 the Isas had left for Raleigh, North Carolina, where there still is a substantial Palestinian population including men from Beitin. One of the Nijmehs who had married Maria's sister Irecema in Brazil had relocated here. While Maria worked in a factory, Irecema watched her newborn, Leilah. After a few months the Isas moved again, because Zein disliked being a street peddler of tablecloths and bedspreads in Raleigh. Irecema and her husband had moved to Paterson, New Jersey, another area with a pool of Palestinians. The Isas joined the couple there. Each time he uprooted his family, Zein told Maria to leave everything behind and buy new clothes and household furnishings.

After eight months in New Jersey, Zein moved Maria and the baby to Puerto Rico, settling in Arecibo, where Zein sold clothes door to door. They bought a house near those of other West Bank emigrés, many of whom were taken with Maria's prettiness and warmth. After a few years in Puerto Rico, the Isas returned to where they had started—Rondonópolis, Brazil—with their two little girls, Leilah and Mona, who was born in late 1965. After two years in Rondonópolis, Zein moved his brood to Cáceres, where their third daughter, Soraia, was born in 1967.

Five years later, still in Brazil, Maria awaited the birth of her last child—the one she would call her easiest, yet the one that would destroy her family.

During the fall of 1972 Zein told the very pregnant Maria, "I need a son."

"You already have one," she told him. "I don't care if I have a boy or not."

On December 3, 1972, in Mato Grosso, Brazil, Maria gave birth to a fourth girl. "I'll name this one Palestina," Zein said, after the homeland where he planned to return, and where the name was in vogue. In Arabic, Palestina is pronounced "Fah-lah-steen-ah" after the ancient coastal tribe of Philistines who gave the region its name. Of all Maria's children, this one most resembled their father, with her black almond eyes and dark skin. Like him she was stubbon and bright. In linguistic ability, curiosity, sense of adventure, openness, warmth, and vivacity, she took after her mother. She had her own special charm.

Zein became so attached to this winsome creature that when he went on a business trip to São Paulo, he brought home an elaborate gift for her—an English baby carriage of red velvet decorated with flowers.

"How could you spend so much money?" Maria asked.

"Because no one else here has something like this," he said, beaming.

The baby not only was paraded in style, she was dressed in the best the Isas could afford. The last of the lot did not suffer in hand-me-downs. Maria and her older daughters hand-painted all of Palestina's clothes—each diaper, T-shirt, and dress. The three older sisters, nine, seven, and five, fought for the privilege of pushing her baby carriage, but the infant would fuss, allowing only her mother or Soraia to touch the handle. When the baby awoke at six A.M., she would whimper until Soraia took her in her arms. Five-year-old Soraia became closest to the baby, a deputy mother.

Palestina had the easiest disposition of all Maria's girls. "She was always good-natured," said her mother, who breast-fed her. "She was always laughing," said her sisters. She progressed rapidly, too. Although it sounds incredible, when Palestina was only three months old, she would whimper as she wet her diapers, so her sisters began potty-training her. Two months later she was in underpants. At one year, she started walking. By eighteen months Palestina chattered in sentences. Soon she spoke in three languages—Portuguese, Arabic, which Zein had taught his family, and Spanish, once they moved back to Puerto Rico.

As a toddler Palestina became the adorable pet who made everyone laugh with her jokes, and then would chortle along herself. She was special to everyone, even to her half-sisters and brother when she visited Beitin. At home the family called her *mea amor*, "my love," and *meu santa*, "my saint," in Portuguese; and *Chica*, "little girl" in Spanish.

Palestina's love was her father. When she saw him, she would cry "Daddy, Daddy," and run up to hug and kiss him. As she grew, Zein continued to indulge her. Every week he bought her a treat. And when Zein visited the homeland, which he did every year for unexplained months at a time, he brought back gifts for his girls. "Each of us older girls got three to four dresses, but for Tina he brought back five or six," Mona said. Leilah added, "When I needed money, I'd send Palestina in to my father and she'd get it."

Zein would promenade through the Arab quarter in Puerto Rico showing off his Palestina. "See?" Zein exclaimed holding up the toddler for the men to admire. "This is my jewel, my treasure."

As if on cue, Palestina would coo and smile. The Nijmehs and other men from Beitin would laugh as Zein strolled by with Palestina: Old Zein was so proud of his last baby, even though she was his sixth daughter, not something to brag about among Arabs.

In Puerto Rico, Zein made a lifelong "business" contact with an angry Palestinian who said his real name was Mahmoud El-Abed Ahmad El-Abed, but whom the Israelis called Mahmoud Atta. Atta was from Dir Abu Mishal, a West Bank village near the Israeli border. He now lived in Vega Baja, a coastal town about twenty-five miles west of San Juan and about thirty miles from Isabela, where Zein later moved. He and Zein, as well as many other Palestinians, would discuss ways to get back at the Jews.

In Puerto Rico there were scores of Palestinians from the West Bank. Zein was popular among them for his wit and was respected for his mind; others would seek him out for advice. Most of his countrymen peddled dry goods door to door. Others more established drove vans of clothes, household goods, and jewelry to factories, where the workers would buy on credit. Such practices were so commonly associated with Arab immigrants that today, when Puerto Ricans see the vans, they assume Arabs are driving them.

Zein's friend Youssef Nijmeh claims they all emigrated to Puerto

Rico for jobs—a joke at best, as Puerto Rico has an unemployment rate that fluctuates between 16 and 20 percent. In truth, from 1976 until 1989 Puerto Rico was known to be a notorious black market for buying fraudulent American visas and passports. Terrorist organizations scooped them up by the hundreds, if not thousands, for clandestine travel under false names. The U.S. Immigration and Naturalization Service office on the island openly sold passports for cash until a scandal in 1989 forced the embarrassed INS to shut it down. In addition to the bribery and sale of documents, many government papers were stolen, making it easy for a Palestinian to establish a story about himself.

The Beitin villagers, as do most Arabs, preferred living in the Latin countries. The cultures are cousins. The Arabs spent 800 years in Spain teaching their values of hospitality and honor, which were transported to Spanish colonies in the New World. "Everywhere in Puerto Rico or South America you see people, they say hi, they're friendly, invite you in for coffee or to eat," said Youssef Nijmeh. However, some Puerto Ricans do not see the affinity between the two cultures. They find the repression of Arab women bizarre. "While we understand the concept of honor," explained one well-mannered man, "the idea of killing a girl because she shames the family is crazy." In some Latin countries the man who sexually assaults a woman risks being killed by her family. In Israel, the West Bank, and Jordan, an Arab rape victim may be slain by her male relatives for dishonoring their clan.

After a year in Arecibo, Puerto Rico, the Isas bought a three-bedroom, one-bath house in Isabela, a town of about 35,000 on the island's north coast. It was a pretty Mediterranean-style house, cream-colored stucco with red-brown trim. From the backyard Maria and the children would watch the waves roll in, and from the front they could see the tile rooftops of the town.

While living in Puerto Rico, Zein would take one or several of his daughters back with him to Beitin for months, even nearly yearlong stays. Maria, who remained behind with the other children, did not mind: "I send my daughters to Beitin to learn their father's language and culture."

In Beitin, Zein was becoming an important man. He posed for photographs proudly, in his three-piece suit and his checkered *kaffiyeh*, a headscarf held with a coil. Behind him rose the centuries-old white stone house where he had been born. He was donating it to the village to use as a men's social club. Such a contribution proved he had become successful in America. Zein Isa now was a man worthy of respect, and more important, a man of honor.

In his newly completed house, Zein would greet guests as they came through a gate to the screened veranda. The large airy porch was filled with cushioned lawn furniture carefully placed between the hanging and potted plants. The family lingered there with guests over small china cups of coffee. A fragrant garden was off to the side. Flowers were everywhere, blossoming under arabesque verdigris grills (used to keep out burglars) on the windows. The family cat stalked butterflies in the yard.

When Palestina was five, Zein brought Maria and their children back to Beitin, into this new house called al Dar Abu Faisal, the house of the father of Faisal.

It was the house where Faisal and his mother were now living.

CHAPTER FIVE

"Our Dirty Little Secret"

At al Dar Abu Faisal, Zein's co-wives were spending the morning side by side in their new kitchen, boiling rice, sautéing potatoes in olive oil, and braising chicken. They were preparing the big midday meal with cardamom-flavored Turkish coffee and figs for dessert. The two women were accustomed to cooking together for their blended family of eight. By 1977 Zein's two older daughters had married and emigrated to America. For two years Foiziya Isa, the first wife, and Maria Isa, the second wife, managed to live together with their five children—despite their differences in age, culture, religion, and the inherent misery of such conjugal logistics.

Sometimes Maria would work in the little grocery store Zein operated and Foiziya owned—selling sandwiches, soda, eggs, milk, yogurt, rice and beans—and Foiziya would prepare the meals; sometimes, Maria wanted to cook alone in the kitchen.

Not that there were not arguments. "We kids just ignored them," said Maria's daughters. "We'd walk away and tell them, 'You solve your own problems. We're leaving.'" Overall, Foiziya, known to everyone as Umm Faisal, "mother of Faisal" was kind to Maria's children, who consider her their well-respected stepmother. Whatever humiliation and jealousy Foiziya suffered, she did not inflict it upon her rival's children. One can only imagine what she and Maria endured. When her husband took another wife a Palestinian woman said to a British author, "My heart was black against him."

Legally, there was nothing Foiziya could have done with the exception of leaving Zein: Under Islamic religious law, called *Shari'a* law, only a stipulation in her marriage contract forbidding a second wife would have given Foiziya grounds for divorce. When a Muslim couple divorce, the husband is automatically awarded custody of their children. While polygyny is a criminal offense for Jews and Arabs in Israel, it was not for Muslim Arabs in the Occupied Territories. While the Qur'an allows for up to four wives at a time, in practice multiple wives have become rare in the more Westernized Middle Eastern countries surrounding the Mediterranean. Some attribute the decline to the expense of maintaining separate quarters, especially when many Arabs live in near poverty and in crowded cities. Most people in the West Bank wrinkle their noses at what is considered an antiquated custom.

Traditionally, polygyny* has been tolerated only when the first wife was unable to deliver a healthy heir, explained Orayb Najjar, author of *Portraits of Palestinian Women*. Even a rich man does not add on wives to indulge *Playboy* fantasties, she added. Sometimes, the advent of children from the second wife creates a bizarre situation, for example, Hussein Nijmeh of Beitin married a Brazilian, telling her his first wife was barren. When Luie, one of the middle children, was born in 1964, in New Jersey, his father Hussein sent the seven-month-old infant back home to wife number one because "she wanted children, she wanna do something, she is the one who raised me and my older brothers and sisters."

What were Zein's sleeping arrangements with two wives? There were four bedrooms in al Dar Abu Faisal: Zein and his son, Faisal, shared a room in which they always stayed up talking, then sleeping late; Mona and Leilah roomed together; Maria slept with Soraia and Palestina; and Foiziya, alone, had her own bedroom.

"Don't be naive," several Palestinian men pointed out. "Zein had sex with both women."

Palestina and her three older sisters were raised as Muslims, although their mother refused to convert. When her children asked her to do so, Maria replied, "There is only one God. It makes no difference."

It did in Beitin. When Zein and Maria lived in the village, there were about twenty-five other Brazilian wives, including Maria's sister, another Nijmeh wife, and the wife of Zein's elder brother. Most of these women had converted, which made them less foreign within a very traditional, very conservative society. Maria may not have perceived any rejection, but villagers say, "As soon as you get the title of outsider, you never lose it." Another added, "It is less than acceptable to marry a Christian. Palestine is not really that secular." And an academic raised in a nearby village

---

*Polygyny is the practice of taking more than one wife at a time; polyandry, more than one husband; polygamy, more than one spouse.

pointed out that Muslim villagers rarely marry local Christians, although many Christian Arabs—Roman Catholics, Greek Orthodox, Episcopalians, and Lutherans—live in the Ramallah district, the political subdivision in which Beitin belongs. (For example, former PLO spokeswoman Hanan Ashrawi, also a literature professor at Bir Zeit University.)

Maria did learn Arabic taking classes in Jerusalem until she was certified at the fourth-grade level. (Previously she had studied Spanish in night school in Puerto Rico.) And she did all this while working and rearing her four little girls and dining with Zein's first wife, who apparently was still cohabiting with her husband.

In fact, Maria literally could not afford to leave Zein. What could a semiliterate woman with four little girls do in an alien land where it is nearly impossible to survive without family? Where would he be able to take her daughters from her if they divorced? So, what would have been untenable to many American and Palestinian women was acceptable to a woman raised in a poor, remote area of Brazil where females are chattel. To Maria, if she and her children were given enough to eat, that was sufficient. She withstood many abuses. Even violence.

Zein was angry. When he raised his hand, Maria did not flinch. He slapped her across the face. Hard. Maria did not fight back.

She asked for it, he thought, and Maria later agreed with him: "He's supposed to hit me," Maria explained. "I said bad things about his dead mother. All over the world, men beat ladies." Her father, after all, had struck her mother. Maria says she was unafraid of Zein's thrashings. She thought her husband was basically nonviolent—he never spanked the children, never "talked bad to them." The few times Maria turned a child over her knee, the girl would bawl and then Zein would cry, too. Zein was so tender-hearted, according to his friend Youssef Nijmeh, that he could not bring himself to slaughter a goat for a feast celebrating the end of Ramadan. "I can't do it," Zein—his eyes filling up—cried to Youssef. "Look, it's wagging its tail at me."

Youssef says he had to kill the beast himself.

While Maria had little recourse to Zein's abuse, there was a system in place to protect his first wife, Foiziya—the extended family. A Palestinian family acts as a buffer. Living together, several generations at a time, there is so little privacy that relatives are confronted by the sight of a woman with bruises around her eyes and a fractured arm. Before the

Intifada (Arabic for "rising up," the revolt against Israeli occupation that began in December 1987), women in Palestine did not always stay with a brutal husband, according to Orayb Najjar. A Palestinian wife had her family to intercede for her. They were obligated to step in, since her bruises reflected badly on their honor, showing they could not protect a tribal woman. Her family could help without telling the battered wife. For example, this true story told by Prof Najjar:

A young Saudi teenager from a city married a mountain youth who beat her. One day she escaped to her family. Her husband followed. Her father sent his brother, the wife's uncle, to beat her husband, in private. The youth could not return the blows to the older man, for age is respected in the Arab culture. As the uncle slapped and punched his nephew-in-law, he said, "Now you know what it's like to be beaten by someone who's stronger than yourself."

The uncle had gone in place of the girl's father to save face, so the son-in-law would not be embarrassed in the future by his wife's father. The uncle's job done, he returned. The father told his daughter it would be safe for her to go back to her husband. She reconciled with him, noting that he now treated her differently. She never knew why or how, because to save face her family and husband never told her.

Unlike battered wives in America, Palestinian women are usually reluctant to go to the police, because the Israeli authorities had often jailed and perhaps beaten their husbands and brothers for "political association." For many women, it would be shameful to go to the police over a family matter.

An abused wife can seek help in the *Shari'a* courts, family courts founded in Islamic law, which oversee marriage, divorce, custody, and inheritance. *Shari'a* courts frown on wife beating because it dishonors the extended family, and in Third World countries with minimal central governments, the tribe functions as a mini-state, if you will. In Arab cultures, a wayward cousin can destroy the reputation of the entire clan. The result is business deals fall through and women lose prime marital prospects.

Had Maria known about it, there were two alternatives: One, traditionally, a beaten wife can seek shelter with the village *mukhtar*, the administrative head, or with a *sheikh*, a rich, powerful political figure. The second alternative is a net of Women's Centers across the West Bank, offering sanctuary, legal advice, job-training, babysitting, and day care. Several are near Beitin—in East Jerusalem, Beit Hanina, and al Bireh. The foyer of one center featured a poster in Arabic but with an international message: a four-color picture of a woman with a bruised and swollen face.

Women's Centers in an Arab country? Westerners persist in thinking of Palestinian women as these timid veiled creatures walking seven steps behind their husbands. They absolutely are not. What is fascinating about Palestinian culture is its complexity and constant contradictions. From a rigid, repressive patriarchy have sprung a number of feminists. Of both sexes. The women are highly educated—indeed, there seem to be more tenured women academics in West Bank universities than in American schools. Palestinian feminists have been working hard for decades to establish rural work collectives and job training for the poor. Feminisms, with the plural s, as one sociologist called it, pointing out how feminism Palestinian-style is not limited to the middle and upper classes.

Ironically, while women have become politically active in the Intifada, some advancing to leadership positions, the average Palestinian woman is worse off. There have been so many strikes and shop closings that families today have far less money. Poorer parents often educate only their sons. With businesses closed and less schooling available, the average woman has fewer job opportunities. She may be left alone if her husband, father, or brother has been jailed for political association (meaning they were imprisoned for years without trial for what the Israelis called threat of sedition). Such a woman would have no money and no support network.

A Palestinian family that cannot afford to feed all the children marries the girls off at an earlier age. One Palestinian study confirmed more girls were being married off in high school, sometimes because the Israelis had shut down the schools. Teen marriages are equally common in villages, refugee camps, and large cities.

Many families pressure their sons to marry young so that they become more responsible during the crisis and to prevent the youths from fighting with Israeli soldiers. With boys of eighteen taking fifteen-year-old brides, there is tremendous strain. The young husband is home too much, taking out his anger and frustration on his wife. And with the woman's brothers and father in jail for their politics, who protects her from an abusive husband? Rates of domestic violence have escalated since the Intifada.

And with more men jailed for fighting, there is a surplus of young single women. Some feminists speculate there may be a parallel increase in second wives nowadays; however, reporting has been only anecdotal.

With or without the Intifada, the incidence of battered wives, abused children, and incest is believed to be higher in the West Bank than in the United States. More cases are being reported now because victims are turning to hospitals and family abuse centers for help. But too often families muzzle their daughters rather than dishonor their male relatives. A female's private suffering is less important than the public disgrace of her entire clan.

Many rapes of all types go unreported. Social workers say it is difficult getting girls to talk. "They're ashamed, afraid," a hospital worker reported. Rape victims feel they have nowhere to go, least of all to the police. In an occupied land, the police are not perceived as protectors.[*] Overall, things are improving; now there is a rape hot line for advice.

Some violent sex acts are not crimes. "In America, if a woman doesn't want to have sex and her husband does, it's called rape. Here, it's called nothing," a social worker said ruefully.

There is another type of violence against women still condoned in the Middle East that is unheard of in the West: Crimes of honor. Women and girls are killed by male relatives because they appear to violate the sexual code. "Appear" is the key word; perception matters more than reality.

Ask any Palestinian woman in America or the Middle East and she has a story about crimes of honor that she heard growing up. According to an old tale from Bethlehem that may be true or may be apocryphal, two girls went to fill water from a well. As they were walking back, their donkey broke down. A man came to the rescue. Someone saw the girls with the man and reported it to their fathers. The fathers publicly dragged their daughters to the village well and drowned them.

Then there are contemporary newspaper accounts. For example, Marjorie Olster of the Reuters Jerusalem bureau reported the following incident, February 1, 1994:

---

[*]Indeed, human rights groups report that some Israeli policemen deliberately molest Arab women to demoralize their families, thus weakening the Intifada.

[The] jealous guardian of his family honor decapitated his twenty-two-year-old pregnant sister and paraded her head around the West Bank village of Anabta [near Nablus]. Villagers who witnessed the macabre spectacle in July 1993 said a rumor had spread through the village that the young woman had an extramarital affair.

While Zein Isa was growing up, crimes of honor were predictable, as they had been for centuries. For the nomadic tribes, there were no courts to determine the facts, no legal recourse for retribution. There was only vengeance.

Punitive measures keep people in line. News of an honor killing travels quickly, serving as a warning to young girls: A woman with a past is a woman without a future. Gossip moves faster in the West Bank than a story over the radio. As Palestinians like to say, "If someone sneezes up north in Nablus, someone else down south in Hebron says, 'God bless you.' " While Palestina and her sisters were playing with dolls in Beitin, a girl was found in a well in Hebron, her neck broken from "a fall." Her brother first had tried to kill his sister's lover, but he had run away. The neighbors told police that the girl had not died by accident, that her brother had thrown her into the well.

About the same time, in Nablus, a father walled up his teenage daughter. For years people thought she had disappeared, until Israeli soldiers chasing a Palestinian boy down an alley heard muffled cries from inside a building. Thinking the boy was hiding, the soldiers broke in and searched each floor. One soldier discovered the source of the muted wailing—a woman, about thirty, filthy and malnourished.

The soldiers learned her father had imprisoned her fifteen years earlier after she fell in love with a man of whom he disapproved. The girl's stepmother berated her husband, demanding he take action. The father did not have the heart to kill his own child, so he walled her up instead and threw bread in from a window. The soldiers took the pathetic creature to a hospital and guarded her room. But her father, under the guise of visiting his daughter, killed her.

Under the old code these deaths were not considered murder. The crime victim was the family, the tribe, but not the dead woman. She was the perpetrator of the crime—for dishonoring her family.

"This is our dirty little secret," explained a Muslim Arab over dinner in East Jerusalem.

*   *   *

No one knows how much effect these stories had on Palestina Isa, who from age five to twelve lived in Beitin. She adapted herself quickly wherever her father took her. Palestina was a sunny yet stubborn child, laughing as she tried and tried again to master some task. She was such a delight, her older sisters enjoyed caring for her.

On school mornings they helped her dress in the blue-and-white uniform Maria had sewn for her. The little girl gobbled her breakfast of yogurt, swallowed her tea, and hurried out the door of al Dar Abu Faisal.

Waiting at the gate were two older boys from the village—Saif and Luie Nijmeh. The boys worked for the Deir Dibwan Bus Company owned by their father. As the trio would walk along the dusty road, the little girl would chatter merrily. The boys then would put the five-year-old on a bus to Deir Dibwan, where there was a girls' kindergarten. There was none in Beitin.

Little girls have the same freedom as boys in the villages, which is considerable. Maria would send Palestina to buy things at the store, knowing the roads were safe and the older children would look out for her. Even four-year-olds play games in the village streets. Mothers often don't see their little children all day except for meals.

Palestina would ride around Beitin on her tricycle, and when older on her bicycle, wearing tank tops and shorts. That she dressed in such abbreviated fashion—even at the age of twelve—proved how liberal her father was, villagers say. They point out how indulged the Isa girls were, the only ones with bicycles. Palestina would cut through the family cemetery adjacent to their house as though it were an olive grove—an act which terrified her sisters. A tomboy, she liked arm wrestling and play fighting with boy cousins and a half-nephew her own age.

As she grew older, Palestina studied in a sexually segregated public school in Beitin, wearing her upper school's green-and-white uniform. She seemed unaffected by the restrictions inhibiting some of the older girls, such as covering their hair by the age of twelve; her parents did not make her do this.

Had she spent her teenage years in Beitin as her twin cousins Ahlam and Sausan Nijmeh did (their mother was Maria's sister, Irecema), Palestina would have been hindered somewhat by *fellahin*, or villager, traditions. Once a girl begins developing, she begins hearing "no."

The Isa and Nijmeh girls knew what happens to "bad" girls. They still talk about one:

There was a teenager from America who went back to the home-land, to a village near Beitin. She went jogging around the mosque in shorts and sleeveless tank tops. When she wore skirts, they were high above the knee. The old men of the village warned her three times. Three times she ignored them. Then one day she was found barely alive, her legs torn from being whipped with a hose which was still wrapped around them. To this day, no one knows who beat her; their faces were covered with checkered scarves.

Tina's sisters nodded in agreement when they related the story—the girl got what she "deserved."

A male cousin of Tina's shuddered over the recent killing of a woman in Borqa (the village the Isa clan emigrated from about one to two hundred years ago). The woman was riding in a sharing taxi when it broke down. She and the driver, the only ones in the vehicle, got out to see what had happened. A neighbor saw her, reported it to her father, and he stabbed her to death. This story is so similiar to the one from Bethlehem, one wonders if it really happened. True or not, the restrictions on girls and women were and are real.

Tina's cousin Sausan could not spend the night at another cousin's because the girl had an older brother in the house. Once she was an adolescent, Sausan's father forbade her to go alone to the center of the village and see friends. Single village girls a decade ago could not socialize, even in groups; their partying was limited to weddings and university trips. Traditionally reared college students could go to movies in groups only, and only during daylight hours. Good village girls could not work outside the family business; they wouldn't be pro-tected there. Similarly, many were not allowed to attend college. There was nothing to do but get married.

Nowadays more village girls go to college and hold jobs—nurses, secretaries, and saleswomen in Ramallah, along with a handful of doc-tors and lawyers. Matrons like Sausan and Palestina's sisters visit rela-tives after lunch and dinner, and frequent the women's social club in the village. These journeys are usually made on foot; cars are expensive to own and operate, and donkeys are used for hauling and plowing.

Some girls from conservative families—not necessarily fundamen-talist—have been more restricted since the Intifada. The return to tra-

ditional life has been a way of showing support for a separate
Palestinian state, a way of being less like the Israelis and other
Westerners and more like their Arab brothers. For women it is also a
return to wearing the *hijab*, or white headscarf, as well as long skirts
and long sleeves. Such clothing sometimes is more of a political statement than a religious one.

The ruling elite of the West Bank, however, has remained secular in
its practice of Islam and continues to dress in Western style. In their
speech, hairstyles, makeup, jewelry, and clothing (albeit with longer
skirts), many women professionals are indistinguishable from their
counterparts in Europe and America—except that the Arab women
tend to smoke more.

Maria Isa did not allow these social restraints to stop her from sightseeing. Taking her girls with her, she visited the Old City in Jerusalem (*al
Quds*, "The Holy"), as well as Bethlehem, Jericho, Tel Aviv, Haifa, Jaffa,
Galilee, and Amman, Jordan. Five times she planned to take Palestina
and her sisters to Nazareth, but "political troubles" kept them away.

Maria enjoyed Beitin, although Zein was having problems obtaining
shop licenses there. The Israelis did not want to continue renewing his
visitor's visas because Zein was a naturalized American citizen.

Palestina, however, was having more fun than she ever did in Brazil
and Puerto Rico. She had a larger audience: Faisal, her half-brother
twenty years older, adored her. Unable to have children himself, the
pediatrician treated Palestina as his own. She would sit on his lap and
play with his Coke-bottle-thick glasses. He would cuddle her and
caress her hair.

Faisal's position as the only son carried special duties. While he was
the most educated—indeed the only one of his father's seven children
who was graduated from college—and while Arabic tradition allows a
son to inherit twice what his sisters do, there was a reason: Faisal was
obligated to provide for all six of his sisters if their husbands could not.
The custom at the various feast times is for brothers to visit their married sisters to ensure that their husbands take good care of them. (It is
not uncommon for brothers to pick up their sisters, married or single,
after work to take them home, and if the women go out at night, they
call their brothers to come fetch them.)

Palestinian women complain about the inheritance customs. Too often, they say, sisters are forced to sell off or give away their land so that the property remains whole for the elder brother.

But Faisal had other problems. In late 1979, as Palestina walked into the kitchen, her stepmother was crying.

Why? she asked, what's wrong?

Faisal had been arrested by Israeli soldiers, Foiziya explained. This was dangerous. (Faisal was later accused by the Spanish government of owing $30,000 in back taxes. He was not allowed to return to Spain, where he had lived for seventeen years while studying to be a physician and practicing as a pediatrician.)

Over the dinner table Zein was vitriolic in his hostility toward the Israelis. Zein hated Americans, too, for pouring money into the Israeli treasury, money that paid for the soldiers infesting the West Bank. Zein never said anything about the English, who had killed his uncle in 1948.

Conversations among the Isas and their relatives took the tone of "the Jews" this and "the Jews" that. There was no difference between American Jews who bought Israel bonds and American Jews who did not; no difference between the Zionist settlers who wanted to evict all the Arabs and Israelis who wanted a peaceful partition. All were lumped together, reviled, and demonized. And the Isas were not unique in their malice. Another man from Beitin reported how the schools had so carefully taught him to hate the Hebrew-speaking monsters that when he finally saw a Jew for the first time when he was fourteen, he was shocked: The Jew looked like anyone else, no horns. Even some Palestinians who are more educated and rational say things like, "Germans? I looooove Germans," with the obvious connotation about Nazis, who were their allies during World War II. (In fairness, many American Jews and Americans in general are no more rational about Arabs. One Fulbright scholar from the West Bank was constantly reminded just how un-Anglo he was at Washington University, a liberal institution.) However, a lot of Palestinians differentiate between Zionism and individual Jews. They also condemn the killing of Israeli civilians as murder, not as political acts to hasten the emergence of a Palestinian state.

Palestina seemed immune from anti-Jewish sentiment nor did she become racist. In East Jerusalem there is an enclave of what they call "Black Muslims," who are unconnected to Black Muslims in America. They emigrated from the Sudan generations ago. Their ghetto is excused with "the Sudanese want to keep to themselves. They haven't been here that long."

Indeed, a century seems the standard measure of time in such an ancient land. Palestinians say the colony of Greeks in Jerusalem has not been there very long—only 400 years. This sense of time obviously affects one's sense of history.

Palestinians constantly refer to "their" famous leader Saladin as though he had died recently, pointing out his statue and the major street in East Jerusalem, Sa'la din. It is unlikely Saladin considered himself an Arab, let alone a Palestinian. He was, in fact, a Kurd. According to legend, Saladin routed the Crusaders—Henry II of England and his son, Richard the Lion-Hearted, among others—from the Holy Land. But that is a myth. Saladin did fight the Crusaders to a draw, but his descendents decimated the knights in shining armor. The last Crusader stronghold fell in 1291.

That was the last time the Palestinians overthrew the Europeans and other conquerers. Since the thirteenth century, they have been ruled in sequence by the Mongols, Maluks, and Ottoman Turks, and since World War I by the British, the Jordanians, and the Israelis. Meanwhile, they have practiced "the patience of the sands," the cardinal virtue of the Middle East. The Palestinians could always wait for revenge. (In this Middle Eastern trait of waiting, the Arabs do not differ from their archenemies. Every Passover for 1,200 years, until the 1967 war, Jews raised their wine cups with the toast, "Next year in Jerusalem.")

Like many Arabs, Zein had long sought a new Saladin. The PLO and Arafat were too dovish for him and his relatives, although they were popular in Beitin. As always in the Middle East, political affiliations were through the extended family. For example, if Zein's cousin, Tawfiq Musa, joined a cause, he might bring in Zein, who might recruit the families of his sons-in-law. When tracing membership of political groups, always look for connections of blood over ideology.

"Everybody in Palestine is in the PLO, or some group," Maria remarked. There were "a lot of refugees from other countries—Zein knows men from Syria, Libya, Kuwait, Saudi." From his base in Beitin, Zein had traveled to Jordan, as do many Palestinians, but unlike them, he also went to Syria, Libya, and Bolivia. He claimed to have lived somewhere in Europe. Not common stops for an immigrant who told the U.S. government he never made much money.

CHAPTER SIX

"The Match Only
Burns Once"

1981   BEITIN, OCCUPIED WEST BANK

May I marry your daughter Mona? Zein read the letter aloud. Nai'el, a young man from their village who had moved to St. Louis, had written Zein in Beitin asking for Mona's hand. Zein was pleased. The proposed union would strengthen his extended family, for Nai'el's older brother was married to Fayrouz, Zein's daughter by his first wife. While Maria forbade first cousin marriages, she decreed that her girls should wed men of the same village. "You can't marry for yourself," she trained her four girls. "You need your father's or Faisal's permission."

"And it's your luck if your husband's kind to you," a relative warned Leilah, Mona, Soraia, and Palestina.

Zein called Mona into the room and asked if she wanted to marry Nai'el, whom she had known since she was a child. Think about it, Zein suggested to her.

It took her a week to decide: Yes, it was the right time, the sixteen-year-old replied. Yes. Many of her classmates were marrying at sixteen to eighteen, sometimes as young as fourteen. Others finished high school first and even graduate school, and carved out careers, but in the Isa family a woman over twenty-one was past her prime.

To Mona, Nai'el was a good choice. With about one thousand souls in Beitin, plus a thousand more overseas in the Americas, how many marriageable men were there? And Nai'el was not too closely related to offend her mother.

Mona was not allowed the luxury of getting to know Nai'el before deciding to spend the rest of her life with him. Dating is taboo in Palestine, especially in the villages and in conservative areas like Gaza and Hebron, although there are whispers about brave souls who meet in secret

57

for ten minutes trysts. On the grounds of Bethlehem University is a lovers' lane, but two minutes outside the school gates into the village merely holding hands with a boy tarnishes a girl's reputation. In university towns and big cities, some couples go to movies and dinner and sit and talk in cafés. Yuppies in East Jerusalem call each other for parties rather than Saturday night dates. There is plenty of infatuation, but that is as far as it goes. Western courtship is so forbidden that a Catholic sociologist in Bethlehem said, "I won't let my daughter date here, but I would if we lived in France or Italy. If one lives in a certain culture, one behaves by that culture's standards. This anti-premarital sex is secular, not religious."

Does a woman resent not being able to have a dinner date with a man she's crazy about? The question makes some defensive. One Muslim woman from Beitin said she never dated when she lived in St. Louis, nor when she attended a prestigious college and graduate school. "But I've lived a full life. I don't feel I've missed anything having no boyfriends. I have nothing against premarital sex, though I'm not some floozy. I didn't want some venereal disease. It's my body and I didn't want to give it up to anybody. Only to the man I marry. I wanted him to be a virgin, too. If I give myself to only one person, I want the same respect." She wanted equality, too, for she rejected several suitors after they demanded she veil her hair.

A single woman from a nearby village said she'd rather be called an old maid than be married just to be married. She not only has male friends, she has traveled with them in Europe,[*] where she went to college. Yet, she too has avoided dating and premarital sex.

"How can American and European women sleep with a man without a commitment?" asked a pretty Christian Arab from Tel Aviv. "Here there's no flirting, no wasting time, no being used. If he's not serious, he's not going to be around."

No one seems to consider that dating does not preclude virginity. But again, it is the perception of what may go on that condemns the practice. Traditional Arabic thought is that women are such lustful and amoral creatures a man is not safe left alone with one. It is not that he might seduce her, as it is feared in the West, but that *she* might entice him. There does not seem to be a Muslim equivalent of Don Juan, only the male fantasy that all women since Eve are nymphomaniacs. That is why female gen-

---

[*]The woman says no one from the homeland knows about these trips.

ital mutilation is practiced in some Arab countries—to sexually restrain women. The custom is prevalent where men travel to trade, leaving their wives alone. In the West Bank, such torture is non-existent.

Although most Palestinian women may not date, their marriages are no longer always arranged except in Gaza, a stronghold of fundamentalism, and in very small villages. The villages between Jerusalem and Ramallah, such as Beitin, are somewhat less rigid.

Zein Isa was modern in one sense. He never ordered any of his daughters to walk down the aisle to a bridegroom she loathed. Forced marriages still occur, although according to Islamic law, a woman cannot be married against her will. The *Hadith*—the traditions and sayings of Muhammad as collected by his followers, and which govern the minutiae of daily life—firmly state that a woman can say no. When the *ma'zun* from the *Shari'a* court draws up the civil marriage contract, he asks the bride if she has been forced into the union. If she says yes, he turns his back and leaves. "Her father might be so angry after that," Leilah pointed out, "that he won't let her marry anyone else." Mona and Leilah knew that if they liked a particular boy and Zein rejected his hand, then they had an alternative: to refuse every other beau for the next two to three years. After that, their father would give in. This method did not always work, as Soraia was heartbroken to discover several years later.

Even if a village girl and a boy were in love and their families knew they wished to marry one day, the lovers still were restricted to seeing each other only in public. And then only for a quick conversation. They should not even whisper in a dark corner during a village feast. Mona quoted a proverb: "There is a devil between a man and a woman," meaning, "Away from watchful eyes, anything can happen."

"If you walk away together and people know it, how do they know you didn't have sex? Premarital sex is the single worst thing that can happen to a girl," added Leilah. Her sister-in-law, Aisha* grimaced and dragged her forefinger across her throat. To guard against that disaster, Zein, like many fathers, wanted to marry his daughters off early.

How much of chastity is self-protection from gossip, and how much is it a moral lesson of what happens to those who flout society's code? And in a land where one cannot live outside society? Three college graduates recalled how as recently as 1988, "A woman in a village just north of Beitin

---

*Name changed at the woman's request.

was shot or hanged in a crime of honor. All the women in town were rounded up and brought to see it. The whole town was in on it."

Passion in Palestine was not always so reviled. Some women who came of age during the heady days of the sexual revolution in the sixties and seventies not only wore miniskirts and had boyfriends, but also took lovers. "A friend asked how I felt afterwards [losing her virginity] and I said, 'It's like getting out of something confining,'" confided one woman. And when one doctor studied abroad, "I discovered I had had more sexual partners than my American peers." While these women speak freely, they must do so anonymously. Fundamentalist Hamas terrorists might kill them for what they did thirty years ago.

Social pressure now is so strong against premarital sex, even among educated women in Jerusalem, that "women do not even think about doing it because of the scandal, not the threat of being killed," an internationally known photographer said. However, there are always exceptions. A pregnant young woman in the photographer's neighborhood in East Jerusalem was forced to marry her boyfriend. Initially, he refused, claiming he was not her first lover. When her family threatened to kill him, he decided it was time to marry.

This is not to say most Palestinian men come to the wedding night pure in body and heart. Prostitution is popular. Hard-core pornographic videotapes are sold openly in street stalls just yards from one of the three most sacred sites in Islam, the Dome of the Rock, where Muhammad ascended to heaven according to tradition. In late 1992 the younger male set was more interested in Madonna's *Sex* book and her latest tapes than whether George Bush would be reelected, which would affect Israeli settlement of the West Bank.

Women complain about the double standard. "The only way to have a sex life is to get married," an academic said. Numerous well-educated women stay single "not because they're ugly, but because they work to help their families and the political revolution. Why can't they have normal human lives—with sex, which is like food? Why should we deprive them of this while single men have sex?"* asked a woman in Bethlehem.

*If a Palestinian woman has had lovers, then prospective husbands might reject her because she might be unfaithful later. A woman professor also noted that men also reject women they deem too well educated, too Western, too independent. Such women may be ostracized.

However, if a woman has succumbed to sensual pleasure, she can be restored. Literally. Several women whispered that their mothers knew surgeons who can resurrect virginity.

While courtship varies widely, as it does in America, today the average villager—whom we'll call Daoud (David)—courts a wife the same ways as his countrymen have for centuries: His father arranges it, or his mother suggests it, or he falls in love.

The mother of a single girl—whom we'll call Zuleika—takes her along when she socializes with other women. That way, a prospective mother-in-law might recommend the girl.

Or, for example, say Dauod sees Zuleika at a wedding and is smitten. He then considers two things—her father and her family—that is, money, respect, social status, how she was raised, and occasionally her beauty. Daoud tells his mother, "I'd like to become engaged to Zuleika."

Daoud's mother visits Zuleika's mother and they talk over mint tea. Very indirectly. Arabs are the masters of allusion, and their language is rich in metaphors. Daoud's mother drops hints. "Your daughter is lovely. My son cannot stop talking about her." Zuleika's mother might be evasive, knowing her daughter thinks Daoud is dreadful, and say, "Ah, your son is well raised, but my daughter has been planning to go to school in America." That comment saves face. "And saving face is essential," explained a Palestinian. "This is the Orient."

Suppose, however, Zuleika's mother replies instead, "We won't find anyone nicer than your boy." That means, let's see where this leads. Then Daoud's mother tells his father, "Maybe this time next year we'll have grandchildren." (Children are paramount to Arabs and Israelis. Each side tries to outbreed the other.)

Daoud's father drinks coffee in a café with Zuleika's father. The men play the same game as their wives, slightly more direct. "My son," Daoud's father says, "is willing to become engaged." Zuleika's father agrees: A joint alliance would be useful for socioeconomic reasons. (Not unlike some marriages among the American country-club set.)

Next Daoud's mother leads a group of women carrying sweets to Zuleika's mother. Zuleika herself makes a grand entrance to show off her beauty—Arab women can unveil among each other—and to prove she has no limps, no squints, and is good breeding stock.

To show off his status, that is honor, Daoud's father finds a sheikh or someone rich and powerful from his tribe and they pay call on

Zuleika's parents. The women follow, carrying bags of coffee, pastries, sugar, and other gifts. The women visit with the women; the men segregate themselves with the men.

Regardless of courtship style, "the girl is the last to be consulted," the Palestinian explained. "She is at best a reproductive object. We are buying meat here, not linking souls," But, he added, the good father would ask his daughter first. Usually the girl, with lowered eyes, replies, Whatever you decide, Father. You know best. "Which is the mark of an obedient, well-raised daughter."

As Palestinian feminists point out, if young Zuleika never completed high school and has been reined in by custom all her life, how self-reliant and independent can she be? What recourse does she have when she has no means of support and cannot run away? An individual alone in a communal society is different from the lone individual in America. One is a pariah, the other a hero.

Once the fathers of Daoud and Zuleika agree to their marriage, the bargaining begins for the *mahr*, the dowry or bride-price which Daoud's family pays to Zuleika and her parents. No one can outbargain the Palestinians, who have raised it to a cottage art. One man near Beitin gave his bride a *mahr* of $20,000 in the late 1980s. (One wonders if Zein paid a *mahr* for Maria.) Zuleika's father uses the *mahr* to buy her trousseau and household goods. A portion is invested in jewelry, usually gold, to be sold off as needed for money. (Historically, villagers and Bedouins in the desert had no access to banks and used jewelry as portable currency.)

The bride-price is written into the marriage contract which can be broken, since marriage is a civil act not a religious sacrament. Obviously, a high bride-price makes the husband reconsider casting off his wife: In divorce, the wife keeps her *mahr*, her jewelry, and the household furnishings, and her ex-husband takes the children.

Once Mona Isa agreed to Nai'el's proposal, his mother began embroidering a traditional Palestinian dress for the bride. These costumes are spectacular in color and sophisticated in design[*]: eg., geometrics like an Oriental rug, a garden of folkloric flowers, or arabesques in gilt

---

[*]Some patterns need no translation. The "mother-in-law/daughter-in-law" pattern features two brackets back to back:][.

threads. To the motif-literate eye, the design signifies geographic origin. In the north, where the biblical Joseph is said to have lived, women still sew coats of bright-colored stripes.

With this finery are worn masses of gold and silver jewelry, part of the *mahr*. Sometimes the bridal ensemble and headpiece are covered with gold and silver coins to display the magnitude of the bride-price (the same idea as a flashy diamond engagement ring.) Palestinian and Israeli gold is brighter than that sold in America, 22k or 24k. All this layering of jewelry and color sounds garish but in the blinding light over the bland desert, it is not. And it is part of the pomp of the wedding festivities: This day, the bride is queen, a queen bee who will propagate her husband's line.

Mona would wear her embroidered dress only for the first day. For the second day every smartly dressed bride wants a white American-style wedding gown, and her bridegroom wears black tie. The walls of living rooms in the homes often are edged with family wedding portraits of the brides and grooms in the same costumes one would see in Indianapolis.

But there are never any photographs of the bridal couple embracing for posterity. There is no "You may now kiss the bride" in a Muslim wedding. "I was officially married and my husband still had never touched me," Mona later told Palestina. Affection and sex begin on the wedding night. Mona and her bridegroom Nai'el left for Jerusalem on their honeymoon. The teenage bride was terrified. During the ride, she sat remembering what another village bride once whispered to her. "I was scared and ashamed. We got to the hotel room. I wouldn't take my clothes off in front of him. An only child, I'd never seen a boy even in his underwear. My husband, who had never even held my hand before, came out of the bathroom stark naked.

"I told him, 'Get that thing out of my face.' I asked him to wait. Some men are very patient; they won't force you. I was so afraid he wouldn't, I slept on the edge of the bed and almost fell off. He waited two and a half days before It happened. It was worse than going to the doctor."

Sometimes, depending upon age, the bridegroom is as virginal and embarrassed as his child-bride. A famous Palestinian man explains the traditional wedding night that still takes place:

"Outside the bedroom his parents and hers are waiting nervously.

Inside, the couple is a wreck. She's hysterical and he's got psychological problems. Sometimes he's impotent.

"As soon as he is done, he gets dressed and leaves the room. The girl's mother-in-law rushes in. She checks for the bloody dot on the sheet," which may be proudly waved as a badge of honor. "The mother-in-law goes to the window and sings special defloration songs—'Our girl is fine.'

"Well, she isn't. But her psyche matters even less than her husband's." Being veiled since she was twelve, married off to a cousin four years later, abandoned on her wedding night, and undergoing a display that would make even an exhibitionist blush creates some sex-phobic wives. Sex is a communal act, not a private one.

"The bride's fate—and that of her entire clan—rests on that sheet." A nonvirginal bride means her mother failed to bring her up properly. The mother of the bride loses face. The father of the bride loses honor. And the bride could lose her life.

"Virginity is everything," the Palestinian explained. "It's the holiest concept in the East. Virginity is like a match. The match only burns once."

CHAPTER SEVEN

The Secret Society

In a three-story stone mansion by the sea in Jaffa was born Sabri al-Banna. He was the son of an elderly rich landowner and a sixteen-year-old housemaid who had been elevated from the broom closet to a second wife. The patriarch's older eleven children despised little Sabri and his mother. When their father died in 1945, they evicted their step-mother as she had once displaced their mother. Eight-year-old orphaned Sabri, who remained, was so neglected he never mastered reading and writing.

Three years later the Palestinians refused to accept the United Nations partition of the land under the British Mandate into separate Jewish and Palestinian states, triggering the 1948 war with Israel. When Jaffa fell, the al Banna children fled their estate and became refugees shivering through a harsh winter in a tent. Sabri spent his childhood in Nablus, clad in rags, begging his half-brothers for odd jobs for money so that he wouldn't be gnawed awake at night by hunger pains. His physical poverty was less traumatic than his emotional suffering. Throughout his childhood his brothers and sisters ridiculed him, mostly because of his mother's lower caste ancestry.

Hardworking and ambitious, Sabri developed into a radical political activist and joined the Ba'ath party as a teenager. Immediately disenchanted, he joined a resistance movement founded by Yasir Arafat called Fatah. Fatah was seeking revenge upon Israel and the Arab countries that ignored their misery. After the colossal loss in the 1967 Israeli war, Sabri became obsessed with regaining Palestine. Politicking was a paltry solution. Only bloodshed would avenge their lost honor.

As so many of his comrades had done, including Yasir Arafat, Sabri took a nom de guerre, renaming himself Abu Nidal, Arabic for Father of the Struggle. It was a romantic title for a vicious psychopath. Abu Nidal swore to murder his former comrade when Arafat renounced terrorism to negotiate peace with Israel in 1974. Arafat in turn sentenced Abu Nidal to death in absentia. Abu Nidal borrowed the name of Arafat's Fatah[*] by calling his faction al Fatah the Revolutionary Council. Abu Nidal has not been seen or photographed for so long that PLO sympathizers call him "the man with no face." This mystique continually blossoms into rumors about his death. "Sabri al Banna has been dying longer than General Franco, but it's a lot of wishful thinking," remarked a former deputy secretary of state.

Abu Nidal's siren song to homesick Palestinians in refugee camps and foreign countries is that his paramilitary group will overthrow the Israelis, and once again the Arabs will control all of the Holy Land "from the river to the sea." He deludes them into thinking he is their savior. But Abu Nidal in reality cares little about the Palestinian cause. He has assassinated many of Arafat's top men, more than the Mossad, including his second in command, Abu Iyad, in Carthage, on the eve of the Gulf war. One of his recent allies has been another terrorist, Abu Abbas, who as mentioned earlier was responsible for the attack on the *Achille Lauro* in 1985, in which an elderly Jew from Philadelphia was murdered. At best, the Abu Nidal Organization (ANO) is a band of fanatics and mercenaries. At worst, they are the sadistic thugs of the Middle East, "the most vicious terrorist group in the world," according to the U.S. State Department.

They are devoid of ideology or religion. They even turn on themselves. Abu Nidal purged his organization of "traitors" through the mass execution of 600 young soldiers in his training camps from late 1987 through 1988. Those troops were lucky. Abu Nidal's level of torture is unimaginable. At least one prisoner was restrained while his sexual member was fried in oil in a skillet.

Abu Nidal typifies the Arab proverb, "I and my brother against our cousin; I and my cousin against the world; I against my brother."

Abu Nidal's death toll is beyond that of most terrorists. His henchmen have murdered more than 300 innocent people and wounded more than 600 in the last twenty years, many of whom were American citizens living or traveling abroad. What purpose does ANO gain by

---

[*]Arafat and his men originally named their group Hataf, the initials for the Organization for the Liberation of Palestine (PLO) in Arabic. Realizing that the name Hataf lacked panache, they reversed Hataf into Fatah, which had the added meaning in Arabic of "conquest" or "victory."

attacking Americans and other foreigners who have nothing to do with the Palestinian conflict? ANO seeks revenge on any friend of Israel and any nation willing to negotiate with it. Abu Nidal has threatened retaliation against nations holding its members in prison.

About 75 percent of ANO attacks are outside Israel and the occupied territories. Attacks on civilian tourists were prevalent in the 1980s:

- November 23, 1985. ANO hijacked an Egyptian jet en route from Athens to Cairo and savagely murdered six travelers. Sixty more lost their lives before commandos recaptured the airline.
- April 17, 1986. An ANO recruit convinced his pregnant lover to carry a bag onto an El Al flight from London's Heathrow Airport to Tel Aviv. She did not know until police arrested him that he had loaded the sack with Semtex plastic explosives. An Israeli security agent at Heathrow, not the British authorities, became suspicious and made the search, saving hundreds of lives—including that of the pregnant woman. (El Al uses its own highly trained security everywhere.)
- September 5, 1986. ANO hijackers took over a Pan Am 747 at Karachi Airport, Pakistan, en route from Bombay to New York. More than twenty passengers were killed in the melee when troops began firing at the gunmen.
- July 11, 1988. The United States became involved when five ANO operatives machine gunned and hand grenaded nine vacationers to death on the Greek cruise ship *City of Poros*. Eighty other tourists were severely wounded in the savage attack. Americans were among the hundreds of holiday seekers.

ANO members like to brag that the organization is proletarian. "Abu Nidal is an honored member, but you have what he has. There is no difference between him and you," Zein's cousin, Tawfiq Musa, announced in a meeting in the United States. That was the Big Lie. Sabri al Banna had millions stashed away under the names of his wife and children in BCCI accounts, while Zein Isa's nephew, Saif Nijmeh, who traveled for him, lived on welfare. Al Banna lives in comfort, if not luxury, in his many estates in the Middle East and Yugoslavia, while his former henchman for the New World, Mahmoud Atta, suffers in a squalid jail cell. Abu Nidal is milking the organization, and if any member protests, that man is labeled a traitor and put to death.

Abu Nidal has funded his group and lavishly endowed his family through extortion of host countries and protection and bribery rackets. For example, as of 1993 ANO was extorting $15 million a year from the Saudis to protect their London casino. Abu Nidal also generates money through kidnapping and ransom, arms sales, and freelance killing. The proceeds are funneled through BCCI accounts. His headquarters have been in Baghdad (recently), Damascus, Tripoli (1986), elsewhere in Libya (1993), and Sofia, Bulgaria. He's run two offices in Warsaw, where he has extorted millions of dollars and was guaranteed safe haven and logistical support, including sophisticated weapons. In return he attacks the enemies of his patron states. As of 1994 Abu Nidal was receiving sanctuary in the Sudan, according to Robert Kupperman, the nationally renowned expert on terrorism. Also in 1994, President Assad of Syria "persuaded" the Lebanese to shut down two ANO training camps—one in the Bekk'a Valley and another near Beirut.

Abu Nidal was dealt another blow by the fall of the Soviet Union. His rather substantial connections in Eastern Europe were revealed when the records of the East German Stasi and the Soviet KGB were opened up. His safe havens in Eastern Europe were taken over and general operations curtailed. But only curtailed. There is no evidence he is out of business in Eastern Europe, "any indication that ANO is totally disbanded would be naive," an FBI expert said.

With ANO operatives in the United States fund-raising may or may not be as crucial as it is with the IRA (Irish Republican Army), for example. Some CIA consultants say ANO doesn't need money, while State Department officials say it does. Among Zein Isa and his group, raising money was a major concern.

Palestinians living abroad certainly need the funds, especially those in the wretched refugee camps in Jordan and Lebanon. While Abu Nidal provides unlimited money to his pack of assassins, he allocates nothing to his committee overseeing the hundreds of thousands of Palestinian refugees and emigrés formerly run by Samir Darwish. What offices did Darwish administer? There are no ANO facilities for Palestinians dispersed throughout the world.

Despite this minimal funding for his committee, Samir Darwish was a powerful man. So powerful that the U.S. State Department wanted him arrested. Darwish served on two other branches of ANO government: the Central Committee and the Revolutionary Council. He traveled constantly and spoke frequently with Zein Isa and Isa's extended family.

Darwish, ironically, is a naturalized American citizen. Born Ali al Batma, he is also known as Abu Samra and El Weher,[*] he met Zein Isa's extended family when he was introduced to the Nijmehs in Albuquerque, New Mexico, decades ago. Since then, Darwish has lived in Los Angeles (1988); Paterson, New Jersey; Raleigh, North Carolina; Manhattan; and Puerto Rico. It is a mystery whether Samir's friendship with Zein Isa cost Samir his freedom or whether their alliance cost Zein his life. Whichever, Zein rejected everything to belong to Samir's violent secret society.

After the *Achille Lauro* hijacking in 1985, the PLO began working with the CIA to break up Abu Nidal. (They had been exchanging information since the 1970s.) The operation accomplished much, but ANO cells continued to proliferate. Some are "sleeper cells," dormant until the overseas leaders order an attack. While many Americans thought of Abu Nidal operatives lurking in the Middle East, Belgrade, Athens, and Madrid (one of their fronts for Western European operations), counterterrorist specialists realized that ANO had long penetrated the Western Hemisphere in Puerto Rico, Brazil, Venezuela, Peru, and the U.S. "We believe there is an ANO infrastructure within the United States," explained former FBI director of counterterrorism Oliver "Buck" Revell.

With the arrest of an upper-echelon leader like Samir Darwish in Lima, ANO's Latin American missions halted. Especially after agents seized papers listing members and future attacks. Mahmoud Atta, the master recruiter, had expanded his territory into the mainland U.S. and Latin America before he was jailed.

Ironically, had Atta not gone to Mexico City in 1987 to meet with Zein Isa, he might have eluded the authorities for years and consequently aided and abetted the growth of ANO in the continental United States. Photographs of Atta's meeting with Zein Isa and others were taken by the Israelis.

---

[*]ANO men, like Mafiosi, have numerous nicknames and aliases. Zein said, "I have a hundred names, plus the organizational one." Most are puns on Zein, which means "most beautiful" in Arabic. Other nicknames include El Helou (Sweet One), Abu Faisal (Father of Faisal), Aaraj (Lame One), The Crippled One, and Abul Banat (Father of Daughters).

The FBI has long been working on tracking ANO cells in the United States, but how widespread these cells are has yet to be made public. What is known is that sympathizers in Brooklyn, Chicago, Manhattan, Washington, D.C., Raleigh, Detroit, Paterson, Jersey City, Miami, Washington, Kansas City, St. Louis, L.A., Milwaukee, Cincinnati, and Puerto Rico were being watched carefully by the FBI, Secret Service, and various local police intelligence units. When the ANO collaborators went overseas, they may have been surveilled by the CIA, army and naval intelligence, and the NSA (National Security Agency), who monitors the satellites. The FBI has been the lead agency in counterterrorist intelligence.

ANO in America is said to function much like any multinational company: "Business reps" would establish a network of small stores in the Midwest, New York/New Jersey, and Los Angeles areas. As these corner grocery and liquor stores became profitable, the men could afford to open more shops—often buying existing stores in bad neighborhoods for as little as $25,000, which relatives and comrades could be brought in to run. Legal ownership is often impossible to ascertain. Whenever a new "business district" say in Lima, Peru was needed, leaders would fly there to see whether that store could support new members. As one cadre said, "If a man's family is starving, he won't be a good worker."

Think of a chain of family-owned stores without the infighting. In a communal culture, individual control of stock shares is unimportant. But the shops are a chain of sorts, because the owners loan or give each other money when necessary. "A cooperative association," Tawfiq Musa called it. Another advantage of working with a brother-comrade was that if one had to suddenly depart for two weeks in Lebanon, the brother could run the shop.

The organizational work ethic was strong. Tawfiq Musa explained, "The comrades who were with us in Iraq are on the executive committee today." His wife Hanan added, "If a person worked well, he will rise up." It is unclear whether Tawfiq was referring to Iraq during the time Abu Nidal moved his organization there, or whether this was during the Iran-Iraq war.

When these men had to make a business trip, they submitted their expenses and a full report of what they did and whom they saw. Like some business travelers, some considered womanizing a perk of their jaunts. As Zein bragged, "And it's my fault that I go to some woman in Greece and grab her?" (This conflicted with Abu Nidal's odd strain of puritanism. Not only did he constantly admonish his men to abide by a strict sexual code, technically adultery was a capital offense within ANO, and punishable by execution.)

Whenever a comrade needed to fly back to the home office in Damascus (or wherever it had been moved to), his boss would call ahead and tell whomever was picking up the traveler what he would be wearing. The two comrades would also link up by speaking in code. But unlike business colleagues, ANO contacts were forbidden by organizational rules to discuss their assignments. Only the cell's head was to be briefed afterwards. Real names were verboten.

Security was paramount, as in any large firm, to prevent closely guarded secrets from leaking to the competition—in this case, intelligence agents. Zein explained to a friend, "It's categorically forbidden to tell another person anything. One cell lost seventy-three people. . . . Everyone is being watched." Tawfiq yelled at Luie Nijmeh for making a phone call at Lod Airport. No one should have known he had even been in Israel. Worse yet, a comrade in the United States sent a fax to Israel that Luie was coming to the West Bank for a visit.

As a security precaution, ANO cells are kept small and each one only knows a little, so that if a cell is "rolled up," its members cannot talk. Similarly, when there is an assassination or bombing or kidnapping to be performed, ANO works in secret teams, each not knowing what the other is doing and not knowing who belongs to the other teams. One team stakes out the victim, another kidnaps him, a third team transports him to the fourth team, who guards him, and a fifth makes the ransom calls.

The major concern for ANO was infiltrators from the "competition." For example, Saif Nijmeh fretted about a friend in America whom he had heard was paid by Jordanian intelligence. (What governments often do is pay the agent's family living in that country so that the informant is not compromised per se.) Saif said, ". . . if he knew that we knew, he would leave town immediately. He knows we would kill him."

Another friend sounded so sadistic, he made the Mafia's treatment of snitches look gentle: "Torture, I swear to God, I'll make him eat him-

self. . . . I shall make them eat each other's meat before they die. I swear
to God I would cut their limbs and fry them, barbecue them, give them
each other's legs for dinner . . . feed them each other while they are still
alive. . . . I cut his nose and his ears and his mouth. . . . when he isn't
able to talk and is disfigured, this is the Palestinian leader who is an
agent, throw [him] at the side of the road and let the rats eat him!"*

As many American multinational corporations provide scholarships,
so did ANO offer financial aid for higher education—in medicine, engineering, whatever—to sons of members. Universities in Vienna,
Athens, and Madrid are among the choices Zein promised a nephew in
North Carolina preparing for college. Students on ANO scholarships
are said to lay the foundation for overseas spying.

As ANO copied American-style business practices, it also adopted
American political savvy. Tawfiq Musa exhorted his men to "raise the
consciousness of the masses." Tawfiq also borrowed American
rhetoric, telling his comrades: "Just like Kennedy said, 'Don't ask what
your country can do for you, ask what you can do for your country.' "

Like other grassroots groups, ANO asked members to discuss its
policies with trusted relatives, send them "campaign" literature, and
invite them to meetings. If they seemed interested, they were asked to
help with phone calls and fund-raising. What name should the fledgling
group use in the Midwest? During a meeting in Milwaukee, Tawfiq's
wife suggested al Nidal Association for Immigrants. No, no, no! shrieked
one member, that would not only scare off prospective members, it
would trigger surveillance by federal agents. How about the Association
to Assist the Needy in the Occupied Territories? he asked. No, no, no,
said Tawfiq, that would cause the PLO to investigate. In fact, like the
PLO, this ANO cell raised money to take to West Bank residents who
were out of work from business closings during the Intifada.

Overall, most Palestinians in Israel and the territories have long
despised Abu Nidal. By early 1994 their contempt deepened. Hamas,
the fundamentalist terrorist group, joined with secular ANO to subvert
the Israeli-PLO autonomy accord signed in September 1993. Hamas—
which proudly took credit for the early 1994 bombings of Israeli buses,

*Arabists say this harangue is merely boasting, that Arabs commonly speak in
hyperbole. Snitches are not tortured, they are routinely shot, while collaborators often
are axed to death in public.

killing and injuring schoolchildren—has terrorized many moderate, secular Palestinians by attacking PLO sympathizers as has ANO.

To thwart the peace process, Abu Nidal Organization again vowed publicly to assassinate Arafat. No one knows whether the attack will come in Arafat's old headquarters in Tunis or his new ones in Gaza, during a meeting in East Jerusalem or in Cairo. It could be anywhere.

Traditionally, ANO attacks have not been within Israel or the occupied territories, but there have been some. A seemingly small ANO attack on an Israeli civilian bus in a tiny West Bank village had ramifications across the globe:

Three cousins waited through a spring dusk, on April 12, 1986, in an olive grove near the ancient Arab village of Dir Abu Mishal. Their faces wrapped in *kaffiyeh*, they poked at a small bonfire by the side of the road. The men had planned this assault carefully, staking out the intersection five times. As the Israeli Egged bus came barreling toward the junction, one man stepped out of the dark, lit a Molotov cocktail, and hurled it on top of the bus.

A second man fired an Uzi at least sixteen times into the bus, shooting directly at the terrified passengers. The third man fired what sounded like an automatic revolver.

An Israeli student sitting in front yelled back to the other passengers, "Lie down!" As he turned back, a bullet hit him in the right shoulder. A second later the bus driver shouted, "I've been hit!" He fell back, dropping the wheel, which the sixteen-year-old boy grabbed. Working in tandem, the boy and the driver made it to Aaubd, an Arabic village.

The teenager begged for help, but the Arabs shrugged and walked away. Desperate, the boy flagged down a car—with yellow Palestinian license plates*—but the driver refused aid. In the next car, with blue Israeli plates, the boy joyfully recognized an acquaintance.

Surgeons were able to save the boy hero. But the twenty-eight-year-old bus driver died.

---

*Driving a car with blue Israeli tags through an Arab village can lead to stoning, while a car with Palestinian yellow plates can provoke assault in some Israeli quarters. It's safer to take a sharing taxi with the politically correct tags. Everything in the Holy Land is politicized: An Israeli cabdriver chided an American for wearing a Palestinian embroidered vest—such finery symbolized allegiance to those who murder little Jewish babies, he said.

By then, the Voice of Lebanon radio was broadcasting from Beirut, "The Abu Nidal Palestinian group has announced it used machine guns and Molotov cocktails . . . April 12, 1986, to attack a bus transporting Israelis."

In August a man from Dir Abu Mishal confessed to the bus terrorist attack. Then he ran toward the village well, shouting, "I'll take the secret with me to the grave," as he hurled into its depths.

The well was dry.

Police fished up the would-be suicide, a forty-three-year-old naturalized American. He and the second suspect—both cousins named Salah Hariz—were separated during interrogation to avoid later defense arguments that they concocted the story together to save themselves. Both told in videotaped confessions how the third cousin in the attack, Mahmoud Atta, had planned the incident. Atta had prepared the Molotov cocktail and threw it at the Egged bus that night, they said.

The second suspect, Salah Mohammed Hariz, described recruitment and training in ANO guerrilla camps: Atta had conscripted Hariz to ANO, Al Fatah the Revolutionary Council in 1984, in Puerto Rico. Atta had wanted Hariz to join because he was a naturalized American with an American passport who could go anywhere in the world for Abu Nidal.

Atta introduced Hariz to his recruiter, a man from East Jerusalem using the alias of Farid. Before Atta went to the West Bank for more "conscription," he sent Hariz for military training in Syria.

In June 1985 Hariz flew from New York to Amsterdam to Damascus, where he spent days writing a voluminous personal history, with the names and ages of all his relatives, for ANO's files. A requirement for new members, akin to filling out employment forms. Then Hariz and six students from the West Bank were driven covertly to a hidden guerrilla camp in the Bekk'a Valley in Lebanon. They trained on revolvers, hand grenades, M16s,[*] and Kalashnikovs[†] and learned to make Molotov cocktails. They rehearsed ambushes on moonless nights.

---

[*]The M16 is a military weapon, a small automatic rifle that was used in Vietnam.

[†]The Kalashnikov is the basic Russian automatic assault rifle. The Chinese copy of it is the AK-47.

Once trained, Hariz was given back his real American passport, plus two forged passports, and dispatched to the West Bank for active duty. Hariz rushed to Atta's house in Dir Abu Mishal. "I've been in Rome," Atta explained. "We've been ordered to carry out attacks in this area. I told them if they see anything about it on television, they'll know we've carried out 'the action.' " After eight failures at their first task, they began plotting the bus attack. When that was successful, Hariz said Atta flew to Switzerland to inform ANO leaders of their hit.

It was a year before Israeli intelligence, working with foreign agents, could track down Atta. And then, it would be across a sea, an ocean, and a continent.

Zein Isa seems to have unwittingly led the Mossad and the CIA to Mahmoud Atta.

CHAPTER EIGHT

The Girl Without a Country

FALL 1984   ST. LOUIS

Palestina slowly peered around the school in South St. Louis. The other kids at Dewey Junior High already knew each other, while she, the new girl, could barely speak their language. Her school counselor had sent her to the ESL class—English as a Second Language. Palestina noticed a thin fair-haired girl watching her. Sensing Palestina's loneliness, the girl walked over and introduced herself as Helena Mylanos.* She, too, was foreign-born, from northern Greece. Helena spoke three languages and Palestina four. The only one they had in common was rudimentary English.

Palestina had no motherland, no native tongue. Not yet twelve, she had lived in Brazil, Puerto Rico, the West Bank, and now St. Louis. Her father spoke Arabic to his friends, her mother Portuguese to her family, her Puerto Rican chums played games in Spanish, and her friends in Beitin sang songs in Arabic, which she had struggled to learn. Now she needed English to make friends. Despite leapfrogging from continent to continent, Palestina tested a year ahead of herself. She was enrolled in the eighth grade.

Palestina seemed to relish being uprooted like an army brat. This time her father had wanted to permanently emigrate and open a grocery store in the United States. He was not coming to America for any of the reasons the huddled masses waited stoically at Ellis Island: Not to escape religious persecution. Not for political freedom. Not for a better life for his brood. Unlike most Palestinians, Zein wanted his girls to live exactly as he had, albeit with more money. He did not encourage them to follow the American Dream and become what they wanted. They were to become wives and mothers. Period.

*Name changed at her request.

77

Why was he willing to leave his beloved homeland now when he had been a naturalized American for four years? All Zein told his wife was that he needed to leave the West Bank because the Israelis would not renew his work permits.

Zein and his ilk did not intend to become Americanized, joining the PTA and the neighborhood anticrime watch group. They made no plans to settle anywhere. Indeed, they were more like the nomadic Bedouin* grazing for a while here and there, and as their animals destroyed all the grass, folding up their tents and moving on. They talked of making enough money in America to return to the homeland one day and build their dream houses.

Zein, Maria, and their younger two daughters, Soraia and Palestina, had immigrated to St. Louis of all places, which has a small Arab population—5,000 in the five Missouri counties in and around the city—compared to the huge pools of Arabs in Detroit, for example. Zein claimed he picked St. Louis because he had three married daughters there—Mona and her half-sister Fayrouz, who had married brothers in the grocery business, and Leilah, who had recently wed a taxidriver from Beitin.

The husbands of Fayrouz and Mona had moved to St. Louis where they owned corner markets, as other Arabs had done throughout the Midwest, especially in Detroit. Many of these mom-and-pop shops were in ghetto neighborhoods, cheap purchases in the wake of white flight. Compared to other businesses, little English was needed to run a grocery or liquor store.

Those sons-in-law chose St. Louis because it held the largest community from Beitin (about 200) in the New World. Many of the villagers lived in new ranch-style houses in a northern suburb settled by the French called Florissant, while they worked in rotting inner-city neighborhoods with horrendous crime rates. The Isas were an exception; they also lived in a tough section of town. Had they gone home every night to safer surroundings, perhaps Zein would have been less obsessed with blacks and violence. Maria and Zein bought Alliance Market at the corner of 4200 block of Shaw Boulevard in South St. Louis. Zein's English was so poor twelve-year-old Tina translated the negotiations between her father and an American man named Flowers.

*From the Arabic word *bedu*, "to wander."

Neighbors claimed the Isas constantly violated health standards: Maria knocked bugs off the meat, onto which she would dab red food coloring. Maria and Zein sold cream cheese past the expiration date. The rice was loaded with weevils, and the back of the store was roach-infested. "The only things safe to buy there were soda, wrapped candy, and booze," one customer said.

But they, or at least Maria, did work hard. At seven A.M., Maria would unlock the shop doors and unpack boxes until seven P.M. in the winter and until nine in the summer. While there was little time for pleasure, Maria tried to drive out with her girls and see what St. Louis had to offer. Maria liked the city, visiting the Arch, Forest Park, and her favorite, the giant lily pads at Missouri Botanical Gardens, known colloquially as Shaw's Gardens, after its nineteenth-century benefactor. While Maria feasted her eyes on the verdant lushness of St. Louis, the six-story oaks, and five-story fragrant, flowering catalpa trees, and the jonquils and tulips along the highways, and appreciated the friendly Midwesterners, Zein was too busy or too ill to go sightseeing with his family. He suffered from diabetes, with its attendant disorders of the kidneys, heart, and circulation. Unlike other emigrés, he did not seek religious affiliation. His was not a familiar face at the mosque.

For Zein it was home-to-work-to-home-to-work, with few breaks for socializing and little time for anything except meeting with groups of Palestinian men as fanatical as he in their hatred of "the Jews." And like Zein, they were contemptuous of the United States for supporting Israel.

Americans were barbarians, he thought—a bunch of rowdy, promiscuous, bastard drug addicts, murdering each other with assault rifles. Too many were blacks who shot the immigrant grocery store owners. "So many Palestinians come back home in coffins, killed by inner-city blacks, that it looks like an epidemic over here," one Palestinian journalist remarked. Before the Intifada began in 1987, more Palestinians were killed in America by black criminals during robberies than were killed in the West Bank by Israeli soldiers, he added. If a Palestinian girl were to take up with a black boyfriend, it would be considered a family disaster.

Zein was typical in his racism. Like many Palestinian-Americans, he could not make it back home, so he had to live in an American slum with blacks from the housing projects and white trash up from the

Ozarks. With his conservative roots, he initially retained his sanity by isolating himself from what he saw as a dissolute society. But as he pulled inward, his soul festered into paranoia against blacks and Jews and Americans. More and more, Zein evoked the patriarchy he had left behind in Beitin. Not the village of the 1980s, but the one he had been raised in—or, to be accurate, the village he thought once existed. In reality Zein was as much an outcast from the emerging Palestinian society as he was from American culture. He belonged nowhere and was an immigrant everywhere.* He was an alien.

But Zein diligently followed those vengeful tribal taboos that had been fading away for more than half a century. And he tried to prepare his two youngest children for the time when they would return to the homeland and have to live under that code of honor. Soraia dutifully plodded along in the worn path of her father's traditions, while Palestina listened instead to the siren song of American youth.

Helena Mylanos, Palestina's chum, and their classmates immediately nicknamed the new girl "Tina." Tina and Helena began their best-friendship by practicing their musical instruments together, Tina loudly on the saxophone and Helena quietly on the flute. Emotionally opposite—one adventuresome, the other timid; one merry, the other melancholy; one resilient, the other fragile—Tina and Helena became lifelines for each other.

Helena frequently joined Tina at home for supper, which in the Isa household meant television, talking, listening to Arabic records, and enjoying platters of heavy, hearty food, sometimes simultaneously. The family would sit in the tiny dining alcove off the little kitchen where Tina had cooked, sautéing a fancy-shaped brown rice, then adding white rice, and frying chicken. "She could cook anything," Helena remarked in awe. Apple strudel, fettuccine Alfredo, lasagna. Maria and Soraia cooked infrequently.

---

*Zein was stereotypical of many first-generation emigrés, a Muslim Arab sociologist pointed out. Zein refused to assimilate, although Arab intellectuals of all social classes easily glide between different cultures. He refused to learn the language. He refused even to socialize with his neighbors, nor did Tina's sisters. This professor found the family's isolation from their neighbors abnormal. "How can they put down roots moving around like that? The big question is why?" Arab parents don't like changing school districts any more than Americans do, added a Palestinian graduate student, in St. Louis.

"Basically, Tina was a little slave" at home, Helena noted, and at Alliance Market where customers said the Isas overloaded the girl with heavy manual labor. When she wasn't stocking shelves in the store, Tina was baby-sitting her nieces and nephews. Tina was always help-ing people, especially children—carrying groceries upstairs for a neighbor, and slipping penny candy to her tiny tots.

What she was not was a good Muslim. "You know when those other Arab kids at school kneel and pray?" Tina confided to Helena. "I don't even know the prayers." Instead, in December, Tina passed out Christmas cards from a large stack to all her pals and teachers. To Helena and other friends, she gave small gifts. Tina adored American holidays and customs. A girl without a country, she adopted America. She desperately wanted to belong somewhere.

In her eighth-grade class photograph, Tina captures the eye with her blazing smile. In another group picture, she becomes the focal point by laughing. In the soccer team photo, she is up in front performing a split and beaming. Yet Tina was no show-off. She was so effervescent, everyone and everything gravitated toward her. By thirteen she had finished growing—to five-foot-four—and was a fully developed nat-ural beauty. Quite fully. She was Rubenesque compared to her gawky girlfriends.

Her classmates would marvel at Tina's energy. She still would be running laps around the basement gym with the girls' physical educa-tion class, while braced against the walls were the sagging bodies of classmates who could not keep up.

Despite her foreignness, Tina adapted quickly to junior high school. She loved math, languages, sports, and anything fun. Not keen on reading, she never picked up a book for pleasure and only thumbed through that bible of teenage girls, *Seventeen*. She and Helena and two black girlfriends would hit the movie theaters for the comedies.

Tina most relished a laugh on herself: As athletic as she was, surpris-ingly she also was a klutz. Their first time on ice skates, Helena caught on, while Tina flip-flopped about like a fish, laughing hysterically. She was still giggling when she fell on her ankle hard, so hard that the guard had to carry her out. Tina chuckled despite the pain that she had been so clumsy she had fractured her ankle.

The two friends did not spend the night together the way most teens do; Tina's parents were not familiar with that American custom. Zein, the quiet one in the family, forbade slumber parties and boy-girl parties. That would be shameful, he said. Good girls never sleep anywhere but with family; good girls are modest and don't dance with boys. But Maria was fun-loving herself and almost always approved the invitations, as long as there would be no liquor or drugs.

However, when Soraia went back to the homeland, Tina was basically grounded by her parents. She was not allowed to go out alone or with friends. "They felt Soraia was some sort of bodyguard," Helena commented wryly.

The Isas did relent on the dress code, allowing Tina, now in high school, and Soraia, who had already graduated, to wear jeans and makeup and to attend rock concerts. Tina's favorite bands were Poison (she would play over and over their song "Every Rose Has Its Thorn") and Bon Jovi (she loved their "Living in Sin"). Tina literally would "Never Say Good-bye," an old Bon Jovi song; instead, she would say, "See you," because she believed "good-bye" triggered bad luck. Tina and her family were quite superstitious. Perhaps rightly so.

Sometime in 1986, as Tina was developing into a popular high school freshman, a "witch" in the West Bank put a curse on Zein and Maria. "The witch wanted to tear our family apart," Tina's sister Mona explained. "Most people who do that are jealous." She recalled a case back home: Two girl cousins who were born hours apart grew very close. A third girl cousin bitterly resented being excluded. "Her mother made the girl go to a witch. The witch put a death curse on the two other cousins. The pair were taken to my brother [Faisal, the pediatrician] with shortness of breath, their hearts pounding. He could not figure out why they were sick. The mothers of the two close cousins took them to another witch, who removed the curse.

"Sometimes it takes years for a curse to work. A good spell from the heart can get the curse taken out. No one knows why a curse was put on my parents."

Curses carry considerable weight in the Middle East,[*] where charms and amulets to ward off the evil eye or to encourage conception are sold in bazaar stalls. And within the culture of the Isas, it is per-

---

[*]Cursing is a sophisticated system of retort, perfected during the Ottoman Empire, when the sultans employed a court curser to hurl maledictions at their enemies.

fectly rational. Nowadays, some educated Palestinians scoff at such things. Others are believers, much like Americans checking out their horoscopes in magazines.

"No matter how educated and modernized people are, they like to hedge their bets," said Professor Victor LeVine, a Middle Eastern political scientist at Washington University. "In the back of our minds lurks this atavistic sense that we're not the masters of our fate, that there is some angry deity we must appease. Like much in the Holy Land, contradictory things co-exist amicably. As the Red Queen said in *Alice in Wonderland*, 'I daresay you haven't had much practice . . . Why sometimes I've believed as many as six impossible things before breakfast.' "

About this time, Tina and Helena were sipping sodas one afternoon at Alliance Market when a black man came in, asking for Zein. Tina pointed him out. The two girls watched as the man offered to sell Zein a case of soap. "It's stolen," Tina whispered nonchalantly to Helena, who was shocked. Zein and the man bargained back and forth before concluding the deal.

Like many other poor, uneducated newcomers, Zein quickly learned the petty criminal street tricks. Feeling oppressed by loutish Americans who look down on them, some immigrants figure, Why not rip them off in return? As Zein said, "When you come to think about this, you can cheat all the people in American stores."

Tina never discussed the soap incident. Nor did she seem unduly worried about another criminal matter concerning her father. "He's not allowed back into the homeland," she confided to a classmate. "He's in trouble with the Israelis for some reason. He did something." She never said what or did not know. Her closest friends wondered.

Maria was driving to North County, with Zein beside her in the front seat; in the back were Tina, a soccer teammate, and Soraia. Maria drove to Dunn Road and Hall Street, to a Shoney's Restaurant, where Zein slowly eased himself out with his crutches. Inside were a group of Arab men.

Later, Tina explained matter-of-factly, "It's a meeting about the country, about the liberation of Palestine." Again, she said, "My father is in trouble with the Jews." Tina told another chum her father hung out with terrorists.

*   *   *

Seated on the sofa and chairs in the Isas' living room were men Tina
knew well, including her father's friend Hussein Karitti, his cousin
Tawfiq, and Saif and Luie, the husbands of her twin cousins. Tina
served them cardamom-flavored coffee ground from beans from the
homeland. Then she returned to the kitchen to bring in platters of
fruit* prepared by her mother and sister. As Tina wandered in and out,
her father was telling the men how he had eluded Israeli intelligence
officers while on an ANO mission. Tina had heard this tale before—
old Zein relished reliving his overseas escapades. To sneak past officials, Zein said he had come for gambling, dancing, and "to make fun."

Zein would bring along Tina or Soraia as cover on these "business"
trips and whenever he was stopped, Zein would say he was on a holiday with his daughter. Often the girls and their mother refused to go,
complaining about his trips and what he was doing. While Tina provided the best subterfuge, because she was a child, she was potentially
dangerous. No one knew what the spunky girl might blurt out to a customs official, who might be undercover Shin Bet.

One night before bedtime, Maria and Soraia sat her down in the living room to coach her about where she had stayed in Mexico and what
she had enjoyed there.

"But they don't ask!" Tina protested.

"But if they asked," Soraia lectured her little sister, "what are you
going to tell them? You don't know anything!"

But what she did know! That her relatives were involved in food-
stamp fraud, and worse. "One time he left for Venezuela. Do you know
what for?" Tina said to Mona. "Someone gave him something, like
your index finger, something the size of a pencil, plastic, wrapped very
well. Someone gave it to him here to take to Venezuela. Where did he
put it? In his throat? . . . Mother showed it to me, we tried to think
what is this thing—a drug, cocaine, a letter? What if he's caught and
this thing is on him? Won't he go to jail?"

---

*Arab hospitality is legendary. In the desert a guest faced dehydration and starva-
tion if his host did not provide succor. A man of honor is always hospitable and generous to guests. At minimum he offers small cups of strong coffee. The area around
Jerusalem is so dry that one must drink twelve glasses of water a day, plus all the tea
and coffee offered.

"Smelling the Air"

DECEMBER 1986   ISRAEL

At first it had been a game. Zein was arrested by "the pagans"—the Israelis—for questioning at Lod Airport outside Tel Aviv, in late 1986.

"Old man, where are you going?" Israeli security agents asked.

"Listen," Zein said, "I want to stay to watch cute ladies while I smoke a cigarette."

But they interrogated him for three hours, relentlessly asking him, "Why did you travel across the world to come here and then stay only two days?"

Each time Zein told the tale to his comrades, his detention grew longer, with the Israelis finally holding up the plane for four hours. The police told him it wasn't his looks but his talk that made him appear radical—"like . . . the blood-thirsty Abu Nidal." How Zein relished that little frisson of fear that accompanied his clandestine adventures.

He laughed each time he recounted his story, reliving how he played up his limp, how he conned other passengers into helping him. He "got the Jews." After the Israelis strip-searched him, Zein looked them in the eye and cracked, "There's one thing you left out."

"What's that?" asked the official.

"My ass," snapped Zein.

Zein loved traveling. In two years, he had been overseas fourteen times. "If I didn't go to smell the air, I'd go crazy," he was fond of saying. Yet, with his leg ulcerated by diabetes, Zein could not always follow the demands of Mahmoud Atta and Samir Darwish, who would phone him to leave immediately for Brazil, Amman, the West Bank, Madrid, or Athens. Between the fall of 1986[*] and spring of 1987, Zein

---

[*]Zein's U.S. passport shows the following activity over one three-month period: August 1, 1986, enters Madrid; August 2, leaves Madrid and enters Athens; August 15,

had flown to Caracas, had been to Israel twice, and had spent fifteen days in Athens, fifteen in London, and four in Zurich. There was a stopover in Paris and a jaunt to Madrid, where he finally hooked up with Atta.

The man-about-town loved Madrid, "bumming around" there with his son's in-laws (who later sent Zein leaflets describing terrorist attacks on three Israeli settlements on the West Bank). During this last trip Faisal's in-laws warned Zein he was being watched—from the airport when he landed to the hotel where he registered. It wasn't easy traveling, Zein told his comrades, with the myriad eyes of counterterrorists everywhere, always looking.

And for good reason. Abu Nidal Organization ran commercial operations in Spain as well as Eastern Europe. Most of these businesses were in armaments, which were quite profitable. The companies were quietly shut down in the late 1980s by the counterterrorism division of the U.S. State Department. That clobbered ANO financially: Despite ANO's millions extorted from various Middle Eastern despots, the organization really did need the money. Especially if it wanted to recruit Palestinians, many of whom needed subsidizing since the Intifada had shut down shops and schools.

Alerted through the Mossad and Shin Bet, Israelis began intense questioning of Palestinian-Americans caught trying to bring tens of thousands of dollars into the country.

Zein willingly underwent the annoyance and danger from the intelligence agents, he said, to help Palestinians mired in Lebanese refugee camps and those starving in West Bank towns. He turned over the donations from America to a committee in Beitin, an ANO front, that allocated the money to "the mothers of martyrs"—those killed fighting the Israelis. He continuously reminded his colleagues he could not say more. "My position is one of great secrecy."

Zein was always telling whomever he spoke with to "be careful—my phones at home and the store are dirty." When a cousin informed him that the FBI was listening in, Zein quipped, "We are honored."

---

exits Athens and enters Tel Aviv; August 27, leaves Israel and enters New York; October 26, enters Caracas; October 28, leaves Caracas; November 4, enters Madrid; November 6, leaves Madrid and enters Tel Aviv; November 13, leaves Tel Aviv and enters Madrid; November 14, exists Madrid and enters New York.

Yet, he and his relatives frequently discussed Abu Nidal terrorist attacks in Europe and the one in a West Bank restaurant, ANO conferences in Algeria, and details of the ANO hierarchy. A comrade reported to him how an ANO faction from Zein's town machine-gunned the American ambassador and his staff in Cairo, but no one was killed. "So, we didn't have the honor then," commented Zein, who when he was naturalized in 1980 had taken an oath to uphold the U.S. Constitution. That oath implies one will not perform seditious acts.

And if Zein and his nephew Saif Nijmeh believed the FBI was recording their calls, why did they propose attacks on American soil?

"We have exported numerous massacres in order to silence atrocities," Zein said.

Saif replied, "If we Arabs really want to hurt the American and Jewish interests abroad and here in America . . . if they want to commit criminal acts, they can place a bomb. . . . They [the Jews will] just howl, howl, howl."

Later that day Zein announced to a cousin, "I am one of the people who spread corruption on Earth. There is nothing left [to] be afraid of losing. . . . Let the world burn."

His daughters had long worried about Zein's ANO activities. He said he had been a member for twelve years, a hundred years, "a long time," while Maria had told her girls he had joined up about 1983. At a family party Mona argued with her father over his ANO membership. Abu Nidal promotes betrayal between fathers and their children, wrecking homes, she said.

To which Zein screamed in public, "Spit on you and your despicable family and those who don't defend the homeland!"

"He's crazy," Mona whispered later to her sister Soraia. "He'll get killed over this. It's beyond the law."

"My father is the dirtiest man I know," Soraia responded. "I swear, he's a liar." She explained she couldn't talk with him about Abu Nidal for fear he'd slap her in the face.

"I feel ashamed of him," Mona said.

Their eldest sister, Leilah, questioned her father as to why he wanted to be involved with Abu Nidal at all, adding that she did not approve. She preferred George Habash's Popular Front for the Liberation of Palestine (PFLP). Zein had attended a PFLP meeting in

Chicago with 3,000 attendees, including American intelligence agents. Comparing PFLP to ANO, he said, "Abu Nidal is the largest striking force in the world . . . organized in Washington, D.C., all over America, and in Europe . . . we are a power to reckon with.

"Abu Nidal Organization takes care of its own," he told her proudly. "If any member cannot feed his family, ANO will give him a monthly payment and fund his children's education. . . . If your husband is in battle, you will receive your living expenses."

"But what about your family and your store?" Leilah asked. "Every time they ask, you go. You leave my mother by herself [at the store]."

"Ah," Zein replied. "To liberate the country, oh Leilah, shit over the store and the house."

Zein hung up the phone one afternoon in early April 1987, and turned to his youngest, Tina. "Just a smell of fresh air, and I'll return after two days."

"What's this about?" Tina asked.

"Would you like to go to Mexico? We'll leave on Friday and return on Monday."

Tina was noncommittal. But Soraia interrupted. "By God, if you go, I also go." Soraia was still miffed that her father had traveled recently to Paris, London, Athens, and Madrid and had not brought her along. Her little sister was not going to vacation in Mexico if she could not.

Zein's old friend from Puerto Rico, Mahmoud Atta, had phoned him from Venezuela, April 3, 1987, asking him to meet in Mexico City later that month. Atta told Zein to bring his two teenagers. Expenses would be no problem. If you can't bring both, bring Palestina, Atta said, adding, but come—"the firm" needed an operable "store" by December.

Zein discussed with his older, married daughters which of the younger ones to take to "the most fearsome of the feared [who] is in Mexico." Fayrouz recommended Tina. Zein argued that she wasn't ready yet "for work." He would bring Soraia, who was mature enough. But his business trip "to open a store" in Mexico City did not coincide with her spring break. After protracted conversations about who would accompany him, Zein left alone to meet Atta at the Hotel Marine in Antonio Caso, near the Mexico City airport. His nephews, Saif and Luie Nijmeh, also flew down for the meeting.

Tina, who surreptitiously eavesdropped on these conversations, wondered aloud to her sister what it all meant. "Atta told Mom that they needed Dad, and all that stuff."

This meeting was an important one: Atta gave his underlings a set of "taskings" to perform back in the States. Zein Isa and Saif and Luie Nijmeh were to raise money for ANO through fraud, theft, and extortion. They were to smuggle the funds abroad to finance terrorist operations. To transfer ANO members around the world, Zein, Saif, and Luie were to lie to U.S. Customs and apply for passports under various names. Tawfiq Musa, Zein's cousin from Beitin who now lived in Kenosha, Wisconsin, near Milwaukee, had men who could readily make up fake driver's licenses and other documents. Last, Atta wanted his soldiers to compile information on Jewish groups in America that might be vulnerable to attack. Overseeing these taskings would be Tawfiq.

Unbeknownst to the participants, a photograph of their business conference was taken by the Mossad.

A few days after his meeting, Zein called his wife from Mexico City to pick him up at Lambert-St. Louis Airport on April 26. He and the others all arrived home safely and returned to their jobs.

Mahmoud Atta did not. Zein Isa never saw him again.

While she loved to visit foreign cities, Tina found excuses not to accompany her father on his trips. And unlike the rest of the family, Tina was uninterested in Middle Eastern politics. She did not want to live in Beitin, where if you do something different such as wearing sunglasses at high noon, everybody ridicules you, saying, "Oh look, she thinks she's an American."[*]

The problem was that Tina thought of herself as American or hyphenated-American, not as Arab.[†] She begged Soraia to bring her a Swatch watch from a stopover in Europe, when Soraia went to the homeland for a three-month visit. Soraia, who had not known what a Swatch was, complied and brought back a black, white, and red Swatch for her sister. Thrilled to be like the other kids, Tina constantly wore it.

Like her peers at school, Tina daydreamed about a career. By the

[*]If a teenager wears sunglasses on the West Bank, it's a safe bet he or she is Israeli or American; Arab kids squint.
[†]Palestinians usually refer to themselves as Arabs.

time she was in eighth grade, she knew what she wanted: to fly. At first, she wanted to be a flight attendant so she could travel worldwide, but in high school she discovered that women could fly, and raised her sights to becoming an airline pilot. Focusing on her goal, she took four years of French so that she and Helena could travel to Paris. Tina intended to study aeronautical engineering at Parks College, at St. Louis University. "She just wanted to fly, period," Helena explained.

To Tina, marriage and motherhood were way off on the horizon. "I'm not getting married till I'm thirty. If I ever have a baby, I'm naming it Alexis."

"After that guy you had a crush on in Puerto Rico?" Helena giggled.

Tina whooped with laughter. "Yep—boy or girl, it's Alexis."

Maria saw the struggle Tina was having between the culture at home and the one at school. Tina had spent less time in Beitin than her sisters had, less time to absorb *fellahin* mores. And being the youngest, she was less apt to follow tradition. Maria had tried to not interfere with the Americanization of Palestina. She yelled at Tina only once about her appearance, the summer after her freshman year when the girl chopped a section of hair above her one ear so short it looked like a buzz cut.

Tina was still the devoted daughter and a constant delight to her sick father. Zein's diabetes was making him ill with high blood pressure. Unable to perform physical work at the market, he would stand around, telling jokes in English or complaining, "This life is bullshit." By afternoon he would be leaning against the freezer at the store, so ashen-faced he looked like a corpse. Then Tina would charge in, cheeks flushed from sports practice, and he would come alive and smile and hug her. Zein always gave her a big kiss on her cheek after not seeing her all day. Sometimes, when the pain in his injured foot was so bad he had difficulty walking even with a cane, Zein would stay home and lie on the sofa. Tina would cuddle up beside him and together they would watch soccer games, discussing the plays. He would talk with her and be affectionate; yet, to Tina's friends, he seemed aloof, even secretive.

On her dresser Tina kept a treasured photograph of her father when he was about twenty. "Doesn't he look handsome?" she would ask Helena.

As much as she adored her father, after she turned fourteen Tina began to rebel. She had no intention of stunting herself to fit Zein's ideal of an obedient Palestinian girl. Zein complained when she took to wearing a lot of black—as many preteens and teens did at that time in St. Louis—even to an Arab party where the other girls and women dressed in traditional Palestinian embroidered gowns. "Do you belong to some satanic cult?" he screamed in disgust.

She and Zein began to fight openly in front of outsiders at the grocery store. "No!" she screamed at him as she walked out one day, knowing he was too crippled to follow. She was marching off to a friend's house when Maria drove by and ordered her into the car. No, Tina was adamant. Maria hopped out, grabbed her by the neck, and while choking her, pushed Tina into the car.

The next day Tina walked through the school corridors with big bruises on her neck. Despondent, she admitted to her friends, "I had the chance to get her off of me and kick her in the stomach. But I don't care anymore. I want to die."

At first Tina would report such incidents in passing to a friend as if they had happened to someone else. Her way of coping was to ignore her angst and focus on having fun as an antidote. She could wring enjoyment from the most mundane activity: One rainy afternoon, Tina and Helena were walking to Tina's when they became soaked. Tina could change at home, while Helena would soon be shivering. Tina saw a laundromat, dragged Helena inside, forced her to strip, and tossed Helena's damp clothes and tennis shoes into a dryer. A few minutes later, the two went on their way, laughing about their latest adventure.

Tina was one of those golden kids who appear destined for all the good things American life has to offer. She was beautiful and bright, with an ebullient personality. Her character was one of loyalty and diligence. Best of all, she possessed depth and compassion and was without malice. Without politicking, she went out of her way to be kind to others. She coached foreign students struggling with the idiosyncrasies of English grammar. She undertook training to go to lower-grade classrooms and talk about teen pregnancies. By the time she was an upperclassman, Tina was into the gamut of activities—Spanish Club, the yearbook staff, student council, the National Honor Society, tennis, and soccer.

Tina had everything, including the terminal jealousy of her three older sisters. Especially Soraia, who shared a room with her.

CHAPTER TEN

The Arrest
of the Bridegroom

APRIL 1987   CARACAS, VENEZUELA

Mahmoud Atta picked up his bags at the Caracas airport after his flight from Mexico City. As he went through Venezuelan customs and immigration, he noticed the authorities were treating him differently. He worried, there had been no problem earlier when he had left for Mexico City using a forged U.S. passport—number 5821861, under the name of Mahmed El Abed Amed El Abed. He could have flashed his real American passport, but that would have been too dangerous. Knowing he was being watched, Atta spent a sleepless night in his apartment in Valencia, a suburb of Caracas.

On April 27 the Venezuelan police burst in. They handcuffed Atta and took him to the station, where they continually interrogated him. Two interviewers spoke Hebrew to each other, which led Atta to believe they were Israeli. The Venezuelan police confirmed this was not just an illegal passport case, and an FBI agent arrived, telling Atta he was there to protect his rights as an American citizen. Atta had no idea why he had been arrested.

After five days in a Latin American jail, Atta was handcuffed and dragged from his cell and packed into a car, with a policeman on either side of him. The police refused to tell him where he was being taken. The car stopped at the Tarmac of a Pan American jumbo jet. The Venezuelan police walked him to the ramp to the plane. Waiting at the top were three FBI agents.

As the jet reached Kennedy Airport, the FBI read Atta the charges against him. Sirens wailing from the police escort, half a dozen agents drove him to the FBI office in Manhattan.

*   *   *

"INTERNATIONAL TERRORIST CAPTURED," read the headline in a Caracas newspaper about the arrest. *"Chief of Operations for Abu Nidal in North America,"* reported a smaller headline. The story said Atta had directed the attack at Dir Abu Mishal. Stacks of documents seized by police included precise instructions for future terrorist attacks: to purchase heavy and light weapons, to gather details about Zionists in Venezuela, to recruit couriers as well as comrades to carry out attacks, and to procure passports through theft and false documentation. "It is important to note that this terrorist of international stature was linked to other international terrorists . . . [who] were accustomed to asking his expertise . . . [about] his speciality of acquiring false documents," wrote reporter Freddy Urbino. Atta had been working in Venezuela for the last year, according to the newspaper.

"Remember the bridegroom who invited you to the wedding?" Tawfiq Musa cryptically asked Zein during a phone call. "After he invited you, the groom was thinking about visiting you. On the way, the groom ran into a problem. Those wedding cards that you have," Tawfiq ordered, "throw them all away. Immediately. The phone numbers, anything like that you have memorize them and pitch them."

Tawfiq had reason to be anxious: Zein had a copy of Atta's little black book, a notebook listing members' names, addresses, and phone numbers. It was too late to worry about other incriminating documents for when Atta was arrested, Venezuelans had seized his letters, "all signed by true names," and given them to the FBI.

While Tawfiq was circumspect discussing Atta, Zein was indiscriminate: He told one daughter that Atta had masterminded the bus attack at Dir Abu Mishal. Tawfiq cursed his cousin for his lack of discretion, while Saif defended him, saying, "the old man's just proud." Tawfiq had reason to be anxious about Zein's spoutings. He believed federal agents were tailing them; Tawfiq and others had spotted the feds lurking outside Zein's apartment. One relative suggested they hire an attorney to sue the FBI.

Saif fretted about hiding the weapons he and his brother Luie owned—a brown automatic machine gun, rifles, pistols, and a knife. He called Sausan four times and contacted Leilah's husband by beeper to hide all the guns. Saif complained the machine gun was registered, but now the FBI wanted his Uzi. "I don't have no fuckin' Uzi," Saif screamed, but the FBI insisted informants had seen him with one. Saif felt harassed by the Bureau. He thought someone was watching him, someone was following him, someone might kill him.

But Saif was tougher than some G-man. "I'm not afraid. . . . If I catch one of the motherfuckers, I'll insult his mother."[*]

Counterterrorist experts were convinced that this ANO cell possessed sophisticated battle weapons. For what purpose? The group's tapped conversations were not specific, but apparently these Palestinians were storing rocket-propelled grenade launchers, known as RPGs,[†] somewhere in St. Louis.

A friend told Saif how he had hidden some RPGs in the ceiling above a store and could wipe out the nearby Ninth District Police Station. A comrade remarked how Saif Nijmeh sold him heavy weapons so they could "organize a resurrection [sic]. . . . He [Saif] also recommended 1988 Jeeps equipped with all weaponry."

It was too late for the gang to bomb the police. The FBI had bugged the phones and walls of Saif, Luie, Tawfiq and Zein along with those of other ANO suspects nationwide. After the men reminded each other they were under surveillance, they endlessly analyzed news, gossip, and feelings more than any group of seventh-grade girls at a slumber party. And they repeated themselves over and over in Arabic and English slang: Five-minute conversations about which plane to take to Bogotá to save $50—or whether to fly KLM to Amsterdam and Athens, or Delta directly to Athens. Using the same travel agency— Sinbad Travel in Chicago—was another tip-off to law enforcement.

The cell spoke about Atta in metaphors a Cub Scout could decipher: "The man in the jar," "The man in the hospital," "The mosque that needs repair." Six months after Atta's arrest, they had raised only $1,000 for Atta's defense lawyer Ramsey Clark, whose fee of $63,000 was small considering the complexity of the case. Zein alone contributed $300. Hussein Karitti—a friend from Puerto Rico who lived in Jersey City and later Manhattan—claimed it was wasted money. Stiff the lawyer, Hussein said, give the cash to Atta's wife and five kids back in the homeland.

---

[*]A verbal sexual slur about someone's mother is considered the ultimate of insults in the Arab world.

[†]RPGs are Russian-made portable rocket launchers about four feet long. Resting on the collarbone, they are heavy-duty, shoulder-fired weapons similar to bazookas.

To raise money for ANO, Luie allegedly turned to dealing narcotics, or narco-terrorism, as the feds call it. Abu Nidal is known for massive drug distribution to finance his campaigns. Luie bragged in late 1987 about going to Chicago to sell "juice" (cocaine). While driving one night in late 1992, Luie was arrested and charged with possession of 150 grams of coke, or about 1,500 hits with a street value of $7,200. More than seven hits is high enough to carry charges of drug trafficking. Were they bringing it in from Puerto Rico, a new drug haven? Or from Miami?

Luie told the cops he had just had his Mercedes repaired and the workmen had left the bag of coke in the backseat.[*] Even his lawyer and the judge laughed.

No one was laughing four months later when Luie's impounded Mercedes had not been returned. Luie's attorney called the police again and was told the FBI had just seized the car under drug forfeiture laws. No one explained why until April Fool's Day 1993.

Luie was thrilled when Tawfiq ordered him and Zein to go to the Middle East. He could not wait to salt the West Bank with revolutionary pamphlets and money. A friend suggested more ambitious plans: Blow up the Israeli Embassy in Washington, D.C. The comrade had a number of Arab friends whose stores they could use for practice. "Bring the bombs. . . . I'll do it, I swear," Luie promised.[†]

Zein was more grandiose. He told Luie's wife, Sausan, "Let's teach them how we hit people and slaughter! . . . If they [ANO] would mobilize the trained youth . . . they could slaughter three thousand Jews in

---

[*]Luie was as vainglorious as Zein and not as intelligent. He called his business trip to meet Samir Darwish in Israel "a paid vacation. I've been working for the boss for a year now and got two weeks vacation." Tawfiq gave Luie a box of cigars—Luie was to smoke one so that Samir could recognize him at Lod Airport in Tel Aviv. But Luie lost the box when he changed flights in Amsterdam and was too cheap to buy another for $15. Once he landed in Tel Aviv, Luie was to look for a tall, thin man—Samir. But Luie, tall himself, looked only for someone taller. Finally, Samir found him. This cell sounds like the gang that couldn't catch a plane, let alone blow one up. But the same was said about the group that dynamited the World Trade Center, especially the fool who returned to collect his van rental deposit, claiming someone had stolen the vehicle.

[†]Luie obviously had never been to the embassy, where even someone with an appointment must clear three sets of guards, the last of whom has acquired a dossier and photograph of the guest. A couple living near the embassy says they needn't lock their doors at night because there are cops literally hiding in the bushes.

America. . . . Let them go to their prayer in their temples and their churches, and kill them with machine guns."

Oval-faced, with a camellia complexion and chocolate velvet eyes, Sausan's comeliness belied her ugly heart. When told how armed Zionist settlers were scaring Palestinians, she proposed, "We have our men here in America . . . kill two hundred Jews here. Let 'em kill ten of them [Jews] here and you'll see if any Jew'll dare kill another Palestinian."

Apparently, Sausan and her relatives failed to see the irony in voicing anti-Jewish sentiments while wearing Levi's. Some of her countrymen chant anti-American rhetoric while wearing leggings, jeans, T-shirts, and running shoes, all made in America.

Although cruel toward his enemies, Zein demonstrated the same compassion to his fallen comrades as do trained soldiers during wartime. Zein would leave no one behind, especially his former leader Atta, saying, "The mosque will be ruined if no one cares about it" and, "I am committed to the preacher's instructions until death." Zein's generosity extended to another friend hunted by the Israeli police for killing a settler. "This man is our man; he is from our group . . . We must come up with money to help. . . . I am ready to kneel until I'm bankrupt." Zein lived up to his name of Most Beautiful of the Believers: He truly believed in the organization and cared for its people. In his mind he was a patriot, a martyr. "There are many problems, but when one considers that the homeland has rights . . . that supersedes everything."

Zein added prophetically, "There's a complacency I can't understand. [It's] as if the leadership just trains the individual and throws him abroad and then they want nothing to do with him."

Zein and Hussein distrusted each other. When Tawfiq Musa suggested using the old man to courier letters too dangerous to mail to the Middle East, Hussein said Zein was a risk because he was known worldwide. "But he's enthusiastic to a level unimaginable," Tawfiq protested. Send him, Hussein said, but he won't return; he'll be arrested at the airport, for intelligence agents had seen him in Mexico City with Atta. In fact, let Zein go, Hussein advised, but distance yourself—neither of us should take responsibility.

Tawfiq was astonished. How did Hussein know this? Hussein refused to explain, saying only that foreign intelligence had dossiers on both Zein and Tawfiq; that when Atta was arrested, intelligence agents had seized his papers outlining plots to destroy embassies, which led to the arrests of three other men. Atta was known worldwide, Hussein said, various countries had set a trap for him.

Besides Hussein Karitti, Zein lacked faith in overboss, Samir Darwish. Samir was forever promising to wire expense money from a Madrid bank through Tawfiq's account at First National Bank of Wisconsin in Kenosha, or through Zein's at Boatmen's Bank in St. Louis, but nothing was ever transferred. Samir, at least, tried to help Atta.

Samir wanted Zein to fly to Athens in April 1988 to discuss "the mosque." From there, Zein would go to Israel and Lebanon to funnel $25,000. Samir wanted Zein to bring Tina or Soraia along as cover, but the girls refused, saying they were busy.

Samir would await Zein in his hotel near the Athens airport and seaport. If they missed each other, Zein would relay information through Maria to Samir. (When Zein called his wife, he displayed no feeling, never asking how she was, never calling her by any endearment. When Maria said, "I miss you," Zein replied, "How are my grandchildren?")

The next leg of the trip was arduous. With all the strikes and road closings, Zein could not give Atta's wife in Dir Abu Mishal the donations from America. The Israelis followed him everywhere, accusing him of smuggling in large sums of money to incite riots and warfare. The brave revolutionary was terrified he would be caught and tortured. When he departed, the Mossad detained him, questioning him about people from Beitin living in St. Louis. Zein tensed up when an agent hopped on the plane with him, trailing him all the way to Athens, where he watched Zein change to a jet bound for America.

At home at last, Zein was not greeted with a hero's welcome. Damn you, Tawfiq rebuked Zein. I've had complaints from twenty men that you blab about your trips and brag about the money you're paid. Keep our secrets to yourself. Zein was in disgrace.

Yet Zein confided details of this trip to his daughter Mona: He had brought in $25,000 in cash and checks to Lebanon and the West Bank to arm the revolutionaries. He had met with ANO leaders in Lebanon.

"What did you do with all the money?" Mona asked.

"Let me tell you, this is a secret—we are not supposed to—" Zein began.

But Mona interjected, "America is the money country," she said.

CHAPTER ELEVEN

El Peru Pilgrims

Zein fumbled for the ringing phone. He wasn't fully awake, it was only 8:30 A.M. At first he barely understood what his leader was saying. Samir Darwish was urging, leave today, meet me at El Concord Hotel in Lima, Peru. Samir had long hinted at a "pilgrimage." Before Christmas 1987, he had called from Bogotá, asking Zein to fly down, but the old man had pleaded that his leg was in a cast. Now, six months later, Samir tried again.

"I may go smell the air in Lima," Zein boasted afterwards, his Technicolor swashbuckling fantasies playing in his mind.

Samir was busy that day phoning Tawfiq Musa and the Nijmeh brothers, asking them to fly down as "pilgrims," too. Samir asked Saif three times if he knew anyone in Peru as Zein did to use as intermediaries. And bring a Sony multi-band, eleven-channel, medium-sized radio, please, Samir asked. In all his calls Samir dialed from coin phones on the street, never trusting a private line, never wanting to give out his phone number.

The next day the lengthy plans continued, with Zein repeating his itinerary like a mantra: He would bring along his nephew from Raleigh, North Carolina, then fly to Puerto Rico and then Lima.

Tawfiq warned Samir, "Keep the old man here. Don't move him. He has a loose tongue and talks too much. Don't even phone him. He may cause you personal troubles." Tawfiq had already tried advising Zein to memorize all important numbers and flush them down the toilet.

"Oh my God," Samir said. "I have an agreement with him."

"Using the old man involves a seventy-five-percent risk," Tawfiq warned.

As if to prove Tawfiq's point, Zein meanwhile was describing insurrections within ANO leadership to his nephew in Raleigh.

Four days later, after numerous calls, travel arrangements through Sinbad Travel in Chicago were complete for Tawfiq, Zein, and Saif and Luie—Samir referring to Saif and Luie as the "fat man" and the "thin man," respectively. Samir ordered Tawfiq to bring his address list, a plate of hors d'oeuvres to whet the appetite of any FBI agent listening in.

And just in case a spook wanted to bug their hotel rooms, the men constantly called home to relay messages: Zein called Soraia from Lima and told her that if Samir phoned, he was in the Hotel Concord, room 1006. Maria repeated the information to Samir later that day. The next day, Zein called Sausan and left his whereabouts so she could give that to Luie when he checked in with her. Then Saif called and told Sausan that Luie was at Calle Chácria, Cicero area, and his phone number there was 229-140. After which Zein phoned Sausan, who repeated the data to him. Tawfiq told his wife Hanan how much he owed at his hostel and to please relay that and his phone number to Samir, who phoned Hanan ninety minutes later. Saif called his wife, asking her to tell Samir or Luie that he was at Hotel St. Martin, room 31, 285-337.

Saif wanted his wife, Ahlam, to join him in Lima as a cover—she could even bring their two children. "Is it very, very important?" Ahlam asked. "Can you not take care of yourself without me?" Saif answered, "We want you to come, but if you can't, tell the man you can't. Are you afraid?" he asked gently. Ahlam told him, "This business is scary. I don't know what to do." Saif also asked Ahlam to phone ANO members in Manhattan and Miami with requests to ante up money they owed him.

So far, the trip had been "one hundred percent success," as Tawfiq liked to say. Samir had given Luie money and mail to deliver to the West Bank villages. On July 13 Saif had met with Samir about buying a new store. They were to meet again the next morning.

But Samir did not arrive on July 14 or thereafter, and Saif did not know where he was staying. None of them did.

Two days later, a mysterious man from somewhere in the Middle East called Zein with some news: Samir had been jailed. Zein who had returned to St. Louis was to hire a lawyer for him and bring Saif back immediately. There was much danger. Zein tried but could not find Ahlam.

Nearly three hours later, an older Palestinian woman phoned Ahlam. "So how's Saif?" she asked.

"Oh, in Peru," Ahlam said, chuckling. "You know his business. What can we do? I don't tell anyone about Saif. I don't know why I'm telling you."

"Don't they go to Peru for training?" the older woman asked, adding, "there's something going on there now . . . do they pay him?"

"Where else could he get the money? He doesn't have a job," Ahlam sighed. She worked part-time and received welfare. (It is doubtful that she declared money received from ANO on her food-stamp application.)

By the next morning, Zein had phoned Ahlam and she reached Saif. "Take the first plane out."

"I don't have the money to pay the hotel bill," Saif grumbled. "Have Zein call me right away." When Zein told him Samir had been captured, Saif was angry. Why didn't he know when he had been there for four days?

Zein tried to wire Saif the money for his hotel, but all the banks were closed that day. Saif did not care; he was leaving anyway.

Zein's anonymous call had come from a man with the nom de guerre of Osama Abu al Adhama, "the Dark One." Osama spoke with Saif after his return and said that a relative would come to St. Louis to bring what was needed to recoup their losses. But nothing could be regained. Another of their leaders was jailed, and counterterrorism agents now possessed incriminating ANO records, including copies of the airline tickets of Zein, Saif, and Luie.

"The business of stores in South America is not working out," Zein told Tawfiq, who replied bitterly, "The man slaughtered us good. . . . May his God be cursed."

Through electronic surveillance, U.S. intelligence agents had discovered that Samir Darwish was meeting in Lima with another Palestinian who had settled there and married a Peruvian woman with whom he had a family. That information made the State Department suspect that ANO had planted this second man in Peru for a long-term operation. There was also a third man meeting with Samir and ANO's plant.

During their arrest police seized automatic guns and personal papers. And what was in those papers! Documents describing how ANO was to bomb the American embassy, the Israeli embassy, and

other international Jewish organizations. When the U.S. State
Department learned this, its officials asked the Peruvian police to continue detaining Samir and the other two men. But for some unknown
reason, Peruvian authorities let them go. Today, what happened to
Samir Darwish is classified information.

Again Hussein Karitti immediately knew details of the arrest—
Samir and two students, one Colombian, one Puerto Rican, had been
nabbed on the street. And a fourth man, from Ecuador, was somehow
involved also in Samir's Lima operation. That Samir and the others
had been caught by counterterrorist agents was no suprise.

"They set a trap for him, the man is well known. He may have been
known a long time. He is known as El Peru," Hussein bitterly told
Tawfiq. "They" were the Mossad, Hussein believed, who had wanted
Samir since his birth, who had recently destroyed his new house in the
West Bank and who had been following him from Madrid. They had
concentrated their manpower on getting Samir.

The spies had given newspapers a list of all Samir's aliases over his
lifetime as well as information about his various ANO missions and his
Egyptian, Algerian, and Lebanese passports. Hussein also knew all
about the documents Samir had been carrying. Hussein claimed he
had gleaned all his information from CNN and from Spanish- and
English-language newspapers in Lima. Was he lying? Hussein had
been in Peru when Samir was caught, and had fled to Israel, where, as
he said, he kissed the Holy Land upon his arrival.

Did it not occur to Zein, Hussein, Tawfiq, any of them, that there
was an odd coincidence that both Mahmoud Atta and Samir Darwish
had been arrested just after meeting with Zein and his nephews? Just
after making numerous phone calls about where to meet in foreign
cities to Zein's phone, which they believed to be "dirty?" Surely
Hussein Karitti, who lived in New Jersey and Manhattan, knew about
the "pilgrimages." When asked whether the phone taps on Zein provided the leads to tracking down Atta and Darwish, or whether it was
Hussein, too, the FBI says, "No comment."

Tawfiq Musa was holding an hourlong organizational meeting January
14, 1989, in which he reiterated the need for secrecy about Abu Nidal,
whom he constantly mentioned by name. Recruiting members was to
be done, Tawfiq explained, by strengthening relations with the people

you could trust—your closest relatives. These were the men to add to the membership lists to receive mailings of brochures, these were the ones you could ask to help with the typing, to come to the next meeting. Never, never, talk about the group with someone you didn't know, he warned.

We have enough trouble as it is with informants, snitches, and collaborators, Tawfiq said, let alone all the intelligence agents watching us. Indeed, one comrade had turned out to be with Jordanian intelligence and had turned over lists of prospective Abu Nidal members. This was a clandestine group, "therefore, the most important thing you must commit yourself to is secrecy."

Betrayal was a constant concern, Tawfiq said. Their organization had been founded on betrayal: In 1947 their land had been given to the Zionists; in 1974 "Arafat betrayed our trust. Our goal is to liquidate Arafat from the minds of our people." Liberating Palestine from the Jews would be the birth of Arab Unity, true Arab Brotherhood. ANO would become an example to the other Arab governments of all for one and one for all.

"What we make is not ours," chimed in another member during this meeting. "It is written on the wall, 'Whatever is left over after your needs and expenses belongs to the freedom fighters.' "

And remember keep this all secret, Tawfiq ranted. "Secrecy is the most important thing." This was "an armed struggle against the imperialism of the Americans, the Zionists, and the imperialistic presses, who have an alliance."

Tawfiq reminded his men again, "Don't ask what your country can do for you, ask what you can do for your country."

During these meetings no one discussed the number of members in the Midwest or on both coasts. But others were said to run ANO in Puerto Rico, overseeing about twenty-five to thirty men in about eight cells or groups. "But Puerto Rico is a drop in the ocean," one man proclaimed. "Here [in the U.S.] is the field where the chance for activities exists."

Living in the United States and being self-employed provided an opportunity to cheat on their taxes, which authorities believe was widespread among Zein and his ilk: On Zein's 1988 tax return, listing himself, Maria, and two dependent children, he stated that his net earnings from Alliance Market were less than $15,397. His total gross, he said, was $16,100; gross receipts were $57,205 and the gross profit, $21,844. And that was just his federal tax return. All of the men could cheat on various state and city taxes, too. The money saved could be plowed back into ANO, sometimes by sending funds to Latin American banks, where it could be withdrawn to buy arms in the Middle East.

Zein was still traveling and talking. When Tawfiq learned how Zein had been bragging he had been paid to go to Mexico to meet Atta who gave him $4,000 to bring back a tape, Tawfiq lectured him again and again about secrecy. As always, Zein repented hysterically and spent a week moping, lamenting how he had been "frozen out." As always, Tawfiq softened.

Tawfiq, however, was in trouble. A relative of Mona's husband warned that Jordanian intelligence officers had interrogated a comrade about Tawfiq, and the other men in his group. The investigation seemed to center on Puerto Rico, where Tawfiq often traveled. Worse yet, a recently detained operative reported the Israelis had issued a notice barring Tawfiq and another member from entering the West Bank after the Shin Bet discovered Tawfiq's name during an investigation. The friend closed the conversation with, beware, your phones are probably tapped.

Tawfiq seems to have ignored the warnings. In early 1989, when he arrived at the airport in Tel Aviv, the Israelis threw him in jail for several weeks on charges of belonging to the ANO. Tawfiq's cohorts blamed Zein's big mouth for the trouble. Indeed, Zein had announced proudly that Tawfiq was "from my Abu Nidal group," and went on to name other members.

With their leaders Mahmoud Atta and Samir Darwish both imprisoned, Tawfiq's group was temporarily lost. Osama Abu al Adhana, who had tipped off Zein, wanted to replace Samir's lost Lima project—although it would cost a lot of money to "reopen the store," he said. Osama wanted to use Arab passports instead of American ones and promised to send some to Tawfiq. He also preferred his men use driver's licenses issued from Arab countries. Osama asked Tawfiq to send someone to "smell the air" in the Middle East.

Tawfiq was reluctant to send Zein after his disastrous trip in 1988. He not only divulged too much, the old man was terrified of being beaten. What if he were arrested at the airport as a friend had been? Zein wailed. At least that man had "nothing in his stomach or up his backside"—that is, drugs or letters or contraband such as gold. And Tawfiq had to nag Zein constantly to write up his travel reports— whom he had seen, where he had gone, what he took over. Zein had never finished writing up his business trip to Turkey. Cross, Tawfiq dispatched another comrade to the Middle East.

Hurt and angry, Zein confronted Tawfiq. People were whispering, especially in St. Louis, saying he had been kicked out of the group, that ANO had suspended his membership for two years.

"Did you make this news that I am frozen out?" he asked.

"No, no," said Tawfiq, who was genuinely shocked.

"That's what makes me go crazy. It must mean I've fallen," Zein said miserably.

Empty talk, his cousin commented. But privately he said Zein was wrong but too stubborn to admit it. The word on the street was that everybody knew Zein belonged to the cell. As Luie said, "Nothing is secret about Abu Faisal. Everybody in town knows everything he does."

Tawfiq tried reprimanding the old man again. Before Thanksgiving, he yelled, "People have a bad impression of you. Contain your emotions."

Tawfiq held Zein responsible for many of the group's problems, and there were many and many were due also to Hussein. Tawfiq did not know it yet, but Hussein was bragging how he had manipulated Tawfiq.

Meanwhile, Muhamed Ghannam told Luie how he had recently attended a Palestinian demonstration in Chicago. Looking at the Palestinian flag, the green, orange, white, and black flag that was illegal in Israel and the territories, Muhamed became angry. He wanted to spit in the faces of Arafat's people, and of Arafat himself, who collaborated with the Jews. The crowd began chanting, "Arafat! Arafat!"

"Fuck peace!" Muhamed had screamed. "Abu Nidal! Abu Nidal!"

As Zein babbled about secret meetings, his mentor Mahmoud Atta was languishing in a prison cell in Brooklyn for three and a half years. Whatever else happened to him, Atta had a great piece of luck: His case attracted the former United States Attorney General Ramsey Clark who possessed a first-rate legal mind and a left-wing, liberal heart. The extradition case was complex, involving civil and criminal law in three countries plus international law. Venezuelan officials argued Atta could be yanked off the streets over a passport violation. Because Israel did not have an extradition treaty with Venezuela, but did with the United States, Atta had been "forced" to leave Venezuela—kidnapped—and return to the United States. Atta, an American citizen, was being extradited from New York back to Israel to stand trial for the murder of the Egged bus driver on April 12, 1986.

Worse yet, the Israelis were not just accusing him of murder, they had affidavits stating that as a leader in Abu Nidal, Atta was guilty of crimes against the state. They knew intelligence agents had taken surveillance photos of Atta's get-together in Mexico and had trailed Atta back to Caracas. Counterterrorist squads were fascinated that Atta had four illegal passports, three of which were foreign—Algerian, Egyptian, and Lebanese. Atta told the authorities that he possessed so many, and under so many different names, because he kept losing them. He did not explain why his driver's licenses in New York and Puerto Rico were under a different name, Mahmad Ahmad Josef. But counterterrorist experts firmly believed that Atta was an artist at creating false documents. Atta had told his cousins in Dir Abu Mishal that he recruited for ANO in New York.

Counterterrorism agents from all three countries were intrigued with all the entries in Atta's passports. From the night he allegedly threw his Molotov cocktail at the Egged bus to the day Venezuelan intelligence officers handcuffed him, the "self-employed salesman" had spent much of his time in the air: He had fled Dir Abu Mishal for Zurich and briefly stayed in New York before going on to Caracas for a day, finally reaching Madrid by late fall 1986. His U.S. passport does not indicate exactly what happened next, but Atta left Madrid only to return a week later, then flew back to Caracas. In January 1987 he went to Colombia for two weeks and disappeared—according to his passport—before surfacing again in Madrid. In one day he entered Madrid again and entered and left Bogotá. Then it was on to Cyprus, Barcelona, Madrid, Caracas, and Bogotá before meeting with Zein in Mexico City. Yet his passport does not show that he went there or returned to Caracas, where he was arrested. It was obvious he was using multiple passports.

Atta claimed, in documents, that he traveled so much because he was the "Goodwill Ambassador" for the PLO. However, he never called anyone from the PLO to testify in his behalf. And he himself never testified in any of his trials, which disappointed Assistant U.S. Attorney Jacques Semmelman, who had relished the prospect of cross-examination.

A federal magistrate agreed with Clark's arguments that what the Israelis wanted Atta for was a political crime which was not an extraditable offense for an American citizen, and that Atta, as an American, had been kidnapped in Venezuela, and faced torture in Israel. It was a clever theory, one bolstered by an impressive array of Palestinian lawyers—including the noted Israeli legal expert Leah Tsemal—and Arab newspaper stories.

Semmelman appealed the verdict (which the feds can do). In a new trial, he called his former Harvard Law School Professor Alan Dershowitz as expert on the Israeli legal system. Dershowitz's testimony, described in his book *Chutzpah*, was that the Israelis do not use torture—physical force—to obtain confessions from suspected terrorists, though both sides like the public to think that.

U.S. District Judge Jack Weinstein noted that torture had been disproved when one of Atta's cousins had reenacted the bus attack in a videotaped confession. The judge agreed with Semmelman that Atta should be extradited to Israel to stand trial. The Second Circuit Court of Appeals upheld this noted jurist and the U.S. Supreme Court denied *certiorari*, i.e., refused to review of Atta's case.

On Halloween, 1990, Federal marshals brought the handcuffed Atta back to JFK Airport, where he had landed three years earlier, and loaded him onto a jet for Tel Aviv. In a civil court, not a military court, Atta was convicted and sentenced to life in prison for the murder at Dir Abu Mishal; there is no death penalty in Israel and its Occupied Territories. There was no chance of parole. But unlike other convicted terrorists, Atta, as an American, was allowed to select the civil prison where he was to be incarcerated.

Yet, Atta's life imprisonment lasted only four years. The man that Zein spoke of in awe as "the most fearsome of the feared" was spotted walking the streets of Ramallah and Beitin in the fall of 1994. Why he really was released remains a mystery.

CHAPTER TWELVE

Sweet Sixteen

Tina and Soraia were performing their elaborate ritual before the bathroom mirror. The band Poison's "Nothing but a Good Time" was blasting on the radio. It was the night of the Poison rock concert, and the sisters and their friends from school had tickets. Tina was moussing her silky straight hair—again. "You go through a bottle of it a day," Soraia sniffed, reminding her sister that she had bought a $70 cartful of hair spray and mousse on sale at Wal-Mart. When Soraia reported the bill to their mother, Maria shrugged, "If you don't use it all, then we'll sell it in the store."

The girls fussed endlessly over their toilette and wardrobe. "Me and Tina, we hate brown and green," Soraia said years later, talking about her dead sister in the present tense. "Her favorite, favorite color is hot pink, fuchsia. Everything she wears is fuchsia—T-shirts, sweatshirts, jogging pants, and socks. Her favorite, favorite lipstick and nail polish is fuchsia. Not that Tina has nails to polish. Her favorite, favorite scent is Xia Xiang by Revlon."

Tonight, as they jockeyed for mirror time, Soraia and Tina agreed they would never marry an Arab. They wanted American boys. Back in their bedroom they discussed who were the cutest rock stars as they scrunched down to wiggle on their tight jeans. Between their bunk beds and their posters of Poison, Bon Jovi, and a Puerto Rican rock group, Menudo, there was not a spare inch of wall space.

Tina's ally in the family culture clashes was Soraia. "People think we are twins," Soraia said. "We went everywhere together. We were always together after school. We swam together, played tennis together, worked out together, went to movies together, and shopped together. Tina was fun."

Palestina won't go, Zein told Tawfiq. "She doesn't want to work with us." Zein's "relatives" in Geneva had called him in late fall 1988, asking for "help" because they were "ill." But Zein couldn't come unless Tina accompanied him for cover.

Zein was angry with the recalcitrant girl. How dare she disobey him? And if Tina refused to accompany him, how would he travel for the organization? Tawfiq wanted to send Zein overseas, and Osama wanted Zein to come to California, bringing a letter too dangerous to entrust to the U.S. mail. That was not possible Tawfiq had to report to Osama, for Zein was having problems with Tina. Damn, Osama cursed. "She can't work with us—what is this case?" Osama was firm. "When he comes, he must come with her. . . . By December 20, he should be in Geneva with her. You tell him so."

Tawfiq called Zein immediately, "Your cousin in California wants to see you." Had Zein spoken with Tina? Tawfiq asked again. Yes, Zein answered, but it wasn't possible for her to go. No, Tina had told him, No, it's too close to Christmas and my birthday. She planned to celebrate her upcoming big birthday at home.

The family usually ignored Tina's birthday, but this year her sisters wanted to acknowledge her rite of passage. Soraia knew that turning sixteen meant a lot to Tina, who wanted to be a Sweet Sixteen because this was a landmark age to American girls. Soraia and the others shopped carefully, presenting Tina with her "all-time favorite, favorite" piece of jewelry on her birthday, December 3, 1988. It was a gold herringbone chain with gold cutout letters spelling "Sweet Sixteen."

Two months later the two sisters broke apart, each blaming the other for having changed. Once they had seen themselves as Palestinian-Americans. Now Soraia was becoming more traditionally Palestinian and Tina more contemporary American.

Soraia, who had vowed she would marry an American, who took college courses, who wore pointy-toe punk rocker shoes with silver tips, a black leather jacket, and tight jeans, who moussed her hair to the max, who applied layers of eye makeup and lipstick, who fought encroaching cellulite at the health club, who had once been in love, who had had several boyfriends, who had been seen smooching with a Chinese whom she told she was a terrorist, would now be marrying and spending the rest of her life under a *hijab* and ankle-length skirts—and with a dictator of a husband.

Her intended, Amjad Salem, who was from Beitin fancied himself some hotshot terrorist, spouting, "I swear on the honor of Abu Nidal."

One sulty spring night he whispered to his beloved Soraia, in an hourlong long-distance call, "Do you know what I'm going to do? I want to go to Mexico and blow up the Jew's restaurant* . . . . I'd like to kill their kids, their women, their men. I'd like to kill them all, I swear. Make them targets and practice on them. . . . They had a chance with Hitler, but with me I won't give them no chance—no survival, no kids, no old, nobody, oh baby, oh honey, tell me, honey."

"He comes here a lot," Tina whispered to Helena one afternoon as Amjad strolled into Alliance Market. The young man made a point of going over to the girls and chatting with them before he left to talk to Zein.

"He's very mean-looking," Helena commented. "You'd think he was a criminal. He is fat and ug-leeee. What does your sister see in him?"

"They're pushing her into marrying him," Tina answered, rolling her eyes. "He's an asshole. They're telling her—my parents and he, Amjad—that she's an old maid at twenty-one."

Blinded by the promise of a gold wedding band, Soraia could not see how restrictive it would become. To her, accepting Amjad's hand meant more than a husband and children. He bestowed family approval and cultural sanction. Soraia, who had barely graduated from high school and doubted she could finish college, did not see much choice. Amjad swore she could continue her classes at Forest Park Community College, but later ordered her to drop out. She obeyed him. That was the harbinger. (Later, he would also force her to give up her best friend because she was black.)

"I don't want to end up like that," Tina confided to Helena one night on the phone.

While Soraia began to veil herself emotionally and intellectually, Tina was becoming more forthright, more of her own person, more private, more independent. "We were always one soul," Soraia said bitterly. "But she changed a lot after I got engaged in February. She started acting weird; she didn't want me to get married. She never had one secret from me. She always used to come and tell me everything. But she never told me she was seeing Cliff. That she didn't tell me about. *Never!*"

*   *   *

---

*It is unknown to whom Amjad was referring.

Sometime in early 1989, while Soraia was looking for something she found her sister's handbag and opened it. Ahh, she thought, What are these folded pieces of stationery? Letters? Look more like love letters. Love letters from whom? Cliff. *Cliff!* Soraia combed through Tina's dresser drawers to discover a secret cache of letters, photos, buttons, and key chains, all of which she later turned over to her mother.

This was not aberrant behavior. Living in a collective society, Palestinians do not see privacy as a primal right nor independence as a sacred virtue. In the harsh desert where the Bedouins[*] roved, a person could not survive without the support of the entire tribe. A Palestinian attorney said her neighbors would not hesitate to rifle through her handbag. Female relatives are supposed to police inside the home; they are the first barrier to keep the rebellious from public shame. A love letter would "murder" any single woman's reputation and shame her entire family. Romantic love, which by nature is intimate, individualistic, and therefore private, is antithetical to a collective society.

With Tina receiving love letters, Soraia felt betrayed. Tina had never so much as hinted that she and Cliff were sending messages back and forth. Soraia tore up the love letters and threw them away. When Tina asked why she had snooped in the first place, Soraia said, "to save your honor." Soraia felt obligated to tell their mother to bar Tina from scandal.

Cliff, that black kid that hangs around the store? Maria asked Soraia incredulously. Tina's involved with him? I thought they were just friends, Soraia answered, but not if he is signing his letters "L.A. Cliff"; "L.A. means Love Always."

Zein was told, as were Leilah and Mona. Half-sister Fayrouz was notified. Cousins Sausan and Ahlam were called. The family hot line lit up.

Soraia harped on how Tina sneaked candy from the store shelves and gave it to Cliff. Mona and Leilah reported how Tina offered handfuls of dollar bills to him. Maria did not require convincing. "I don't

---

[*]Arabs romanticize desert Bedouins—and therefore Bedouin mores—as do Americans with cowboys and their values of independence. Arabs watch soap operas about Bedouins, flock to buy Bedouin jewelry, and sightsee at their encampment near Beersheba, as Americans proudly wear denim and cowboy boots and watch Westerns.

like this boy," she said. And Zein's rabid racism had so festered, he could not differentiate between a black gang member and a decent honor student.

"Soraia's just jealous," Cliff and Helena told Tina, who felt Soraia had betrayed *her*. Tina had a boyfriend who was her soulmate and a sky's-the-limit future, while Soraia faced a domestic tyrant and a loveless marriage.

Cliff loved to talk about the first day he had met Tina years earlier: He was fourteen, a freshman who had just moved into the neighborhood with his mother. He was so shy and unassuming, it took people awhile to learn that Cliff was in a special scholastic program with advanced college prep courses.

Aesthetic by nature, on his "quiet days" Cliff wrote poems and short stories, and sketched and painted. He was published in the high school literary book. He was gentle and patient, and took pleasure in listening to Tina talk about her goals. He idolized her. He never pushed nor demanded. The traditional Romantic Lover, he was the opposite of the strutting, macho Mediterranean male, different from what Tina knew at home.

One fall day in 1985, as Cliff strolled into Alliance Market, he had spotted this winsome child-woman with almond eyes sweeping the floor. He was struck by her exotic beauty. He worked up his nerve to buy a candy bar as an excuse to talk with this fetching creature. "I really liked her, but I didn't know if she liked me. For about a year I would go in and say 'hi' to her and her sister and they'd say 'hi' back, and they'd laugh. I wondered why." Finally, he asked. Tina quickly answered, "You look like Michael Jackson"; they both broke into laughter. After that, Tina and Soraia would call him "Mike" and they'd all laugh. Cliff began stopping by almost every day, talking to them for twenty minutes, then for half an hour. Soraia was friendly to him back then. He liked Tina a lot. As he hung around more, he could tell Tina liked him, too.

After more than three years of joking around, right after Tina's sixteenth birthday Cliff took a deep breath and asked Tina for her phone number. "Fine," she said. "Give me yours and I'll call you."

"I was surprised. I liked her style. That night, she called me. We talked on the phone for two hours. Her parents were home. Another time I called her and they answered, so they knew all along I was calling."

Feeling comfortable, Cliff asked Tina out. "I said in a weird way, I said in a question way, 'I have this problem. There's this girl I call A [another girl] and this other girl I call B [Tina] and I call myself C.' I said, 'C likes B, but A likes C. I was wantin' to know does B like C?'

"And she said Yes." His face lit up, recalling that night, "She said Yes!"

For a month he met her after her last class at Roosevelt High School and walked her from there to Alliance Market and then went home. Tina would phone him from the store. Sometimes, if Tina did not have to work, they would stop and eat at Taco Bell or McDonald's. Then he would put her on a bus and he would walk home.

One warm January day, as Cliff waited, Tina skipped up to him with a wide smile and some good news. "Today you can walk me home," she said. They walked up to her door and, as she turned her key, she invited him in. "Soraia and my parents are at the store," she said. They talked for two hours.

"After that, I walked her home every day. I never saw her on week-ends—unless she didn't have to work. I liked being alone with her and talking. Back then I was real shy and introverted—I still don't like going out. Tina was the outspoken, outgoing, pragmatic one. If I wasn't working, I'd go over to the house, talk and watch TV. Her parents did-n't like her keeping company with boys. She'd say, 'You have to leave before they come home.'

"We weren't too serious in the beginning. We just liked each other a lot. Friends. For Valentine's Day I gave her a card [he designed a huge heart with a banner across it spelling out Tina's name in big letters] and she brought me suckers she'd made at school and a fuzzy cutout heart that said, 'I Love You.' By March we felt closer. I was falling in love. She was the first girl I ever loved. As I got to know her, I appreciated how we liked the same things, how friendly and outgoing she was. How she laughed a lot. I even became more extroverted.

"When I talk about her now I can't stop smiling."

One night in March, Cliff dialed the Isas'. Soraia answered and yelled through the tiny apartment, "Tina, it's your honey-bunny. Cliff's on the phone." Cliff thought she was just teasing. A few weeks later, when he tried to talk to her, Soraia was monosyllabic and refused to tell Tina she had a call. Other times Soraia would tell him not to phone anymore, and slam down the receiver. That hurt Tina's feelings, for she had not tattled when Soraia had surreptitiously dated non-Arab boys.

*　　　*　　　*

Cliff and Tina were laughing, sitting in the Isas' living room on a warm April night. Tina felt safe, her parents would be at the store until nine P.M. at least.

"Just let me check, in case," she said, and dialed Alliance Market.

No answer. She called again. No answer.

"You'll have to leave," Tina said, walking Cliff to the front door. As she opened it, Cliff behind her, they could hear Maria talking downstairs. As Cliff tiptoed out, he glanced at Tina's cousin Sausan, who lived in the building complex, chatting with Maria. He kept walking.

"Isn't that the guy from the neighborhood?" Sausan asked Maria. They looked at each other and marched up the steps to confront Tina.

"Who's been in this house?" Maria demanded. Tina said nothing. But Soraia—who had been sitting in the car—knew; she saw Cliff creeping out. She told Maria. Leaving Zein at home, Soraia and Maria flew down the steps and back into the family car. They raced around the neighborhood, confronting Cliff on Grand Avenue.

"They rolled down the window and pulled me over, very angry," Cliff said, "and asked, 'Did you just come from our house.' I didn't want to get Tina into trouble, so I said no. They—mostly Soraia—kept after me. I kept saying I'd been to a friend's house.

"Soraia looked at me and said, 'Don't come to the store. We don't want your dirty money. Don't go out with my sister. Tina is not supposed to be dating because of her religion.' " Speechless, Cliff stared at her.

Maria looked at her daughter, then at Cliff. "You can come to the store," she said slowly. "You can call Tina. You just can't take her out."

As they drove away, Soraia yelled out, "You keep doin' dis, you and Tina'll be dead meat."

The next day Maria, Leilah, Mona, and Soraia ganged up on Tina and held her down on the floor. While Tina shrieked and struggled, they punched and kicked her. They pulled out a knife and held it to her throat, as Soraia screamed, "Better stop seein' Cliff. If someone else finds out, you two'll be dead meat."

The embarrassment the Isas felt over Tina's behavior with Cliff centered on *Shari'af*, literally "honor." The word does not mean honor in the conventional American sense of one is only as good as one's word;

has integrity; is loyal; has achieved professionally. Arab honor stands for generosity, manliness, courage. *Shari'af* more closely corresponds to the Western sense of shame. There is less guilt in Islam per se, because a nasty thought or ugly emotion is known only to the individual. In Islam human emotions are accepted; it is no sin to think licentious thoughts as long as one does not act upon them. "If no one knows about it, it's okay," Tina's sisters explained.

"But if everybody knows, or thinks they know, it's shame. Even wearing shorts is shameful. The number one cause of shame is a girl dating," Mona said. Shame in the West is over some act an individual has done. In the Middle East, shame is collective, some horror rotting within the group that exposes them to public ridicule and gives the group's enemies something to use against it. Shame is more than losing face. Shame means the family is no longer honorable enough to do business with, not respectable, not good enough for marriage. Shame ruins the extended family.

Shame most often is sexual in the Muslim Arab world. An Arab man loses his honor and is shamed by the sexual behavior of the women of his family. Like dogs, his women must be restrained. In traditional societies, East or West, a father protects his daughter from making mistakes. This in turn prevents her from developing fully; then she really needs a man—father, brother, or husband—to protect her. If Tina Isa was considered "loose," then Zein had failed as a man for not protecting her. The best way to prevent a wanton woman from shaming her family by premarital sex was to marry her off during adolescence.

If other methods do not bring back the unrepentant, one way for a man to redeem himself is to commit what Arabs refer to as a crime of honor: A male relative of the wayward woman—her father, brother, uncle, nephew, or even a son if she has one—is the one who must do the deed. And almost always it must be a male of the woman's natal family. A woman thought to be adulterous shames *her* family, not necessarily that of her husband, although sometimes the husband will fatally stab his wife in a crime of honor.

It is almost irrelevant whether a wife is in fact sleeping with another man, or a single girl is holding hands with her sweetheart. The girl or woman need not have committed fornication or adultery. It is the appearance of impropriety that matters. Explained one Palestinian woman, "Rumors can kill. You're ruined here if you're out late at night."

Usually the rumormongers are the women, who police immodest behavior. They inhibit through the threat of gossip. If that doesn't work, they function much like Mafia enforcers. Then the men take over. A father like Zein is berated and ridiculed by other men; his manhood is at stake if he cannot control his women. Once an Arab man is publicly accused, even by his own wife, he is forced to take action. While the men perform the killing, Arab women are guilty, too; similar to the driver of the getaway car who assists to bank robber.[*]

Only tradition encourages honor killings. Nowhere in the Qu'ran are crimes of honor mentioned let alone sanctified; nowhere in the Hadith does it say, put a fallen woman to the knife. Most Palestinian families will do anything to avoid such bloodshed. Palestinians have a myriad of socially acceptable solutions they will try. But then, most Palestinian families are not fanatics in league with Abu Nidal.

The Isa family blamed Cliff for their problems, refusing to see how their restrictions chafed Tina who only wanted to be an average normal American teenager. For example, Tina wanted to join her junior year American history class on its May field trip to Washington, D.C. Leilah called Tina's counselor and asked whether one of Tina's sisters could come along as chaperone. When school officials said no, the family refused to allow Tina to participate, although Maria argued that Tina should go. When Tina was honored with a scholarship to a summer school program at the University of Missouri at Columbia, Tina thought her parents would allow her to go. They refused, saying she would not be sleeping under her father's roof and that would shame him. Soraia was driving Tina and Helena home one night when Tina announced, "I'm going."

"No, you're not," Soraia shrieked, and became quite nasty.

"She's just jealous," Helena told Tina the next day, trying to mollify her best friend.

"It makes no sense," Tina cried. "Lots of Palestinian girls go away to school and no one talks about them. Even girls from Beitin!"

---

[*]A story is told of a twelve-year-old girl from America who went to live with her grandparents. It was harvest time and their house was empty, everyone was working in the field. The girl went home for something, and while she was there, a village boy came by. As they stood talking, the grandmother walked in. Shocked, the grandmother ran to report this transgression to the grandfather, who hurried home and killed his grandchild.

Being denied such privileges might have crushed the spirit of another girl, but not one as strong-willed as Tina. She continued being sociable and generous. She liked chatting with the neighborhood children while she worked behind the counter at Alliance Market. One afternoon, working at the store, some tots were a few pennies short of the price of the candy bars. "That's okay," Tina told them. "Take it and pay me next time." Maria overheard, came over, and slapped her in the face.

"Nigger lover. Get those niggers out of here," she yelled at Tina.

Maria had learned this epithet from Zein. Cliff thought the entire family was racist: "Soraia and Maria did something to a black lady's little kid," he said. That woman came up to the store with a friend, and the next thing Cliff saw was a fistfight between the four women. "Soraia's nose was bleeding and she was yelling racist names at the black ladies. Another time some black teenage girl was bothering Soraia in the store. Soraia came out from behind the counter and called her 'black nigger.' I was shocked she'd do that in front of all the black customers."

One May night Tina's sister Mona awoke from a horrible dream. She had no trouble remembering it, for the imagery was prophetic: "The whole family—Mom, Dad, all the girls except Tina—were running down a long alley and fell into a large hole. We all got inside and couldn't get out. The only one who didn't get in was Tina. She looked down at us and smiled. We were screaming for help. But the way she looked at us, it was like, 'You deserve it. I won't help.' "

Mona cried when she recalled the nightmare. "My bad dreams always come true," she said with wet eyes.

By early June, Soraia was frantic. What if Amjad's family found out how Tina was dishonoring the family? Instead of announcing the betrothal, his parents would call it off. "The night before the men of my husband's family came to formally ask for my hand, Tina did it [she went to her Junior Prom.] She saw Cliff to make us break the engagement. She was grounded, but she did it."

Tina had been beaten and sentenced to house arrest that night. Her family claimed they had seen Cliff leaving the apartment. Or rather Soraia scurried to tell Maria she had spotted him there. "They lied," Helena said. "That was the excuse they gave. The real reason is Soraia panicked them. Soraia told them it's a tradition on prom night for couples to rent hotel rooms after the dance and to have sex there." Yet the Isas had permitted Soraia to attend her junior prom.

Tina was determined to attend her prom. The afternoon of the dance, she took her dress to Helena's, called her mother, and said, "Mom, I'm going to the prom," and she hung up. Soraia called around to find where the dance was being held. "We sent Dad home before he had a heart attack," Soraia said. With Amjad driving, Maria and Soraia went to the prom at Stouffer's Airport Hotel. Soraia and Maria found a guard outside the ballroom and asked him to retrieve the wayward child, one Tina Isa.

"But Tina wouldn't give him her last name," Soraia said. "She said, 'My name is Tina.' He asked her what about her full name. She said, 'My name is Tina, and it's my only name. I don't even know these people.' He asked her for her parents' name. She said, 'I don't know.' Then the guard called the police, who told her, 'You're only sixteen.' " Tina walked to the car and got in. She was terrified of her family's revenge.

Leilah joined the family fracas and she, too, combed through her sister's drawers. "I found the letters and pictures of her and Cliff," Leilah said. "My mother saw them together at Cliff's prom [which was impossible, for Cliff did not attend it] and at Kmart. It was not good for her honor. My cousin's husband and others saw her and him together. She acted with disrespect in public, and did not listen to our parents, and screamed at them.

"My parents didn't beat her. Nowadays if you slap a child, it's child abuse. The only time Tina had bruises was when she was wrestling with her brother-in-law and he got her accidentally with a belt." But amongst themselves, the sisters spoke of Tina being beaten with a shoe and Zein's crutch, as well as having a cup of scalding coffee thrown in her face one morning at the store.

While Tina may have comprehended the Arab code of honor, she could not understand why it was operative for an American teenager in America. All she had done was encourage a gentleman caller, a custom going back centuries in the West.

"I love my family," Tina told a friend. "I'll always forgive them for beating me. I just wish to be happy with them again." She tried to gain her parents' approval by spending evenings reading English to Zein and Maria. She would frequently visit her half-sister Faiza and her wealthy husband Amir Darwish (no relation to Samir Darwish) in

Chicago. On Friday nights she often would pick up Leilah's eldest daughter who was quick and lively like herself or go to Mona's and pick up her little girl—and take either niece back home with her until Sunday night. "She was a perpetual baby-sitter for her sisters, who treated her like dirt," was a neighbor's comment.

As many American teenagers do, the more her parents restricted her, the more Tina resisted. And the more she fought back, the more punitive they became. Customers at Alliance Market were disgusted to see the Isas hurling cans of food at Tina and cursing her for such infractions as wearing headphones while she stocked the shelves. Her parents' attacks and vitriolic anger scared Tina, making her think they would kill her.

So, on August 14, twelve days before Soraia's wedding, Tina did what thousands of physically abused American children do. She ran away from home. To her father, that damned her forever. It proved he could not control his women. Zein was humiliated as a man.

Her mother was so distraught that she called the police within the hour. Maria told Officer Robert Sanneman that after a fight that evening in the family market, Tina had run out, saying she was going to commit suicide. Tina was already depressed, Maria said frantically. She guessed her daughter went to her boyfriend's home, a Clifford Cortez (Cortez is his middle name) on Detonty Street. The officer took down a physical description of Tina, including the clothes she'd last been seen wearing—a white shirt, red shorts, and white tennis shoes.

Two days later, Fayrouz, who was raising teenagers herself, was trying to soothe Zein over the phone, but Zein liked to nurse his ire. He became hysterical with Fayrouz for being reasonable and hung up on her. She called back.

"No, Father. This is not the way. Patience brings relief," Fayrouz said.

"Do you want me to hang up again?" Zein demanded. "As far as I'm concerned, this one is burned forever. A whore for the niggers."

Fayrouz suggested she talk with Tina's friends to try to find her.

But Zein was no longer interested in resolution; he wanted revenge. "The glass, when it becomes dirty and broken, is there any way to repair it? Is there a way to cleanse my name?" Why was Fayrouz being so sympathetic, so understanding? he wanted to know.

"I don't know, but I'm telling you, still sisters," Fayrouz said. "We remain sisters."

"For me this one has become a burned woman, a nigger's whore" he repeated. "There is no way to cleanse her, except the red color that cleanses her."

"People's talk is not going to hurt. When we find her, no one will dare open his mouth."

Zein protested that not only in Beitin, but in all America and Brazil, people will say the daughter of one from Beitin ran away. Already everyone in the Beitin Association in St. Louis (a group from the village) knew. Gossip tells the truth, he added. When a girl leaves her parents' house, there is only one reason: whoring. "She gets fucked and you come telling me that she is our flesh and blood."

An hour later Soraia called her half-sister Faiza Darwish in Chicago. Where Fayrouz counseled reconciliation, Faiza demanded blood vengeance as much as Soraia. "By God, when she comes back, a person should shoot her and throw her into the sea."

After three days and four nights, the prodigal daughter returned. Her family had beseeched Helena, calling her constantly, crying how much they loved Tina. When Helena reported that, Tina laughed and said, "You believe that?" Helena explained later: "They act like saints in front of other people. They wear these masks." Tina wanted to come home only to avoid ruining Soraia's wedding, but was afraid, confiding in Amjad Salem after he tracked her down at Helena's that "they want to slaughter me. My father raised a knife at me and my mother choked me. It isn't a matter of beating, it's a matter of life and death."

Oh, he's just trying to scare you, Amjad told her. Then Amjad begged her parents to stop the beating; Zein gave him his "word of honor" five times. And Amjad gave his "word of honor" to Tina that she would be safe.

That was a lie; he had intended all along to betray her.

When Tina came home and walked into her room, all her posters were gone; Soraia had taken them down. "The day Tina came back, she got a letter from Cliff," Soraia said sourly. "And another two days later."

Soraia was angry with Maria, who had agreed to stop assaulting Tina and let her play school sports. And when Zein yelled at his wife for acquiescing, Maria countered by threatening, "If you say any more, I'll go rent an apartment for me and my daughter."

*   *   *

Amjad Salem, Soraia's betrothed, lectured his future father-in-law: "Most important of all, more important than all the money you made in America," he told Zein the next day, "more important than anything else is that you must handle Tina."

"By God, dear," Zein sighed, "if one can control her. But . . . the world doesn't lack guns." Tina needed discipline "at the hotel under the ground," Zein added.

Amjad offered his help. Whatever was needed, he would do.

"This girl should be taken to a doctor," Zein said. "Is she [a] virgin? Is there a disturbance in her mind that makes her do this? I don't want to hide anything from you."

Amjad, exhausted from negotiating Tina's return and worrying about the effect on his wedding, next spoke to his fiancée. Soraia said she wanted a family conference, the works—her parents, all the sisters, their husbands, the cousins Luie and Saif Nijmeh, and other relatives in St. Louis. They would confront and admonish Tina for this scandal. Only Fayrouz and Maria felt sorry for the girl. Only they seemed to love Tina for herself, not for how obedient she was.

Amjad replied that it was Zein's decision alone to restore his honor: Zein must murder Tina. But that Zein could not bring himself to do. So Amjad volunteered to perform the grisly chore. Why, he announced to Soraia, he could buy an unregistered gun.

My father doesn't have the courage to use one, Soraia whined.

"I do," her fiancé promised, "on my mother's honor."

For close to thirty minutes he and Soraia discussed ways of dispatching Tina.

"This is a duty," Amjad said. "I would do it while I smoke a cigarette . . . No more Tina. Tina's gonna be history."

Amjad discussed the "scandal" with cousin Luie, who lamented how Tina's disgrace was already known in Milwaukee. "She just wants to live the American way," Luie complained.

He pointed out how the women of the extended family—Maria, her other daughters, and her nieces, the twins Sausan and Ahlam—had first learned of Tina's shame. They had planned to keep the problem to themselves until they had solved it. But they had failed, and now the men of the family had to do something. Or they would be ridiculed by their own women, Luie said.

Luie and Amjad agreed with Soraia's assessment: This one had to be slaughtered. They also agreed that Zein should send Tina to her brother in the homeland, where he would "take care of her." And, Luie suggested, "Send her there and tip someone off that she is a collaborator [with the Israelis] and to shoot her."*

By labeling the dead woman a collaborator, the family avoids the police, because any investigation would have been impossible for lack of witnesses, explained Professor Joseph Ginat of Haifa University, the chief authority on honor killings. If there were an honor killing, however, Israeli police would begin an inquiry.

What Amjad didn't know was that Luie had asked Tawfiq about his talents for use in ANO. He's good, Tawfiq answered, but has required lots of hard work over the last two years and hates to travel. Luie felt the ANO work should focus more on St. Louis, they should do more recruiting there. Luie relished talking about expansion possibilites over coffee and cards at the Village Inn, where he and his friends went every day. The Midwest was the fertile ground for sowing Abu Nidal missions, as one comrade had said. They should contact all Arabs around St. Louis.

While there are some 5,000 Arabs and Americans of Arab descent living in the five counties west of the Mississippi in St. Louis, many are Christian. Did Luie realize that to the grandsons of Maronite Lebanese forced out by Muslims, he and his ilk were worse than pariahs?

Zein, however, envisioned leaving America altogether. "People here are becoming like sheep without a shepherd. The second month of next year, I'll sell the store and dedicate myself to getting away. My home base will be outside America, and from there I'll be ready to be sent worldwide for work," he confided to Tawfiq. His cousin retorted, first solve your problems at home with Tina. Zein wailed, "I'm sick of this life."

---

*The uniform sentence for collaboration was execution. A woman who betrayed her family's honor was a woman who would betray her race. The common wisdom on the West Bank was that Israeli police recruited dishonored women. This was an excuse. Two-thirds of the women killed between 1988 through 1993 for suspected collaboration with Israel were found to be victims of honor killings, according to a study. Researchers found that of 1,000 men and women killed for collaboration, only a third were likely traitors.

The study was made by an Israeli group. No known Palestinian research exists, most likely because of the taboo in discussing it and because in a land fighting for independence, such an issue is considered marginal, though important.

Zein tried to console himself by calling his son in the West Bank. Teach her some manners, Faisal recommended. No, Zein argued. There was no way, no way at all to train this one. "Teaching her, I think, must take place in the hotel under the ground." Faisal said in a low voice to someone standing nearby, "He is crazy." And the man retorted, "Ah, and what did I tell you about him?"

Rarely in his many lamentations about Tina did Zein refer to her by name.

A Palestinian band was singing Arabic wedding songs in a banquet hall at the Airport Holiday Inn when the bridal limousine pulled up. Soraia's $600 wedding dress was draped over the car's leather interior. Her wedding had been chronicled by a video camera and a professional still photographer back at her parents' apartment. The family planned a big feast tonight, August 26. There was a temporary cease-fire with Tina during the festivities.

Nearly everyone in St. Louis's Beitin community had been invited to the hotel reception, more than one hundred. Even Soraia's and Tina's black friends were allowed there, including Cliff. Despite the bride's bigotry, her best friend was a light-complected black from West Africa. According to a guest, the bridegroom became visibly distraught when he saw the black people, and stood in a corner hysterically screeching at his bride. (It was after that incident that Soraia stopped speaking to her best friend.) To Amjad, only blacks from the Sudan, who are Muslim, or those who worked in family stores were socially acceptable. He had sworn to Luie that if he saw any blacks at the wedding, he would leave.

During the reception Soraia and Tina—in a new black-and-white dress with sequins—were giggling with Helena in the ladies' room. Tina had ducked in there to avoid Amjad's twenty-one-year-old brother, whom Zein wanted her to meet.

"Did you see that guy over there, at that table? He came here to check me out. He's got this long beak of a nose," Tina chortled. Tina swore again she would never walk down the aisle with an Arab or a Mexican—"too domineering, too macho." Laughing, Helena peeked out of the powder room to see Zein's idea of a husband for Tina. "Ug-lee!" Helena cackled. "Nobody would want him." Nobody but Zein.

Mona had suggested taking Tina to a gynecologist. If Tina was still a virgin, then there was a psychological root to her rebellion, Mona reasoned, and they could find a psychiatrist to fix her. But if Tina were no longer pure, then they should get rid of her, Mona said. Maria dragged her embarrassed daughter to a physician who was a Hispanic woman—Arab women often search for a female gynecologist rather than reveal themselves before a man. The doctor reported that Tina was chaste and typed up a note of verification, a fact Saif Nijmeh immediately reported to relatives.

Fayrouz, believing Tina could be cured of disobedience, drove her little sister to the psychiatrist. Tina told him, "I don't want to marry Cliff. I don't want to follow in my sisters' footsteps. I want to be my own boss."

The doctor agreed with Tina, telling her to get out of the house as soon as she could. "Your family are the ones with the problems, not you."

Then he questioned Fayrouz, asking how she had felt "when your father abandoned you, your mother, and siblings to marry a younger woman and then chase another one?"

Despite their "word of honor," Zein and Maria continued beating Tina. There were at least two attacks after she returned home: Twice Maria and her daughters held Tina down, stomped and kicked her in the ribs, and throttled her with Zein's crutch and cane. And once Zein joined in the melee, holding a knife to her throat.

Zein was desperate for life to go back to the way it was when nice girls obeyed their fathers and then their husbands. Tina planned for her life to go forward—*her* life, the one she chose as an independent American woman. That September she looked forward to her senior year and graduation, when she could leave the fighting on Delor Street forever.

"If," as she wrote, "if I live that long."

CHAPTER THIRTEEN

"For Myself"

EARLY OCTOBER 1989

Tina and Helena strolled along the curved roads in nineteenth-century Tower Grove Park, past pastel-colored gazebos and lily ponds, and over the cast-iron footbridges. They ambled onto the tennis courts, where Cliff waited for them, as he did every afternoon. The trio would laugh and talk until the tennis coach and girls' team arrived for practice.

That Tina was seen publicly with Cliff—albeit surrounded by a crowd—disgraced her family. Mona bewailed how Tina's dishonor had already spoiled the chances of Mona's toddler daughters to make marriages. Others worried that Tina would never find a husband. Leilah explained, "In our village, if somebody knows, everybody knows. It would be hard for a girl to kiss a boy without him thinking, If she kisses me, she can kiss anybody else. It would be hard for her to get married in that village, though she can marry into another village."

What if the girl refused to marry? Leilah's sister-in-law drew her finger across her throat and roared with laughter. But Tina no longer lived in a village in the West Bank. Didn't that mean anything? "It's hard for us to come from a culture existing for hundreds of years to change in one day," countered cousin Sausan.

To protect Tina's honor, Zein announced he and Maria would take an apartment wherever she went to college so that she could live at home. "It would be unusual for a Palestinian girl to live in a dorm. I mean, a lot of girls do it, but Arab people talk. Even if the parents are not embarrassed, other members of the family are," Leilah said.

This is untrue. Palestinians are famous for collecting advanced degrees. For this they are known, ironically, as "the Jews of the Middle East." And as sexually oppressive as they are toward women, Palestinians and Israeli Arabs more than encourage women to go to college and graduate school. Financial assistance is available through PLO and foreign university scholarships. For decades large numbers of girls have been sent overseas to American and European universities. Often the coed leaves home without speaking English. And often, she cannot afford to come home for four years, so she won't see her parents until after she is graduated. Generally speaking, educated Palestinian women students are far more independent and self-sufficient than their counterparts in America.

After her summer of torment, Tina was unable to concentrate on her homework, and her grades plummeted. Compared to February, when she was eligible for honors in French and received praise as "extremely conscientious" from her teachers, Tina was performing poorly. Roosevelt High School counselors sent Zein and Maria an "Academic Deficiency Report," notifying them that Tina was in danger of flunking the first quarter of her senior year. The school officials asked the Isas to attend a parents' conference day on November 28.

By the time her parents received the letter, Tina was afraid to lie down to sleep for fear she would be murdered. Her father had warned her already, "Don't make me responsible for your blood! So . . . that I, your father, sixty years of age, spend fifteen years in prison or go to the chair electric and you get buried?"

Her parents might throw open her bedroom door at any time and drag her out of bed. Her mother would hold her down on the floor and her father would beat her. Tina began pushing her bedroom chair against the door. She might inadvertently say something so provocative that Zein or Maria would throw another cup of hot coffee in her face. She began leaving for school before they were up in the morning.

I've got to get out, I've got to get out, Tina thought. She could not go to her sisters; Mona had called her a whore and told her to stay away from her daughters. Tina ran into Bruce, a neighbor slightly older than she. They considered themselves pals, not close friends, because the Isas would not allow her to socialize with a man.

"Things are hard at home," Tina told him. "I need to move away from them. I need to hide my stuff. May I store some of my stuff in your basement locker?"

Tina went to her favorite teacher, a single black woman, and begged the teacher to let her move in. Knowing the Isas would not approve, the teacher refused. She did not comprehend how severe Tina's problems were. No one truly did until afterward.

It was hard to tell Tina was being abused. "Even at the end, she was so cheerful," Helena remarked. Another friend, who lived in an apartment over Alliance Market, later realized Tina was trying to cover things up: "She was really a sweet girl, always pleasant and friendly and had a smile, but I could tell she was sad underneath."

On October 12 the Isas barred Tina from seeing her best friend, claiming that Tina used Helena to sneak around to see Cliff. But this was just a ploy—a family usually prefaces an honor killing by confining the girl: locking her up at home, not allowing her to see friends, taking her out of school. By the time the family murders the wayward female, she has been "killed" many times and in many ways, in body and in spirit, according to social workers in Palestinian women's centers.

The next morning, Friday the thirteenth, Maria Isa walked into the office of Tina's school counselor and dropped Tina's books on her desk. Tina's been disobedient and we're taking her out of school, Maria explained to the counselor. Pamela Fournier was shocked, knowing how "very dear" school was to Tina. Maria bemoaned how Tina betrayed her family by dating a black youth without permission—not that they would give it. Maria cried with frustration. The counselor calmed her down and convinced her to allow Tina to return to school on Monday, October 16.

On Saturday, October 14, Zein and Soraia, now married to Amjad and living in Dayton, Ohio, reanalyzed the situation long-distance.

"Whore" was Soraia's pronouncement.

Zein reported that he had taken Tina out of school and torn up her notebooks, but his older daughter urged him to be more punitive. "Tie her down in the basement of the store. Tape her mouth all day, go buy her passport, send her to the homeland, and over there it is neither forbidden nor against the law." (Honor killings are against the law in Israel and in the occupied territories.)

"That means I have to send her in a box like a dead person," Zein said.

Soraia had an alternative: "Get a dirty nigger, one of those who land in prison every two or three days. Tell him, this is a hundred dollars in advance, this girl is such and such, you know, and when you finish, this is two hundred and fifty—"

Zein interrupted. "No, by God, I won't accept it. It is necessary that

I do the story . . . it is impossible to wipe the shame off me that a stranger killed my daughter."

Bizarrely enough, as Zein and Soraia described scenarios on how to kill Tina, they also discussed whether Tina should be permitted to participate in school sports. Maria, Fayrouz, Mona, and Leilah were all in favor of letting Tina play after-school sports. Maria believed if they did not give Tina some leeway, she would run away again. But Soraia obsessively argued against it with her father. Tina, she pointed out to Zein, was cutting tennis practice to see Cliff. She claimed Tina's teacher had called Maria and told her that.

Zein interjected with an idea, a plan to end all these problems, "She threatened me with a knife and I shot her!"

Soraia interrupted again. "This one, this one doesn't deserve to live one year on the face of the earth!"

As Zein started wailing again, Soraia suggested, "As you have said, 'She threatened me and I killed her.' "

Zein added, "She threatened me. And I'll put the knife in her hand after she falls."

There was no alternative; he and Maria had given Tina a sadistic beating in the store, but she had retaliated and almost bested them. "She has a strangely amazing power," he marveled.

Drugs, she takes drugs, Soraia said. That made her unredeemable. But, Soraia criticized, "My mother said things can be repaired."

"My God, haven't I told you? Your mother is overlenient," Zein said, adding, "I can't take problems anymore. If I did something bad, it is not because I wanted to, but because I had to."

Meanwhile, that morning—out of her parents' sight at Alliance— Tina phoned her boyfriend. "Man, I got to find a place to stay at," she told Cliff. "They took away my [driver's] license. They took away all the money I had. I don't have a thing. She took my radio. I broke my phone because she said, 'Just bring me your phone.' I figured if I wasn't going to use it, nobody else was. . . . All my dad does is stare at me."

Tina hoped to leave home in December and go back to school in January, but she would be missing three credits. "I got to leave now, I don't have anybody to stay with. I can't use the phone. I can't do nothing."

Her cousins discussed the Isas' dilemma the next day, Sunday, October 15. Sausan told Luie how the Isas had beaten Tina severely at the store. Afterward Tina had threatened her parents with a meat mallet. The fighting was so awful, Sausan said, she wanted to quit working for her aunt and "Mr. Zein." "They're spoiling her rotten," Sausan added. "They should shoot her before she reaches seventeen," was Luie's verdict. Sausan felt they should give up their honor and let Tina go to Cliff. Or, said the soft-spoken woman, Mr. Zein should regain his honor by killing Tina.

Home from the market, Zein and Maria quarreled with their daughter. "I plead to God for you to take the responsibility of your blood! Don't place the responsibility of your blood on my shoulders!" Zein cried.

"Do you want to marry Cliff?" "No!" "Do you want to leave for the black person?" Zein screamed over and over. "No," cried Tina. "No, no, no!" "If it isn't for the black person, then for who?" Zein argued.

"For myself," Tina said.

Zein thought for a moment, then added fearfully, "What do you want to do? Will it satisfy you to go and accuse me, you and the black person . . . that I am with the guerrillas?"

All Monday morning, October 16, Tina's counselor, Pamela Fournier, watched anxiously for Tina. No one came. Maria had promised Tina would be back in school. That afternoon, Tina, her mother, and her sister Mona came to Fournier's office. Mona often acted as a surrogate parent. Indeed, today Maria did not speak directly to the counselor, instead Mona ran the entire conference, saying, "Palestina is a whore and a tramp. If Palestina were my daughter, I would kill her!"

"Then you would go to jail," Fournier retorted. Tina sat quietly throughout this harangue. The counselor spent the rest of the two-hour session urging Maria to return Tina to her classes. Maria said that would be fine, as long as her husband approved.

After they left, Fournier told her principal, "I think they're going to stone that girl."

An hour later, as they waited on their store customers, Tawfiq and Saif mulled over in Arabic what they should do about the "scandal."

"If you want to do anything," Saif said, "you have to do it to the girl. Don't do it to the other [Cliff], because it's not the other's business. This is a guy who loved a girl and went after her. When the girl follows him, it means it's the girl's fault. Then if you do anything to him, she will go and say we are the ones who did it, because she knows many things. Do you understand me?"

Tawfiq wanted them to assist Zein; the group had to stand together.

Saif grunted. "I expect that because of him, we will bear responsibility."

Mona's heart was corroded by envy. Tina had freedom, while she, Mona, was a house slave to her in-laws, with whom she and her husband Nai'el lived. Mona grumbled to her mother on the phone after the conference with Fournier, "I cannot leave whenever I want now. If I want to go out, I have to leave my house shining!" She even had to clean her father-in-law's room, and had kitchen and housemaid duty twice as often as her mother-in-law, as her father-in-law had decreed.

When Mona called to tell her father about the school conference, Zein launched into his diatribe. "If God makes my wish, I'll put her in the grave."

"May God make her sleep and not get up!" Mona exclaimed.

"Don't you want to listen?" Zein interjected. He griped how he had been so generous with Tina—movies, shopping trips, spending money. And what did he get in return? "The thing she wants, no one is able to give her except Cliff," he said plaintively.

"By God, the biggest rifle," Mona shrieked. "One would shoot her in the stomach."

Zein returned to how hard he was working, and for what! If someone wanted to buy the shop, "[we would] take a break. Here or in Brazil. I am not going back to the country. Do you understand?"

"Why?" Mona said.

"Because I don't want to," Zein said.

"Or you can't?"

Mona complained, "Maybe this one [Tina] doesn't want anything. She wants a dick, a nigger slave's dick in her mouth. By God, my mother made a mistake. She made a mistake when she first saw the black person leaving the house and she didn't follow him. She should have followed him, cut him up in pieces, and told him—"

"Listen," Zein interrupted. "She [Tina] is the one that followed him. . . . Do you go and tell the nigger to 'keep your dick away from her'?"

Mona blamed her mother for allowing Tina too much freedom. Zein agreed, but he had another grievance: Maria had shamed him. Tina, Soraia, and he had been in the store the day before when a twelve-year-old black boy came in. Zein apparently was rude to him, for Tina said, "If you talk to me the way you talk to him, I will get out of here."

Zein was hurt: "That day, instead of hitting her on the face, your mother humiliated me . . . she told Tina to prepare herself to go to Washington, D.C. [for the upcoming school field trip that ultimately was forbidden]. . . . How can she let her go with a group of street kids? She humiliated me! And after that, what she tells me! She tells me, 'I promised her, and I want to send her at the end of this year to Paris.' Ah, Maria, isn't it shameful? Who, among my daughters, my sisters, your sisters, ever went to Paris?"

Zein grumbled, "So as for your mother, she opened the door for the girl to disrespect me and not to fear me. . . . It is your mother who comes to her protection."

On or before October 16, Tina called Missouri's Child Abuse Hotline and reported that a child, one Palestina Isa, was being abused. She did not give her name, she did not need to; all allegations of abuse or neglect, anonymous or not, must be investigated by law. Tina was assured that a caseworker would talk with the victim.

Missouri newspapers are filled with stories and statistics about the grim failures of the Division of Family Services. How neighbors reported a child being thrown against a wall and burned with cigarettes, and how DFS took no action, and the toddler died of internal injuries. How homicide detectives close the cases that DFS leaves open.

When queried, DFS cloaks itself in confidentiality. The only public record of the DFS inquiry of Tina's case is the FBI taped phone conversation on October 16 between caseworker Kent Dickens,[*] who investigated Tina's complaint, and Mona. Zein had called his older daughter to translate for Dickens, who was then meeting with Zein, Maria, and Tina together.

Mona first asked if a man had called DFS about the family. Dickens admitted that it was an anonymous female, who said that Tina was

---

[*]Name changed as the state of Missouri has no record of where he has moved. He was unavailable for comment.

bruised and marked from beatings, that she had been withdrawn from
school and made to work from seven in the morning until nine at night,
and that she wasn't paid for these fourteen-hour days. Mona said she
knew "who's that shit"; it was her sister, who needed to see a psychiatrist.

What about the parents' rights? Mona protested. My sister does not
respect her mother or her father.

"I can understand where he's coming [from]," Dickens said. "I came
from an old-line family myself, from the Deep South, where we've got
some pretty deep-seated roots ourselves when it comes to traditional
respect for the family." Dickens added how he admired Zein for working hard and accomplishing so much.

Dickens commiserated with Mona about how kids weren't being
brought up the way they had been. Children weren't like they used to
be. "There isn't a sixteen-year-old out there for that matter who does-
n't think her parents is making their life miserable," he said.

Mona explained how Tina would be killed in the homeland for having a boyfriend, let alone a black lover.

Dickens, who as a caseworker knew full well that these were poor
people, said that Tina "has no respect for anything because she hasn't
had to earn anything. . . . Your dad is almost excessive with her. Your
dad's made it so she hasn't had to want, to work. . . . It's all been on a
silver platter."

The caseworker did tell Zein that he must pay his daughter for
working and that Tina should be back in school. Apparently that
would be all the caseworker would demand, for Dickens said he was
reluctant to cross cultural lines.

When Mona claimed that Tina ran away only to attract attention,
the government employee paid to protect the rights of children
responded, "Exactly. I don't doubt that at all! I don't doubt that at all!"

Dickens and Mona discussed raising their toddlers; Dickens had
custody of his little girl. "As a matter of fact, my ex-wife married a—
say it! My ex-wife married a black man."

"You ought to be nuts," Mona exclaimed.

The caseworker laughed, "I am real close . . . I am real close."

Did he think her parents would hurt Tina? Mona asked.

While they might hit her, "I don't know if there was a spanking. I
don't know how bad it was. I can't look at your sister to see if there's
any marks." Dickens added, "I do not think it would be abuse now."

Dickens later told the police that he twice visited the Isas, once for two hours. Tina showed no signs of injury, he said. What did he think Tina would reveal with her parents sitting on either side of her?

Dickens closed Tina's file[*] and forgot about her—until a homicide detective called him.

Zein felt doubly betrayed by his daughter. Not only had she reported him to government officials, but she also told Dickens her mother bossed her father around—a problem Luie and Amjad also remarked upon. Zein called Tawfiq for advice. Tawfiq suggested sending Tina to live with a sister. Nope, said Zein, she won't go. Tawfiq recommended, "She needs to be beaten up. She wants to be beaten up mercilessly."

"The stick was used," Zein reported. "She was beaten more than even a mule can take. It seems we have to return to the more difficult method."

Mona called Tina's counselor, Ms. Fournier, on Tuesday, October 17, accusing her of reporting the family to the child abuse hot line. Fournier had suspected the Isas of brutalizing their daughter. One day she saw Tina in dark sunglasses in the dimly lit hall. Rushing up to her, the counselor asked the student, Are you hurt? Did someone at home punch you? Averting her face, Tina denied being attacked. Fournier tried to draw the student into confiding in her, but Tina would say nothing.

Kent Dickens apparently never checked with Tina's counselors or schoolmates about her reported injuries.

Soraia phoned her father, nagging him to do something. He was paralyzed with misery because Tina had shamed him again, telling the neighbors how her parents beat her. Soraia said she had already told Leilah to stab Tina and then say Tina had threatened her. Don't say things like that on this phone, Zein reprimanded.

But Soraia was angry with her older sisters for telling her to let Faisal handle this. Faisal and his wife are low lifes, Soraia said, they ask Tina if she wants to marry Cliff. She doesn't want to get married, Zein said.

Yeah, "she just wants to open her legs to the blacks," Soraia said.

Zein changed the topic. By God, he had just bought two nice ties,

[*]In fairness, DFS has been grossly underfunded and understaffed. Missouri is a poor state.

but he wouldn't have the chance to wear them for he soon would be wearing overalls.

Overalls? What overalls? Soraia asked.

"The overalls the criminals wear."

Talking long-distance about Tina to his relative Nidal in Raleigh, North Carolina, Zein admitted, "Her mom and I beat her to death." The other day, he continued, he had hit Tina so hard with a stick that it broke in two.

"Just hang her and throw her away," Nidal suggested, then asked if Zein were really serious.

"My God, I'm being serious," Zein replied.

"Curse upon her," Nidal responded. "How old is she?"

"Near seventeen years old."

"May God make her into seventeen pieces. This one needs to have her head broken, I swear," Nidal said.

Alarmed suddenly, Zein blurted out, "This talk can't be made on the phone," but continued to detail the beatings. How he had punched Tina because she was seeing a black youth. And that was why the blacks were going to stage "a march" in front of his store on Sunday.

"You disallowed that kind of thing [Tina dating a black]—they're going to make you lose your shirt in that store," Nidal cautioned. Sell it now, the blacks will wreck the business.

"I can't sell it tonight, I sell to those I know," Zein complained. "I hope we will burn up the store and everything." (Arson to Zein's group was a common solution, not a problem.)

Zein went on, "During my lifetime I expected things to happen. I expected killing, I mean I would kill but not here. I expected being arrested, and this is likely to happen any day now."

Meanwhile, Tawfiq was so alarmed, he decided to come down from Milwaukee to be with his cousin. He would try to soothe the neighborhood hysteria over the Isas' racism. There had been talk among blacks of boycotting Alliance Market and maybe even picketing it. "We need to prove to this world that when one of us is in need, we stand by each other," he reminded Saif.

Go to the black church leaders to pacify them, Saif recommended. That would avoid a black boycott. He was tired of telling Zein what to do; if he could run his own house, Zein should be able to run his, too.

But there is no remedy for Tina, Saif told Tawfiq, no remedy except "the last solution. He is the only one who can do it."

Mona and Zein were convinced that the cause of their misfortune was that Tina was sex-crazed. "If it is for a dick, all men have it," Zein said during a phone conversation, October 20.

"The young donkey has it, the cow, the ox," Mona laughed, "but the blacks are larger."

Mona berated her father for not taking a tougher stand with Tina.

Watch your tongue, he warned. "My phone's been 'dirty' for two years."

Tina, meanwhile, wrote an autobiographical essay for French class: She had been a very outgoing little girl, she wrote. She had always tried to help everyone with anything she could. Indeed, whenever someone was hurt, Tina would stop to help them. So she even wanted to be a doctor like her big brother, Faisal.

While she always was surrounded by friends, Tina wrote how she always felt different from them. She implied that was from moving around so much—her first two years were in Brazil, then Puerto Rico. She missed her friends when she moved to Israel, where she felt lost not knowing anyone or the language. No matter. At school she was always the best, despite an accent that created a minor barrier. It was really no problem, Tina wrote, she had learned no matter what. She had almost become like everyone else when her parents announced they were moving back to Puerto Rico. She was pleased, thinking it would be permanent.

It was not, but ultimately Tina was happier living in America. Here she had met people she foresaw as lifelong friends and acquaintances.

While she had many associates, Tina felt she had only two true friends. She noted that she wasn't as outgoing as she had once been.

After graduation from high school, she planned to go to college, where she would study to become a pilot. But, Tina noted, she also wanted to counsel other teens who had problems.

"After college, I want to work until I have enough money to go and see the world. At least France. And then maybe get married—that is, if I live that long."

Her parents decided Tina could not go to college. But Tina was determined no matter the obstacles, confiding in Helena, "If they won't pay my tuition to Parks [College, St. Louis University], then I'll become a math teacher before I become a pilot."

Zein had once yelled at her, "You want to run your life like a boy would. A pilot is not a woman's job."

"Why not?" Tina had retorted.

"Those are like whores. They sleep each night in a different city. If you like to travel so much from one country or city to another, join our organization. Every week they send you to a country to deliver letters, and this will be all you do. You will smell air. You will go for three or four days to the homeland."

What Zein didn't tell his daughter was how unpleasant and dangerous couriering papers could be. One female relative had been detained and strip-searched at Lod Airport where authorities recovered the ANO letters she had stuffed in her vagina.

Stay far away from Dad's politicking, Leilah had long warned.

Fayrouz called her father October 21 to repeat how she thought Tina could be redeemed. Nah, scoffed Zein, one day she's going to try to stab me with a knife.

Two days later, Tawfiq came to town to help. He sent Zein out of the house and sat down with Tina. But Tina refused to talk with him, saying, this is the way I am. See, I told you so, Saif later snorted, this cannot be repaired.

Determined, Tina managed to take Cliff to her Homecoming Ball October 28, with the help of her best friend. "I was driving," Helena explained. "I picked Tina up. At first they weren't going to let her go. They didn't know Cliff would be there. When Tina got home, Maria asked if he were there. 'Why do you want him?' Maria demanded. 'Why don't you find someone else?' " Then her parents took away her telephone again.

The teacher's back was turned in room 106, Roosevelt High; he was writing a trigonometry equation on the blackboard. Tina tapped a girl who sat near her. Pssst, take this, she said, handing the girl a piece of notebook paper. The student, who knew Tina only within the confines of trig class, looked down at the folded, torn piece of notebook paper and then at Tina's eyes. Tina looked like a weary hunted animal.

The girl studied the folded paper. On the outside was written, "To the St. Louis Police Department," and inside, "If anything happens to me, my friend Helena, or my boyfriend Cliff, it is all my father's fault."

"My father's going to kill me. He says he will kill me," Tina had told the girl earlier. The classmate remembered the times Tina had walked into trig class with bruises on her face. Her father beats her, other kids had said. Parents always say they're going to kill you, the girl had consoled Tina.

Tina walked into Ms. Fournier's office on Thursday, November 1, and sat down. "My family is going to sell their grocery store. They are going to leave the country," she said.

"Where will they go," Fournier asked.

"My father cannot go back to Israel, so they're moving to Brazil," she said. Before the counselor could speak, Tina added, "I'm not going to go. Don't worry about me, I'll be fine."

"We can find you a scholarship," Ms. Fournier said. "I'll call your mother and tell her."

"No," admonished Tina. "Don't call. It would be worse coming from an American."

Despite the school year, Zein suggested taking Tina and Maria to Brazil for a few months to visit Maria's mother. "I'm not going with you," Tina cried.

Faisal, her favorite in the family, again offered to send a round-trip ticket for a three-week vacation, but Tina would not leave school. Faisal upped the offer: Come live with me and my wife. He would send her to the superb, Quaker-founded Friends School in Ramallah, filled with culture-shocked Palestinian-American teens. But Tina refused, saying, "Palestine isn't my homeland. I never want to go there again."

"I'm afraid," she confided to Helena. "My family'll have me killed. They think it'll be safer to do it over there."

If Faisal were being truthful and had he enrolled her there, Tina might be alive today. The privately run Friends School takes very good care of its students. Ironically, the Friends curriculum was instrumental in shaping the feminist movement on the West Bank, according to its brochure quoting famous alumna Hanan Ashrawi, former spokeswoman for the Palestinian delegation to the peace settlement.

Friends—with its old ivy-covered stone façade of large arched windows, its afterschool drama rehearsals, its book fairs and newsletters—looks like private schools across America. Friends is no reformatory for the culturally confused, no political correction, but a college prep institution. The teachers are first-rate. The classes are entirely in English. For "transfer" students, some of whom are Tina's relatives, there are

counselors to ease reentry into an Arab culture. Accommodation to a
radically different society is hard, Fayrouz's beautiful daughter said:
"You're known here first as the daughter or son of so-and-so. Your own
name is not important." Echoed another girl, "We come here with terrible adjustment problems."

Indeed, a handful of students there said they were convinced that
had they stayed in America, they'd have been raped, become pregnant,
or addicted to drugs. Their teacher gently told them to think for themselves and to avoid stereotyping Americans.* (Most Palestinians, however, correctly believe that Americans do stereotype them.)

The kids dress in Gap and Guess? and use the same slang as well-to-
do suburban American teenagers, seeing the United States as a cornu-
copia of earthly consumer delights. One teen told how she was "hooked
on dating, staying out till midnight, and football games. None of which
are here. My dad—back in the States—sends me copies of *Teen, Seventeen, Glamour*, and *Cosmopolitan. Cosmo* is very controversial here."

"There are no shopping centers with movies, clothes, and fast food,"
another girl itemized her losses. "I still miss The Limited, Gap, denim,
Keds, Reeboks, all the hair elastics, Burger King. I can't let go of Taco Bell."

One girl shook her head sadly, "Totally, I miss the malls."

Fayrouz saw a way to save both family honor and her little sister's life:
To keep Tina away from Cliff, Zein could sign papers and the juvenile
authorities would lock her up. Zein was reluctant to go to the authorities for anything. Fayrouz pushed her case: This way, if Tina ran away
again, the police might jail her.

The next morning, November 3, Fayrouz called Juvenile Court. A
judge told her that the family could not forcibly take Tina out of the
country; that if she wanted to leave her father, have sex, whatever, those
were her decisions to make after she turned seventeen. And if her parents
kicked Tina out, they were responsible for her until she was eighteen.

Zein and Tina were at an impasse. He had exactly one month to
prove his manhood, to control his daughter before she turned seventeen on December 3.

---

*A popular 1992 joke at Friends illustrates this: "Why was Jesus born in Palestine
instead of America?" Answer: "He couldn't find a virgin over there."

CHAPTER FOURTEEN

The Long Walk Home

The phone rang in Homicide. It was ten o'clock on a Friday night, November 3, and fortunately it was not the Command Post calling with a new case to be investigated. It was Lieutenant Harry Hegger. "Just checking in," he said with his low, cigarette-husky chuckle. He phoned in every night.

"Not to check up on us," Sergeant Mike Guzy explained to a new detective. "Harry's really interested in what's going on. When there's a breaking case, he doesn't leave because it's five P.M.. He'll be here in the office with us till all hours." Hegger was notoriously eagle-eyed; he saw the entire panorama and could point to each tiny piece within it. "If they want a job done, they have to give it to Hegger," explained another officer, so that Hegger was promoted without politicking (unusual in the St. Louis Police Department).* "Energy and dogged-ness beat talent and high IQ every time," Hegger commented wryly when complimented on his latest advancement.

Indeed, when reporters asked him questions at news conferences, he would defer to the sergeants and detectives who worked the case. And that was the only time—and only if the brass were there—that his men called Hegger by his rank. The rest of the time he encouraged informality. "This is a team effort. I just give directions," he chuckled. "And then I get all the credit." Hegger was never derided for being "a suit."

"He gets results because he's so cooperative," said Tom Newman,† the FBI supervisor then in charge of the Violent Crime Unit, who often worked with Hegger. "Harry just wants to get the job done; he's not interested in grabbing any glory." Hegger's mental agility and minuscule ego allowed him to nimbly sidestep intra-agency feuds.

---

*The police department also uses tests for promotion.

†Name changed at the FBI supervisor's request to preserve anonymity in working cases. Newman later became supervisor of the Counterterrorism Unit for the FBI and oversaw the federal portion of the Isa case.

Earlier in the year Hegger had been transferred to Crimes Against Persons, where he served as deputy commander. He liked cleaning up those violent cases—the department was and is first-rate, and has achieved a high rate of arrests. "Usually, and I emphasize usually, murder is an easy crime to solve. The most important piece of evidence is the body. Then's it's not hard to establish motive, time, and opportunity. And that leads to your suspect."

In the biggest case of Hegger's career, the most important piece of evidence would not be the corpse.

Tina hunched over as she filled out the employment application at the Wendy's restaurant on 3800 South Grand Avenue. She wanted to work as a cashier. She currently was a cashier at Alliance Market, she wrote, but "it was a dead-end job." She explained she wanted to work as much as possible—at night, after her classes, *and* eighteen hours over the weekend. It would be hard to find time to see Cliff, but she knew he would adjust to her schedule.

"The person to notify in case of emergency"—Tina thought about this one, then wrote "Helena Mylanos" and her classmate's phone number. She felt depressed but pushed herself to smile. "I need a job. I want the money so I can move out, get my own place to live," Tina had told Helena. "Then I can save for college."

She was to start Sunday afternoon, November 5. Her parents would be at Alliance Market then, unable to stop her. Tina wrote a note to them: "I'll be back after work late tonight," and she stuck it to the television set in the living room.

For hours that Sunday night, Tina and her manager worked side by side. They both were nervous. It was the first night on the job for her boss, who had just been promoted to assistant manager. Tina was trying very hard to work quickly, keep up with the orders, and foremost, not to spill coffee on the customers. But she did not need to worry about making a good first impression on her boss. The woman looked familiar.

It was Colleen Flowers, now Winterbauer. Their working together was one of life's little coincidences. Nearly five years earlier, when Zein had bought Alliance Market from Colleen's father, he brought along twelve-year-old Tina to translate. "I remembered this little girl speaking all these languages," Colleen said. Tonight, Tina impressed her again. "She was really good at work. She picked up things awfully fast. And I found out she had had a four-point grade average at Roosevelt [until her recent problems with her parents]. She was so smart."

Tina was confiding to Colleen, "I don't get along with my father. I need the extra money. I might be moving out of the house around my seventeenth birthday in a few weeks."

Toward the end of the exhausting evening, Colleen looked out the window. Here it was nearly closing time—past eleven o'clock at night—and there was this guy standing outside by the drive-through window. Does anyone know who this dude is? Colleen asked. Tina smiled broadly. Yes, he's my boyfriend, she said. Colleen wondered why he was there. It was so cold that night. Cliff waited patiently for Tina, who had quickly changed clothes, throwing her brown Wendy's uniform into her bookbag. She rushed out to join him.

It was long past eleven P.M. when they slowly began the long walk home.

Tina walked through the front door at a minute to midnight and entered the apartment. The door slammed loudly as she closed it. Maria and Zein had been sitting silently in their darkened living room waiting for her. "Where were you, bitch?" her mother yelled at her.

After almost ten minutes of haranguing her, Zein drew out a butcher knife. Maria held Tina by her hair.

"Listen, my dear daughter," Zein said. "Tonight you're going to die."

PART TWO

"HELL WAS WAITING"

CHAPTER FIFTEEN

"Such a Cold Tale"

"Homicide requested. A cutting at 3759 Delor, apartment C," the police dispatcher said at one A.M.

Twelve minutes later Sergeant Michael Guzy and his Homicide crew, Detectives Billy Qualls and Timothy Richards, met on the apartment steps. The First District officer who had responded to the original call was waiting: "I've got a guy inside who says his daughter attacked him with a knife and in the struggle she was killed. The mother is the witness."

Ironically, this officer, Robert Sanneman, had interviewed Maria in August when she reported Tina as a suicidal runaway. Now, three months later, Sanneman was staring at the teenager's corpse. "Maria Isa was more emotional the evening she reported her daughter missing," Sanneman told Guzy.

As the Homicide crew opened the door, Detective Qualls took a deep breath; on the floor lay a young girl soaked in blood. The paramedics were finishing up; they had run an EKG line which was flat. As his daughter was pronounced clinically dead, an old man sat blank-faced on the sofa.

The girl's blouse and bra were pulled away, revealing pools of blood from numerous puncture wounds. Detective Qualls thought it odd that the wounds were grouped together; nobody stands still to be stabbed. Sergeant Guzy counted eight large lacerations. The smaller ones were too numerous to count now, when he was busy calling the medical examiner's office for an investigator. Then he dialed the Command Post to find interpreters in Portuguese and Arabic so the police could interview the man leaning back on the dirty sofa and the woman sitting in a shabby, cheaply upholstered chair.

The couple were in full view of the body, though both ignored it, later walking around it as if it were just some obstacle in the room, Qualls thought. Two large knives lay by the girl's side. An evidence technician covered the hands with plastic bags to preserve any hair, fibers, or blood from her assailants. The body was still warm. Around the girl's throat lay a gold necklace spelling out "Sweet Sixteen."

Bare footprints in blood formed a path from the body down the hallway to the bathroom to the toilet. A bloody handprint stained the wall, droplets grouped about the light switch. There was blood all over Zein Isa's feet as well as on his hands and chest. His clothes were soaked in blood. The seasoned Homicide crew looked at each other: Could this really be his own daughter?

The memory of one of his first murder cases flashed in Detective Qualls's mind: He had been driving home after witnessing the autopsies of two little boys. Distraught, he pulled over to a pay phone and called his father, a retired detective. "Dad," Qualls said, his voice breaking, "those bodies reminded me of my own two babies."

"Help their family as much as you can, son," his father answered. "Thank God they're not your little boys. And move on."

People often think Homicide detectives are these big tough guys in dirty trench coats, swilling syrup-thick coffee and dragging on unfiltered Camels between their thumb and forefinger. While they do not pin up embroidered samplers about sharing and caring, Homicide detectives are rarely distilled machismo.

Yeah, they drink from mugs imprinted with such adages as "OUR DAY BEGINS WHEN YOURS ENDS." Yeah, they have to wrestle with thugs, but they also must be able to talk to people—encourage reluctant witnesses to open up, make defendants want to confess, and soothe the grieving families. Families, plural. Many of the bodies outlined by the evidence unit's chalk marks are not those of upstanding citizens. "Remember, even the worst drug dealer now dead was once someone's bouncing baby boy," Sam Lackland, now a retired Homicide lieutenant, said. "And his killer, another dealer—that was also once somebody's child."

"No matter how many murder scenes he has to investigate, a good cop has to keep his or her humanity or he or she is worthless," Qualls remembered being trained, by Joe Burgoon, a legendary Homicide sergeant, to be nice to people.

But when an innocent person, especially a child, has been murdered, the cops react differently. These were victims who were helpless, stripped of their humanity, according to Qualls. And the police double their efforts, sometimes to the level of obsession.

*   *   *

What came to Sergeant Guzy looking at that teeny apartment—with its plaster-board walls, tacky furnishings, lack of cleanliness—and nondescript, gray, middle-aged Zein was Hannah Arendt's "banality of evil." Guzy is *very* proud of his master's degree in English literature. "The devil works in such ordinary ways. Zein was an evil son of a bitch," Guzy later told his lieutenant. "He was very disdainful of his daughter, even in death, saying, 'There she is, take her away.' He and his family—who kept arriving in droves—continued to portray the incident as psycho teen attacks dear old daddy. I didn't buy it from the gut from the git-go."

The physical evidence did not match the father's story. The victim looked larger than her assailant. Tina was clearly big-boned, full-breasted, and wide-hipped. Even in death his daughter appeared more robust than Zein did limping around the apartment.

While the Homicide detectives and the evidence technicians were busy measuring where the body lay in relation to the furniture, scraping up samples of blood, and checking the knife drawer, the living room telephone rang. Guzy answered. It was Amir Darwish, Zein's son-in-law, the owner of a sporting goods store in Bensenville, Illinois. Amir asked to speak with Zein. "He can't talk right now," Guzy said. "You'll have to call back."

The police separated the couple for interviews to see if their stories meshed. Qualls took Zein. Guzy and Richards questioned Maria whose English seemed limited. "She refused to converse in English. Very uncooperative," Guzy told Qualls. Finally, Guzy allowed Mona's husband, Nai'el, to interpret.

"I didn't exactly see how Tina was stabbed," Maria said, emphasizing repeatedly, "I never stabbed her." Nai'el added that Maria had called them about one A.M. hysterically demanding that they hurry over. His in-laws had problems with Tina, he said, over "issues of independence." The girl had run away several times. The police thought how runaways are often abused children.

Zein rose from the sofa and reenacted the murder scene to Qualls. He hobbled to the kitchen, opening the drawer from which Tina had taken the two knives. "She came at me with a knife," he said furiously. He showed Qualls a small cut on the top of his hand. "My daughter attacked me," he repeated self-righteously.

A man defending himself against a blade slashing away would have at least several deep gashes. But Zein's cut was so superficial that he refused to be taken to a hospital (and signed a release form). Instead of sympathizing, the police took him and his wife downtown for questioning at the station.

Some of the family stayed in the bleak house after the detectives led Zein and Maria away, busily calling relatives and cohorts. At 2:30 A.M., Nai'el started phoning relatives and friends. He first checked in with Tawfiq long-distance.

"I'm in the house of the old man, Abu Faisal," Nai'el said. "We . . . need you here. . . . There's a problem we want to talk to you about."

Tawfiq asked, "Is something the matter?"

"The girl took care of herself. They took her father and mother to jail."

"I'm coming," Tawfiq said.

Tawfiq called Rabih, Leilah's brother-in-law in St. Louis, who asked, "What happened?"

"She went to hell," Tawfiq said.

"She died—and how is her father?" Rabih asked.

"Nothing."

"If she suicided, they will get out, and if they killed—oh, gosh, how?"

"God knows," Tawfiq said. "The important [thing] is that hell was waiting for her."

Nai'el told Jamal, Zein's brother, in Wisconsin, "I want to inform you, the old man has a problem." "The girl" killed herself after demanding $5,000 and attacking Zein and wounding his hand, he said.

Before she left for the police station, Fayrouz phoned Leilah. "Don't mention what you told me about late this afternoon to anybody! All I know is, forget what you know," Fayrouz warned.

Leilah cautioned Fayrouz, "He [Amir] said that we all stick to one story." And do not mention Amir's name, she added.

At 4:34 in the morning, during a three-minute call to the West Bank, the family notified Faisal that his favorite sister was dead.

Zein and Maria could not understand why they were being bundled up into police cars. Their attitude was, What else could you do with such a wayward child? She's been so much trouble. We knew she'd do something like this. "Her" and "she" did not seem to have a first name to the family.

The cars pulled up in front of the St. Louis Police Headquarters. Downtown St. Louis was dead quiet. The 1927 pale gray stone fortress in the Government Moderne[*] style, with its foyer of Art Nouveau brass and glass globes and cream-colored marble, was silent, too. The detectives bundled the Isas inside the shining brass doors of the elevator and went upstairs.

Homicide's warren of sergeants' offices with frosted glass panes set into darkly varnished wood resembled the set from any 1930s cop shop movie. Qualls and Richards walked Zein down the sad brown linoleum floor to a spartan interview room, sat him down on a plain wooden chair, advised him of the charges against him, and read him his rights.

Zein agreed to being interviewed. Why? "The Isas saw us as allies," explained Sergeant Guzy. "They were talking to us, like 'Hey, we all have teenagers and know what a pain they can be.' "

Qualls thought, "Initially, Zein seemed forlorn. But then a degree of hardness came out. I can't imagine killing a child rather than knocking him out if he attacked me. I love to analyze cases, although it was hard with the Isas. I had no frame of reference. Theirs was such a cold tale."

Zein's version was that he and Maria had come home at 2:30 that afternoon from work to an empty apartment. Where was their daughter Tina? A note was on the TV that she had gone to work and would be back before midnight. Upset and angry, the Isas ate dinner and spent the evening watching television, Zein said, waiting for their errant child.

The front door slammed open at 11:30. "Hi," he said to Tina. "Hi," she snapped back as she trotted into the kitchen. Quickly, she returned to where her parents were sitting on the sofa. Brandishing a butcher knife with an eleven-inch blade, she demanded $5,000. Her father thought she was crazy. The banks were not open. Where was he going to get that kind of money? Maria asked what she needed the money for. Tina held the knife out and, looking at her beleaguered father, said, "Give me five thousand dollars, you son of a bitch."

Defiantly, she walked toward him. He stood up and asked, "Are you doing drugs?" Her parents thought she might be in some satanic cult;

[*]Government Moderne is the hybrid of Art Deco and Moderne popular with government then, according to the Landmarks Association of St. Louis, Inc.

she wore black a lot. She continued to walk toward her father, holding the knife out. He reached up to take it from her and cut the inside of his left hand as she pulled it away from him. She came toward him again, trying to stab him. He grabbed her hand and wrist. They struggled for the knife, but he overpowered her and turned the butcher knife inward. He thrust the knife into her chest, once. She fell forward onto him. They battled for the knife. He yanked it away and thrust it into her chest a second time. She fell to the floor. The knife dropped beside her.

He fell onto his knees over her. As he pulled himself up, he saw she had a second knife, the one with the eight-and-a-half-inch blade, in her left hand. He picked up the first knife, the one with the eleven-inch blade, and stabbed her in the chest once or twice more. Then he dropped the knife to the floor. He stood and walked down the hall, where he urinated. And without washing Tina's blood from his hands, he called the police.

Qualls and Richards handcuffed Zein and took him down to Booking, where they charged him with murder in the first degree and armed criminal action—using a weapon in the commission of a felony. Guzy called downstairs to the lobby and told the officer on guard duty to send Maria's son-in-law up to fetch her. She could go free. Later, Guzy said, "My initial guess was Zein killed Tina while Maria stood by watching and did nothing. She kept saying, 'I never stabbed Tina.' I was right on the fence. Why book her?"

By eight o'clock that morning, Lieutenant Harry Hegger had been working for half an hour at an old battered desk with a picturesque scene through his casement windows of the French Renaissance Revival–style City Hall[*] behind him. Not that Hegger took the time to look outside much. The frosted glass door to his office was open in case anyone wanted to plop down on the ripped vinyl settee and talk with him. The lieutenant was more than available; he was always there.

"Put Harry in charge, and he's the first one in in the morning putting on the coffee. Whatever his job is becomes the focus of his existence, he becomes obsessed within the moment," a sergeant once told a reporter. The root of that obsession was curiosity: Hegger always wanted to know why, what was the answer to the secret, how all the pieces fit together in the puzzle.

[*]St. Louis City Hall is modeled after the Hôtel de Ville in Paris.

As a little boy watching "Dragnet," Hegger had no interest in becoming another Detective Joe Friday. When he had recovered from his Vietnam War wounds, in 1969, he enrolled in night school at a community college and started work on an automobile assembly line. "I quickly realized I wouldn't enjoy being the fourth generation of Heggers at the Ford plant."

Wondering what he wanted to do next, the twenty-two-year-old remembered how he had been impressed with police recruiters at the military base back when he was a marine ready to be shipped off to Vietnam. With not much else to do on his days off, Hegger underwent the tests and interviews at St. Louis Police Headquarters. They told him they might call back in four to six months. A week later the phone rang: You've been selected for our next Police Academy class. It starts Monday, an officer said.

When Hegger finished work that day, he gave notice. Then he walked into his father's office in Labor Relations and told him. Harry Hegger Sr. became very quiet.

"Ford's been good to us," his father said. "You think you're making the right decision?"

"Dad, I don't want to expect the same thing every day when I walk into work. I want a challenge. I want a surprise."

By the time St. Louis University awarded him a diploma in Urban Affairs, Hegger was a comer in the Police Department. Federal agencies offered him jobs that he was sorely tempted to take—more money, lots more; more prestige; often, more sophisticated work. In the end he said no: "If I went with a federal agency, I wouldn't have been based in St. Louis. I'd just been divorced and wanted to see my daughter, a toddler, more than once a month. I didn't want her growing up my daughter in name only."

Several months later Hegger was transferred to the department's Intelligence Unit. It was a perfect fit. He was quickly promoted to detective/investigator, going undercover after big-time drug lords. "Intelligence is proactive. You have to anticipate. You're constantly working," said the minimum-sixty-hour-a-week man who would work up to 100 hours a week during a hot case, overtime gratis. "There's no reason to burn out," Hegger explained to a reporter who asked. He clearly was fueled by the investigations. The more complex the case was, the more his curiosity would trigger the adrenalin.

Hegger and his partner brought in more high-caliber criminals in one year than anybody, according to the U.S. Attorney's Office, where the pair was assigned to the Organized Crime Drug Enforcement Task Force. Hegger had more fun in Intelligence than a kid at a country fair. "It's a challenge trying to outsmart a dealer," he explained. "It's extremely satisfying when you crack a major dealer. If you make a good haul on a search warrant, you can break the back of a criminal organization."

When he was named the National Law Officer of the Year, Hegger's acceptance speech illustrated why he was the detective's detective:

"Though I have been chosen to be recognized today, I know a person's accomplishments are not achieved by only one's self-initiative. Throughout life, one's realization is achieved by the inspiration, encouragement, and association with their fellow human beings. There have been many such people in my life. I would like to take this opportunity to say thanks to them."

Detective Qualls, who had worked overnight, came into Hegger's office and handed him a draft of the sergeant's police report. Hegger respected the crew's opinions and agreed with their assessment for the warrants.

"There's enough for me for murder second. The girl gets hacked to death and there's no harm to him. You might get a murder first," Hegger said.

Qualls lay the evidence photographs over Hegger's desk. One featured Zein's cut hand. Looking at it, Hegger said, "A paper cut isn't exactly a defensive wound, Qualls. I get more than that reading your reports," his laugh husky from cigarettes. "Let's apply for murder one."

At 8:30 that morning, the assistant medical examiner began the postmortem of Palestina Zein Isa. The forensic pathologist found thirteen wounds, six of them mortal. The worst one plunged into her chest wall, breaking her sternum and ribs and piercing her heart. A second gash ripped her left lung. Her liver had been slashed five times, four fatally. Seven times her breasts had been punctured, seemingly with the point of a knife. These wounds formed small circles.

On her death certificate, under race, some bureaucrat typed "Arabian."

At ten A.M. Saif called Umm Leilah—"mother of Leilah," as he referred to Maria—who was staying with her stepdaughter Fayrouz.

Don't talk to reporters, he said. Fayrouz told him that Farid Badran had already warned them. Saif said he was more concerned about all the cops he saw watching the apartment and trailing him. Make certain Maria sticks to her original story she told the police, he added.

At 10:45 A.M., Detective Qualls was sitting in the warrant office, furious, as a prosecutor ticked off the reasons why he could not issue any warrants against Zein: The only witness was Maria; she confirmed her husband's alibi of self-defense; there were two knives on the body; Zein had not tried to run away from the crime scene; and the post-mortem report, with additional evidence, was not in yet.

"You have to issue," Qualls demanded.

The prosecutor, Bob Craddick, took him upstairs to the circuit attorney's office, but he was not in, nor was his chief trial assistant. Next in line was the new first assistant to the circuit attorney, Dee Joyce-Hayes. "T.U.A. it ["Taken Under Advisement," meaning the prosecutors would consider the matter later] for the time being," she said. "It's not my decision alone."

Under Missouri law, police cannot hold a suspect after arrest more than twenty hours without warrants being issued. Zein could go free.

"Wait till Hegger hears this," Qualls thought as he left. He ran into Hegger in a hallway back at the station. They ducked into his office.

"You're not going to fucking believe this!" Qualls burst out. "How the hell can you kill your own kid and not be held?"

Hegger, who had the world's worst poker face, looked profoundly stunned. He grabbed his phone and called Intelligence. "I need a favor: Put Zein Isa under surveillance. I need to know where he is at all times," Hegger said. "I'm guessing that he and Maria won't spend the night in the apartment where they killed their daughter—they'll go somewhere with one of their daughters, in the county [St. Louis County]."

Then he called the FBI, "Please tail Zein for me," Hegger asked. "Fine," the man said. "Some people are working on this." That meant the feds were investigating safe houses. Hegger suspected that there were a group of such buildings in North St. Louis County, where Zein's relatives lived. He wondered whether Zein's apartment and Alliance Market were stopovers for terrorist couriers moving money coast-to-coast and overseas. Places to chill out when things got hot? Were they some sleeper cell waiting the word to help plan an attack

here? There was a lot for a terrorist to hit in the river city, which was
the hub for TWA, world headquarters then for General Dynamics, and
McDonnell-Douglas Aircraft, the location of the Army Record Center
of the entire U.S. Army as well as the Defense Mapping Agency.

He punched in the number of the warrant office for Bob Craddick.
"Hey, Bob," Lieutenant Hegger said. "The crime speaks for itself. This
isn't self-defense. Zein didn't have any real wounds."

"Harry, I'll take it to the grand jury," Craddick protested, meaning,
let the grand jury charge him. "It's just a domestic. She attacked him."
(Hegger never faulted Craddick; "he just didn't know all the details of
the case.")

Next, Hegger called Hayes. "This isn't right, to T.U.A. it," he said.
"This isn't a self-defense issue. How could it be when the dead girl is
chunky and the old man is slightly built?"

The circuit attorney himself agreed with the lieutenant's assessment and
called Hegger from his car phone late Monday afternoon, after Hayes had
called him about the wrath of Harry and the medical examiner's report
which had come in late that day. "First thing in the morning, we'll put the
warrants together," the circuit attorney said. "You'll get murder first."

Hegger was temporarily appeased. He took the murder of the sixteen-year-old girl personally: The perpetrators had to be facing death
row or Hegger would feel betrayed. He walked down the fourth-floor
hall to Intelligence, tucked away in the back, to pick up one of their
two-way radios with its protected surveillance channel.

He had a hunch that the Isas, being foreigners, would try to flee. It
was more than a feeling. Hegger could feel his stomach and muscles
tightening up as though he were back in Da Nang and a battle was
coming: He had to see Zein in handcuffs, before the Palestinian's family could whisk him away.

As Hegger returned to his office, Bill Bryan, the well-wired police
reporter for the *Post-Dispatch*, wandered in. He had interviewed the
neighbors on Delor Street and the Isa relatives—even Zein and Maria
in their apartment.

"Harry," Bryan said, "Zein showed no emotion. There was blood still on
the carpet and he's saying, 'She deserved it. She attacked me.' Maria the
mother was coldhearted. 'I have nuthin' to say.' Her loyalty was to him. And
there were these two guys standing behind him, silent. They didn't smile.
They just stood there. Mean-looking dudes. They looked like terrorists."

CHAPTER SIXTEEN

A Rose for Mourning

Lieutenant Hegger awoke early the next day, downed his I-have-to-count-fat-grams breakfast of a banana and a granola bar with a pot of black coffee, and smoked a cigarette while racing downtown. The phone was ringing in his office as he walked in. It was an FBI agent.

"Hegger, remember back in '86 when you were working Intelligence and we called you in? About how we might need four hundred officers at a moment's notice? This guy that killed his daughter is one of that group, one of the people we're looking at."

Holy shit, this asshole's an Arab terrorist? thought Hegger, lighting up another cigarette. He calmly said to the FBI, "Oh, really?"

"Yeah," the agent continued. "Regarding your murder case, we have some very substantial evidence connected to that. I can't tell you what it is now. We need authorization out of Washington and we're trying to get it. We need to go through the channels. Bear with us. It's a highly sensitive issue. When the time comes, you'll find it very substantial. Title 50, National Security Act."

And just what the fuck is "substantial"? Hegger wondered. "I'm going to arrest this guy this morning," he said. "Getting at-large warrants on him. But I don't want to jeopardize your case." That's all we need, he thought, a stampede of terrorists.

"Don't worry," said the agent and hung up.

At 9:40 A.M. the phone rang again. It was Qualls in the circuit attorney's office. Dee Hayes was issuing at-large arrest warrants against Zein Isa for murder first and armed criminal action, writing "Zein admits third stab wound administered after his daughter was flat on her back on the floor." They would be signed later, at 3:21 P.M., by a circuit judge.[*] Now that the warrants were forthcoming, Hegger knew he could legally make his arrest before Isa fled.

---

[*]Judge Charles A. Shaw, whom Hegger had worked with years before when the judge was a federal prosecutor. Shaw would later preside over the Isas' murder trial.

Meanwhile, at 9:44 Farid Badran phoned Saif Nijmeh, saying he wished Zein would leave town. The newspaper stories were terrible; the police did not believe the self-defense alibi and would be investigating. If Zein didn't flee now, before Tina's funeral, he might not be able to later.

Ah, said Saif, and quickly dialed Tawfiq Musa. Things just got complicated, he said. Tawfiq ordered Saif to move Zein out. It was now 9:49.

At 9:50, over a special radio with a private channel, Intelligence detectives contacted Lieutenant Hegger. "We've got him here, on M-L-K [Martin Luther King Drive] in a liquor store in the three-thousand block."

Pushing the button to talk back, Hegger yelled, "We're en route" as he grabbed his jacket. It was unusual for a lieutenant to make an arrest himself, but considering the sensitivity of the case, he had to go.

He darted across the hall into the cubbyhole office of Sergeant John Roussin. (Guzy and his crew who worked the midnight shift were home sleeping.) The twenty-plus-year Homicide veteran understood what Hegger needed, why they were picking up Zein in such a public place early in the day: "You don't want a suspect picked up where he feels safe. Let as many Palestinians around as possible know that this is an important investigation. Let 'em wonder how the police knew where Zein was. But don't let 'em know how much we already know," Hegger said later to a reporter.

As Hegger and Roussin pulled up in an unmarked police car right at ten o'clock, an old Arab hurriedly walked out of a liquor store. It was Zein. "By God, we've missed him," Hegger yelled, just as two Intelligence detectives ran up and surrounded the man. Zein looked surprised to see the police—two tall, powerfully built men who towered over him, but he was unafraid, in fact, he was arrogant, even disdainful as the officers placed him under arrest.

Hegger handcuffed the prisoner and eased him into the backseat of his car. As Sergeant Roussin pulled away from the curb, Lieutenant Hegger could not resist. He turned around and said to Zein, "How does it feel to be in America now, you asshole?"

Now that he had Zein in custody, Hegger asked Qualls to do some legwork that night: "Please interview Tina's classmates, teachers, coun-

selors, friends—anyone and everyone you could find at Roosevelt
High. Canvass the neighborhood on Delor to see if anyone heard Tina
screaming. Interview the folks down on Shaw Avenue around Alliance
Market. And that's just a start."

" 'You're under arrest' is not as important as TV and movies make it
seem," Hegger explained later. "In the movies the police put the villain
in handcuffs and walk off into the sunset. In real life the system does
not take care of itself. The most important issue is, How are you going
to prove in court that this person did it?" He needed Qualls to make
the case—showing how all the pieces fit together into a chronological
story. He wanted to show there was no excuse, no alibi, no reason for
what Zein did. He wanted all the loose ends tied up so that at trial the
government could demolish any defense Zein's lawyer tried to present.

Intuitive, Hegger also possessed a solid analytical, legal mind.
"Harry has a great sense for how the facts in his investigation become
evidence at the trial," said the U.S. Attorney, Edward Dowd Jr., who
had worked with him on complex investigations. "He knows what to
push. He could walk into the U.S. Attorney's Office right now and try
a case for us." "Absolutely," added a former federal prosecutor.
"Harry's brighter than half the lawyers there." And when he was
called to testify in his cases, Hegger's rugged sex appeal added to his
jury appeal.

As reporters called him for the information about the Isa case and
the other recent murders, Lieutenant Hegger obliged them with
details. Reporters adored Hegger. He was that rare creature, an accomplished person who could talk for hours about his work without constant reference to how he figured into it. To the lieutenant, each case
was a human interest story—some sad, some droll, none were dull.
And when the tale was heartbreaking, like this one, Hegger looked as
though he were crying, even though he was not. Maybe only the really
tough can reveal their soft side.

In a strange way, because he saw the world in black and white,
Hegger was an innocent, although far from naive. No matter how
much gore he saw on the streets, he was always shocked by it. And then
he would point to his temple and say, "I want to know what they were
thinking when they did it. What made them do it? Why?" Once he had
solved that mystery and saw the perpetrator put away, Hegger was sat-
isfied, unlike those baby boomer opportunists his age—cops, prosecu-

tors, defense lawyers, reporters, and federal agents—who saw a big crime not as a human tragedy but as potential career stepping stones.

Hegger was also straightforward and honest without being stricken by self-righteousness. No altar boy, he was pleasantly unaware that most women found him very handsome and very sexy. Partly because he was unafraid of women, he treated them the same as men, professionally. But if he knew one well, he might enjoy flirting with her; Hegger liked to laugh every chance he could, frequently at himself. And what's more unusual, he truly enjoyed funny women.

While Hegger led the police investigation, Tawfiq took charge of the Beitin group. He ordered a mourning rose to be put on the door of Alliance Market; he planned that all of Zein's colleagues and cousins go together to the funeral procession to appear as if things were not unusual. Normal appearances, he emphasized. He wanted no criticism.

That morning of Zein's arrest, in Beitin, during their errand-running, Foiziya Isa asked her son, Faisal, to drive her to a phone so that she could call Tina. Foiziya wanted to console her about the problems she was having.

But Faisal screamed in the middle of the street, "Get into the car, let's go home."

"No, no," Foiziya insisted, "I want to call Tina."

"You can't," Faisal said. "She's dead."

His mother's legs began shaking so hard, he had to carry her into his car.

That afternoon, Maria moved in with her daughter's family in Florissant.

That night, a group of Palestinian men from other midwestern cities came into Homicide pretending to be lawyers and interpreters. "Damage control. They wanted to evaluate and assess what Zein's arrest had done to their terrorist organization. One was from Chicago and the FBI knew him," said Hegger, who asked them for their identification. "Then, I copied it all," he said with his husky laugh.

Cliff Walker and Helena Mylanos wanted something more than a keepsake to remember Tina by—something that would keep her alive for

Beitin. (Rula Halawani.)

The old and the new,
in Beitin, 1992. (Rula Halawani.)

Olive harvest in Beitin.
(Rula Halawani.)

Tina Isa (*left*) and a friend smile broadly
at winning their trophies.
(Courtesy Helena Mylanos.)

Tina and Cliff Walker at Tina's
Homecoming, October 1989, just weeks
before she was murdered.

Tina, shortly after her family immigrated
to St. Louis. (Courtesy Helena Mylanos.)

Tina and one of her favorite teachers at
Roosevelt High School.

The living room on Delor Street just after Tina was killed there at midnight, November 6, 1989. (Courtesy St. Louis Police Department.)

Tina's bedroom. She and Soraia shared the bunkbeds until her older sister married in August 1989. (Courtesy St. Louis Police Department.)

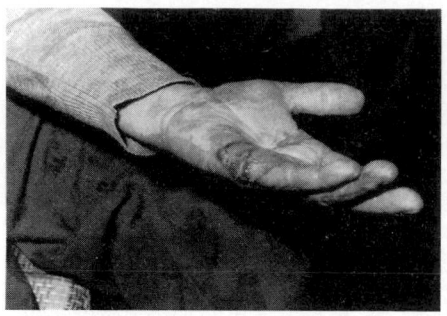

Zein Isa, at home, shortly after murdering his daughter. Police wanted to photograph him with Tina's blood staining his chest, both arms, legs, feet, and hands.
(Courtesy St. Louis Police Department.)

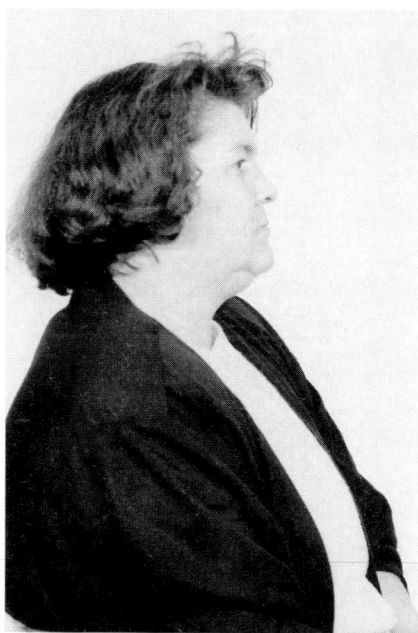

Maria Matias Isa.
(Courtesy St. Louis Police Department.)

Soraia (*left, in hijab*) and her aunt waiting for the verdict in the murder trial of both her parents, October 26, 1991.
(Doug Miner, AP/Wide World Photos.)

When he was the lieutenant in Homicide, Capt. Harry Hegger led the investigation in the Isa case and worked with the FBI. Later, he was transferred to his first love, Intelligence, where he was promoted to captain in 1994. Women almost always found Hegger a fascinating mix of character, sense of humor, and sex appeal. (L. A. Kelley.)

Det. Billy Qualls, later promoted to sergeant.

Sgt. Mike Guzy.

Charlie Shaw (*third from left*) and his World War II bomber pilot squadron. Note the handsome fellow with the ears—Clark Gable. Shaw defended Maria Isa.

The Hon. Charles A. Shaw tried the Isa case. Now a federal district judge.

Bob Craddick, assistant circuit attorney, who cochaired the prosecution of Zein and Maria Isa.

Dee Joyce-Hayes was an assistant circuit attorney when she tried the Isa case and is now the circuit attorney of St. Louis.

Daniel Reardon, former St. Louis circuit attorney, defended Zein Isa.

Luie Nijmeh leaving court in Dayton, Ohio, after his arrest on April 1, 1993. The U.S. Marshal called him violent after Luie screamed threats. (Wally Nelson/*Dayton Daily News*.)

Tawfiq Musa.
(*Milwaukee Sentinel* photo.)

Saif Nijmeh before yelling "Happy April Fool's Day" at reporters as FBI agents in St. Louis walked him down the hall, April 1, 1993.

As the lead prosecutor in the Abu Nidal case, then Assistant U.S. Attorney Jim Steitz spent three-plus years, sometimes taking only Thanksgiving and Christmas off, combing through the FBI logs of the 25,000 hours of taped conversations. Shortly before the federal trial, he was appointed an administrative law judge. Yet, even in late 1994, he could still recall specific dates and quotations from a myriad of conversations. (L. A. Kelly.)

Keith Liberman, defense attorney for Saif Nijmeh.

Neil Bruntrager, a former assistant circuit attorney and defense lawyer for Luie Nijmeh. (L. A. Kelly.)

Linda Murphy, defense attorney for Tawfiq Musa, and the only woman lawyer in the Abu Nidal terrorist case. A former chief trial attorney in the St. Louis Public Defender's Office, she had fifteen-plus years of trial experience. (Karen Elshout.)

them. "You know that picture of Tina in a yellow dress that they used in the [Roosevelt High School] yearbook dedication? They would have never gotten that picture if it weren't for me," Helena said with a deep breath, clearly not used to taking credit. "Tina never even saw that picture of herself. After she died, one night I and Cliff went up to their apartment. It was sealed with police tape. But the pictures had arrived in the mail after the murder and had been stuck in the doorway between the screen door and the front door." Helena took them and ran.

Tina Isa was buried as a bride two days after her gruesome murder. "I wanted my baby in a complete wedding outfit—white dress, veil, stockings, and shoes," Maria later explained, wiping her eyes. "In Brazil single girls are laid to rest that way." Fayrouz agreed, spending $600 for the dress. "That's how I still think of Tina, as a virginal bride—pure and clean. Despite what people said about her," Fayrouz said. The sisters made certain Tina was wearing her "Sweet Sixteen" gold necklace.

While people lined up to give Tina a kiss good-bye, her sister Mona froze. "I felt guilty, but I couldn't even touch her that day." Maria was in a daze, or a trance, people thought; she was turning around and whispering, "Where's Tina?" Zein was in handcuffs. The ceremony at the Sacred Heart Cemetery, in Florissant, was a Muslim service in Arabic.

Only people from Beitin had been invited. To keep Tina's friends from attending her funeral, the Isa family agreed not to put an announcement in the paper. "If Cliff had shown up, for sure we'd break his face," Mona said. "It wouldn't have been one funeral."

As they lowered Tina's coffin into the ground, everyone pulled out their handkerchiefs, and the hidden FBI agents took out their cameras. All of the Isas' relatives and friends from other states came in for the funeral—for moral support, and to raise money for the funeral expenses and the attorneys' fees. They were steadfast in believing Zein had been temporarily insane when he knifed his child.

Yet, back in the homeland, Faisal was practically shunned. "This shame lasts a generation because it's a crime of honor," Leilah explained. Tina's blood sacrifice did not cleanse the family name as Zein had planned. While the villagers supported Zein, most said he should not have killed Tina: "Even if Tina was sleeping with her black boyfriend, Zein should have used his brains and found a solution. He should have sent Tina to Beitin earlier." One young woman who liked the family noted, "Her slaying was a control problem that Zein tried to justify with a cultural context." But three young women added, "No Palestinian woman in America has ever married a black man."

As the winter rain washed away the funeral wreaths on Tina's grave, her father's relatives back in Beitin began whispering. Their words were carried from Bethlehem to Bir Zeit: that Tina's boyfriend was an FBI informant who had used her to gain access to the Isa home so he could install the bugs for the FBI. That Tina was an FBI informant who snitched on her father, that she herself had installed the bugs. Some villagers said Tina knew too much and knew that her father would kill her and that's why she planted the bugs and taps and even surveillance cameras. By the time her parents were sentenced for her murder, villagers were saying Zein belonged to Abu Nidal Organization.

A woman lawyer in Beit Hanina, on the edge of East Jerusalem, heard the stories about Tina's friends with rude manners, and her alleged involvement in a Satanic cult, and that one day Tina told her parents, "The devil is telling me to kill my mother." Another well-educated woman, slightly older than Tina, repeated to a reporter the assorted tidbits of gossip: Tina belonged to a Satanic cult, Tina was pregnant, Tina still was a virgin.

A Palestinian sociologist pointed out that a family needs to villify the murder victim to convince themselves they needn't suffer remorse. But, the professor added, "No Arab would condone killing a child because she was suspected of being an informant to the FBI." (Arabs do murder teenagers/young women suspected of being collaborators, which is akin to being an informant.)

Christian Israeli Arabs judge Zein more harshly, most condemn him. "What I really dislike is the way some families hated Americans, hated the culture, and yet they go there to live and refuse to let their kids enjoy that culture. They want to import our backward culture? Their kids naturally want the American way of life," said an artist outside Tel Aviv.

While this woman prefers living in her homeland, she resents attacks on the West. While studying in America, she heard an imam lecture. Never had she heard the U.S. condemned so badly. The imam hated all Americans. The only way was Islam. "Why is he there if he hates it? It's not like being American and criticizing your own country."

"Tina's case sounds bizarre, like a movie. No one avoids sex here for fear of dying. It's more fear of gossip. My friends with really strict fathers—they'd be more likely to sleep around out of rebellion. They wouldn't be killed."

The Isa case scared a lot of Palestinians. To keep their children from becoming too Americanized, many Palestinian-Americans, especially the rich ones in California, flew their families home and enrolled the children in the Friends School, where one-quarter of the students are hybrids of the culture clash between East and West. Indeed, through-out the Ramallah District, there are groups of teenagers who speak in American slang and black street talk.

Tina's half-nieces and -nephews, Fayrouz's children, were enrolled in Friends after her murder. The two older teenage children said their mother was raising them alone while their father commuted back and forth from America. The breathtakingly sultry sixteen-year-old in jeans told how she had to wait for Dad's visits to obtain CARE pack-ages of Guess?, Reeboks, and Nikes; a $70 pair of tennis shoes in America sold for $120 in the Middle East. She said she liked living in Beitin—this was her country—but she enjoyed visiting friends and buying clothes in America.

Sounding eerily like her Aunt Tina, she added that she wanted to learn French and Spanish and travel around the world.

With four more murders in the city that week, plus the backlog of unsolved homicides, it was the following Monday, November 13, before Qualls's shift hours changed and he had the time to begin the background investigation on the Isa case. He started with Cliff Walker, meeting him in his home at 10:45 that morning. The eighteen-year-old was so shy and withdrawn that to relax him, Qualls—who could be as gentle as a golden retriever when he wanted to be—brought up writing guitar music. That eased Cliff into talking about Tina.

They began dating last January, Cliff said. They never slept together, although her mother was always driving her to the doctor to see if she were a virgin. Her father intended to marry her off before her reputation was ruined. He and her mother would drag Tina out to din-ner, and when they arrived at the restaurant, sitting at the table would be some eligible, older Palestinian male. Tina always balked at such arrangements.

By fall the family fights had so escalated in such violence that Tina feared for her life. She wrote numerous letters and notes which she tucked away in her books and pinned on the inside of her clothes: "If anything happens to me, my father killed me. Call the police." She tried to escape by taking a job to make enough money to leave. Her first day was November 5. Afraid to tell her parents, Tina left them a note saying she was at work. When her shift ended, Cliff walked her home.

"We arrived home about midnight, the apartment was dark. I waited outside fifteen minutes for her to turn the lights on in her bedroom. She never did, and I left.

"Early the next morning I went into a grocery store owned by a relative of Zein's—on Natural Bridge off Fairgrounds Park—to buy some candy. They kept staring at me. I wondered why. I came home and collapsed in bed until the phone jarred me awake. It was Helena Mylanos, crying so hard I could barely understand what she was saying: 'Tina's dead.' "

Qualls set up a series of afternoon interviews at Roosevelt High School. The fifteen-year veteran officer was surprised at what Tina's counselor, Pamela Fournier, reported about her October 16 conference with Maria, Mona, and Tina. The school staffers opened Tina's locker for Qualls. He opened her books, flipped through her papers, but there was nothing of evidentiary value. Where were the written pleas that Tina's friends had described?

As the fifth girl twisted her Kleenex, trying not to cry, Qualls waited patiently, trying to soothe her. Over and over, from each friend, Qualls had heard a consistent story of isolation and violence. Girl after girl said how she and Tina had been friends, but they only socialized at school functions. Yes, this girl dabbed her eyes, Tina told me a bunch of times they hated Cliff because he was black. They told her she had to marry "someone of her own race." Yes, I saw bruises on Tina's face. Once I saw a burn on her chin. I heard something about coffee being thrown in her face. In August Tina could no longer take the restrictions and the beatings and the scalding coffee. She ran away. Can I come stay with you? Tina had asked this girl on the phone.

When the friend opened the door, there was Tina crying so hard she could barely explain what had happened. Again they had beaten her. Again her mother held her down. But this time, her father pulled out a knife, screaming, "I'll kill you if you don't conform to my way of life."

After Tina returned home, she came to classes covered with bruises. "How do you stand it?" the friend asked. "I love my mom and dad. I forgive them," Tina tried to explain.

The next teenager reported seeing bruises. Qualls looked up from his notebook, where he wrote down every detail. Where were they? Oh, on her arms, her legs, her thighs, her stomach. Her mother beat her, choked her and held her down while her father put a knife to her. I saw the bruises, the next two girls said. "Her dad said he would kill her because she conducted herself improperly. She failed to hold to his way of life from the homeland."

Did you save the note about calling the police? Qualls asked another girl, holding his breath. It would be such a perfect piece of evidence for the prosecutor to wield at Zein's murder trial. Talk about premeditation.

"No," said the girl. "I don't know what I did with it."

"Jesus," Lieutenant Hegger inhaled and shook his head in disbelief after Qualls relayed these tales. "Can you imagine what that child must have gone through? What Tina's friends must be going through now?" Hegger shook his head again and drank more black coffee. "Survivor's guilt."

Qualls thought about how teachers must be lying awake at two A.M. wondering "what if." Then there was Cliff.

"Imagine how he's hurting," Hegger said.

Qualls thought of the look on Cliff's face when he talked of how he waited for the light to go on in the Isas' living room.

Detective Qualls had one last interview at the high school, with the person who could tell him the most: Helena Mylanos. Helena was overwhelmed with sorrow. In a voice soft as a whisper, she told Qualls how Tina had been her best friend since the morning they met in Dewey Middle School five years ago. Not only did they meet daily in classes and team sports and the school yearbook office, not only did they talk nightly on the telephone, they went shopping together, to the movies together, and visited each other's homes.

Helena stopped. The detective was reluctant to push her to talk. Helena said Tina and she frequently analyzed Tina's predicament. Tina's soul was more battered than her body. She wanted to do what her parents demanded, but conforming to Old World mores would have been alien to her nature. After talking it over with Helena, Tina would calm down and return to being her normal cheerful self. Until the August night when her mother held her down and her father had pointed a large knife at her stomach and Tina ran away.

This fall Tina regularly reported her parents were planning to kill her. For protection, Tina handed Helena a piece of folded notebook paper in early October. On the outside, Tina had written, "To the St. Louis Police Department." Helena opened it and read, "If anything should ever happen to me or my friends, Cliff Walker or Helena Mylanos, investigate my father." And she had signed it. I gave it back to her, Helena said. She was going to copy it and hide the duplicates in her book bag, around her house, and inside her school locker.

"Did Tina give you a copy of the note?" Qualls asked.

"No," said Helena sadly. She believed that the Isas had found those notes in Tina's book bag that night and destroyed them.

"Did you ever see the Isas or their daughters beat Tina?" he asked.

"No," Helena said. "I only know what Tina told me when I asked about those bruises."

Qualls knew—because detectives must testify in court—that what Tina told Helena about the thrashings would be ruled hearsay. Hearsay is not admissible because the speaker cannot be cross-examined. However, Tina's friends could testify they had seen the black-and-blue marks. Maybe an investigator at the Child Abuse Hotline had some hard proof.

Kent Dickens at DCFS told Qualls he took an anonymous call about a Palestina Isa on October 16. He went to the apartment two days later (he was wrong about the dates) and spoke with Tina, who denied being abused. As Tina was wearing shorts and a blouse with no visible signs of injuries, Dickens said he closed her file. Dickens never told the police about his conversation with Tina's sister Mona when she had said, "Tina had everything handed to her on a silver platter."

Dreams of dead people are a bad omen in the Arab world. And when the deceased speak in a dream, it augurs ill fortune. By day Soraia wept; by night, she dreamt of her dead sister. "I was driving somewhere. I'd look in the rearview mirror and see Tina sitting in the backseat in the white dress she had been buried in. She was stalking me. I was so scared, I couldn't sleep for six months."

A week after her sister was buried, Leilah began having another dream over and over: "Tina was dead, in her coffin. She said to me, 'My back hurts me.'

"I asked, 'Tina, what can I do to help?'

'Put a piece of iron, a jail bar, on my back,' she said. 'So that I can rest in peace.' "

Leilah looked at the visitor. "My bad dreams always come true."

No one knows what wretched night visions Zein had; by day, he was worrying about his defense. He called Luie collect and asked him to "make" his wife, Sausan—who had hated Tina "to an astonishing degree"—write a letter saying Tina had threatened her father. All my daughters have done so, Zein said.

Had the government shown Zein any evidence yet? Luie asked. A man came to talk with him in jail, but Zein referred him to his lawyer. But the man persisted, saying it had nothing to do with the defense attorney, it was about Zein. Ah, Zein told him, I don't know nothing about what you want; all I used to do was go out of town to look for stores. (The man was a CIA agent who posed as an assistant U.S. attorney. In this guise, he tried to question Zein about Samir. Interestingly, he never signed the visitor's registry at the workhouse.)

Luie interjected, they're listening to us talk now!

His brother Saif wasn't so careful a week later when he told a comrade how he had a rocket-propelled grenade in his car, "if you need one." Ohhhh, the friend said. They laughed how a comrade could put the RPG on his shoulder and, from far away, destroy a tank. Their comrade, Farid, they agreed, needed this.

The members of the Beitin Association were meeting, just before Thanksgiving, November 17. There was a heavy agenda this noon—elect new officers and devise ways to help Zein. Saif didn't announce it then, but he wanted the family to give him Alliance Market. The old man was still incarcerated; the judge refused bail. Why? asked Amjad's brother. The government says it has solid evidence that Zein would run away to Brazil, Saif explained. That's why they arrested him so fast—he wanted to fly there.

How do they know that?

Someone told them! Saif exploded.

It's time we started "cleaning," the man snapped.

A few minutes later, Saif's little brother Luie was discussing the same issue with his wife Sausan.

"They say someone has reported on him [Zein] that he plans . . . to buy tickets for Brazil," she said.

"Is the one who reported on him an Arab?"

"Yes."

Sausan went on to explain how the Arabs would hold a rally if the judge did not reduce Zein's million-dollar bailbond.

"Who is the Arab, this son of a bitch who is informing on him?" Luie asked.

"There is one among them who is informing . . . but they don't know. . . . I swear no one knows so far who did it. But they [the feds] know, they told them Zein wants to go to Brazil. Who would know other than an Arab . . . ?"

"Is it possible Tina told them?"

"By God I don't know. I don't know what Tina did," Sausan said.

"It's either her or an American," Luie pronounced.

The feds gotta be tapping your phones, Tawfiq told Saif the next day. Where would they get an informant? Who would do such a thing? Was there anyone that awful in St. Louis?

Many, Luie replied. He would have been shocked and horrified to find out it was one man, one they had all trusted and worse yet, maybe another, one higher up.

CHAPTER SEVENTEEN

Substantial Evidence

THE DAY BEFORE THANKSGIVING

Hegger paced the floor of his office, dragging on his "sissy cigarette" as he called Merits. He was thinking he did not fault the school for not calling the Child Abuse Hotline about Tina. He could imagine a teacher being hauled before the school board: "Did she ever confide in you that she was being abused by her parents?" "No." "Then why did you call the hotline? You interfered! That's against school policy."

This was not the easiest investigation. Qualls had some good evidence, but Hegger wished he had something airtight.

"I need a warrant for Maria Isa's arrest, murder first. I can't say why. Just trust me on this one," Hegger told Hayes over the phone a few days later, on November 30. At first she was reluctant. "Dee, I have enough for probable cause," Hegger pressed on, revealing only the sketchiest details he had gleaned from the federal agents. He did not want to violate their confidences. Calling Hegger back at 5:15 P.M., she issued the arrest warrant over the phone. "The ink's barely dry," she joked. "I wrote it by hand."

Hegger radioed Homicide Detective Willie McCuller who, with his partner, Detective Joe Right, had been maintaining surveillance of the back door of Alliance Market. They and the two Intelligence detectives who were watching the front door had staked out Alliance since early afternoon. One of the Intelligence officers was a woman, Detective Kim Roach, for Hegger had wanted to have Maria searched, and there were no women officers then in Homicide.

"When the four cops walked in announcing she was under arrest, Maria seemed more puzzled than scared," Detective McCuller told Hegger. "She did not understand why." Maria cooperated, submitting without fuss to the handcuffs. She told her relatives at Alliance to call her husband's lawyer. But the two Palestinian women and one man there screamed at the police officers. "Irate—abusive even," McCuller said. Maria was taken to Homicide, where Hegger had an interpreter standing by who read her her rights in Spanish* after Detective Right read them in English. Maria signed the Warning and Waiver Form, yet refused to talk without a lawyer.

On December 2, the day before what would have been Tina's seventeenth birthday, Helena called Fayrouz after seeing the funeral on TV. "I was Tina's best friend since eighth grade and you didn't even tell me about her services," Helena reprimanded her.

"I tried to pick up the phone two times to call you," Fayrouz said. "But if you were such a good friend, you'd have called us. That was the best funeral this country has ever seen." Fayrouz added that the family was angry with Helena: They had found Tina's driver's license authorizing organ donation, witnessed by Helena. "How could you agree to such a thing?" Fayrouz asked. "We're grateful we found it too late for the doctors to take out her organs and give them to other people."

At the end of their conversation, Fayrouz said, "It's her birthday tomorrow and we're going to visit her at her grave with a cake." Helena was sobbing. She so badly wanted to be with Tina on her birthday. "Maybe later," Fayrouz continued, "when I think you should know, I'll tell you where she is. Whenever I feel like it." She slammed the phone down on the crying girl.

It took Helena two days to track down where her best friend had been laid to rest. "It was awful. All dirt in a pile and no grass. Two little plastic flowers—purple and white—that they had bought at some tacky discount store, sticking at the foot of the grave. There was such a small headstone. If I had any money, I'd buy Tina a big headstone." Helena left a $20 spring bouquet on the grave.

On what would have been Tina's day of emancipation, December 3, her cousins Saif and Tawfiq again discussed how their group may have been tapped and bugged. "We've all been under surveillance for a long time," Saif pointed out. There must be Arabs working with the government. They will be exposed one day.

Nah, scoffed Tawfiq. The only source is the telephones. And the feds were stationed in front of Zein's house for five months and they

---

*While Maria's native tongue was Portuguese, she also spoke Spanish.

eavesdropped and watched who came in and who left, he added. Arabs talk too much on the phones. They make things up.

No, Saif insisted. There are Arabs working with them. "This is the story of Arabs. Each sings his own song." A variation on the Arab proverb, "I and my brother against my cousin, I and my cousin against the world, I against my brother."

Hegger's phone rang for the upteenth time the morning of December 11. It was the FBI. Well, Harry, we have the authorization, the agent told him. We walked it through, even hand-carrying it. Went all the way to the Attorney General of the United States, the agent said. Got something for you. Very substantial.

Guessing it must be taped conversations that needed such clearance, Hegger asked two detectives to go down to the FBI office and pick up a package under his name. When they returned, Hegger had already pulled out a Supplemental Police Report, so when the case went to trial, the prosecutors could show the chain of custody of the evidence. Defense lawyers are known to win acquittals based on the mishandling of such technicalities.

Opening the package, the lieutenant realized how literally "substantial" this was. Two Scotch Model 60 reel-to-reel audiotapes. They were marked "T" and "M." One was from a wiretap placed on the Isas' telephone. The other came from a bug inside the paper-thin wall of the living room closet near the short hallway. Both were recordings made the evening of November 5–6. A two-track audiotape of a child being murdered. Outside of Mafia whackings and the live televised shooting of Lee Harvey Oswald by Jack Ruby, Hegger could not recall another federally recorded murder in America.

Remembering that the feds said they might need hundreds of officers at any time, Lieutenant Hegger decided to make every detective in his department familiar with the Isa case. Calling them in, he played the tapes. Only a few words were in English—mostly it was in Arabic and Portuguese; her parents' harsh tones and Tina's screams transcended language.

A group of men walked out midway through Tina's cries. "I've had enough," said one twenty-year veteran. When Sergeant Roussin closed his eyes that night, he could hear Tina begging for help. The recollection awoke him again before dawn. The haunting lasted a week. "If anything sends Zein Isa to death row," Hegger said, "it will be these tapes."

In preparation for his grand jury appearance, Lieutenant Hegger packed up a boom box and cassette copy of the FBI wall bug. He walked to the back of the Municipal Courts building and through the tunnels to the second-floor grand jury room where Dee Hayes was waiting for him. She had yet to hear the murder tape, although she would try the case. Bob Craddick would present it to the grand jury today, December 11. Because Craddick was inside the room with the jurors, Hayes remained seated outside the door during the proceedings.

Hegger walked into the room where the dozen jurors sat on old varnished wooden chairs at school-style desks. He tried to prepare them. "No matter how much you think you've anticipated these tapes, I can't warn you enough about what you're going to hear." He turned on the boom box and played about seven and a half minutes of Zein and Maria yelling at Tina. Intermittently, an Arabic translator explained key phrases. Then Tina screamed and cried, "Mother, please help me!" in English. Maria answered, in English, "What do you mean?" Tina repeated, "Help! Help!"

Zein's attack began. Hegger tried to ease the jurors into it—he played a bit, then stopped and explained, then started up again—but it still overwhelmed them. The interpreter announced, "This is where Mr. Isa says, 'Die, my daughter, die.'" Tina screamed louder and louder. Tina moaned, then cried. Zein yelled harshly in Arabic. Then silence.

The sounds from the boom box carried outside the grand jury door where Hayes sat hearing the murder for the first time, her hands over her face, sobbing. The jurors were very moved. Some were nearly traumatized, some asked if they could leave the room. Several darted into the adjoining rest rooms to escape, but the screams inundated them like high waves. One man thought he would be sick. "Who could get used to this?" Lieutenant Hegger asked Craddick.

The morning after the grand jury, one juror stopped off at a Walgreen's on his way to work to buy a birthday card. As he thumbed through the racks, a two-year-old child behind him flung herself on the floor and "threw a fit. The screaming brought to mind Tina crying. I felt flushed, hot, and began sweating. My arms had tremors. I was shaking inside. I had to leave the store. I couldn't even stay to buy the card."

The grand jury indicted Zein Hassan Isa and Maria Matias Isa, each, with one count of murder in the first degree (premeditated or capital murder) and for one count of armed criminal action (use of a deadly weapon in the commission of a felony.) There would have been no case against Maria without the tapes.

The grand jurors recommended the Isas be held without bond. A defendant accused of a violent crime is incarcerated to protect the community. And in cases where the defendant might flee, no bond is allowed. Bond is to guarantee that the defendant show up in court. Why would Zein Isa want to stick around to go to trial? Maria was a Brazilian citizen, she might return to her mother.

Had they set a bond and had the Isas tried to reach it, the government would be allowed to check their source of income and that of any friend or relative putting up collateral; the authorities would swarm all over grocery sales, gross receipts, IRS filings. The bond hearings would have been a turkey shoot for law enforcement.

However, police Intelligence and other agencies already were investigating the Isa clan's finances.

The extended family continued to worry there might be tapes of their phone calls. "The old man's case is complicated," Saif Nijmeh told his brother, Luie. "It isn't just because of what he did. . . . They're tying this business to that business. It isn't going to be easy."

"For him or for everybody?" Luie asked.

"For everybody . . . for whoever they know about," Saif told him.

"There is nothing against us . . . I mean this business," Luie scoffed.

"He [Zein] told me Abu Samra's [Samir Darwish] papers and Abul Huda's [Tawfiq] papers are present," Saif said, "present here . . . they asked him about things like those."

"By God . . . it is better if they charged him [Zein] with this business . . . than charging him with the other business," Luie responded.

"Why?" asked his brother.

Luie said, "To charge him with patriotic acts is better than charging him with murder."

*   *   *

As the Justice Department continued to declassify more tapes, it became obvious that Zein Isa was not the only member of the family who wanted Tina killed. There was a Cinderella quality to what was revealed in the tale of sour older sisters. And years later a grim plot was unveiled, similar to Agamemnon's sacrifice of his daughter Iphigenia on the altar of political ambition. Political assassination, Hegger called it. Murdering a child so that she could never reveal a great secret.

After it became known that the FBI had recorded Tina's slaying, the Isas' extended family still continued to talk openly on their phones about Abu Nidal and about illegal weapons.

Saif and a friend discussed their guns. "Remove the heavy weapons from the car," the comrade said. "There's nothing [in there] but an RPG," Saif laughed.

Meanwhile, just after the New Year, Lieutenant Hegger drew up a list of referrals for translators from Washington and St. Louis University. While big city police departments often scurry for interpreters for suspects and witnesses (some now subscribe to an AT&T language line that puts tongues as obscure as Urdu a phone call away); they usually do not need translators with security clearance.

Finding people who knew Arabic was not difficult, it was the Isas' dialect that was the problem. Arabic may be spoken all the way from Morocco to Yemen, but there is no common vernacular. In a highly sensitive murder case in which the defense was certain to argue about idioms, colloquial expressions were crucial.

An expert recommended Peter Heath, an assistant professor in Arabic Literature at Washington University, who had taught at Bir Zeit University, near Beitin. Heath provided Hegger, who was always curious, with background on Palestinians. He explained that Palestinians are the most sophisticated of Arabs, quite well educated, with about a 60 percent literacy rate for men and slightly less for women.

Do they still live in tribes? Hegger asked.

The structure is one of extended families, not nuclear families like ours, Heath said. The clan is the basic level of social security in Palestine, providing all medical care, old age support. Very patrilineal, think of nineteenth-century immigrants to America, where the relatives invested in the family and the family took care of each member.

When Heath taught at Bir Zeit, the man who ran the copy center made $250 a month. Yet he and his family had sent $30,000 to the States for a cousin to open a liquor store.* When this man needed money to educate his children, the cousin would pay.

"Most importantly," cautioned Heath, "do not judge a Muslim by Islam, which Americans have a tendency to mysticize, as though it cloaks the minds of the people—though some use it that way. Don't judge a Muslim except by what he or she does. Assume each is an exceptional case. Islam is not important in the Isa case. Zein used religion to justify, 'This is what Muslims do.' What he really means is, 'This is what we do in our village.' It is an unsophisticated use of Islam."

While fewer women are being sacrificed for family honor, obedience to authority is still important. "This system of social controls is critical in the villages, where there are no external restraints on social behavior. Only custom. Without custom, you'd have anarchy. Therefore, these norms are strictly enforced."

The most important thing to Zein Isa is status, said Heath. Education, money, and religiosity are not connected to social status per se. Social status stems from one's honor.

Heath brought with him a brilliant graduate student in history named Mohammad Masad, who had been his student at Bir Zeit University. Masad, who looks like the actor Daniel Day-Lewis and went on to win a Fulbright scholarship, proved to be a first-rate insider. Raised in a village not far from Beitin, Masad understood both the archaic dialect the Isas spoke and their antiquated social mores. Disagreeing with those customs, as do many Palestinians, he drank beer, smoked, ate pork, and socialized with Americans—he had even married one.

There was a third translator—another graduate student—but after hearing the murder tape once, he quit, unable to listen to Tina die over and over again.

Hegger checked their references very carefully. Translating the tapes was in effect like a federal appointment, for Heath and Masad had to be cleared by the FBI.

*   *   *

*Selling liquor is not proscribed by the Qur'an. Just drinking it is. Many Muslims imbibe alcohol just as Jews eat pork and Catholics practice contraception.

Based on what Qualls had discovered and what the translators found in their first forays into the tapes, Hegger decided the Isas should be charged with committing a "Bias Crime." "Maybe they would have killed Tina anyway if she had a white boyfriend," Lieutenant Hegger said. "Her having a black boyfriend exacerbated the problem." The Justice Department tracks patterns of hate crimes—those affected by race, gender, religion, ethnic group, or sexual persuasion—and asks local police to classify violations in which prejudice is a factor. The new warrants were issued against Zein and Maria Isa on January 4, 1990.

Just after this Saif and a friend discussed the Jews on the telephone as Saif waited on customers.

"When the judge is your enemy to whom do you voice your complaint?" Saif asked rhetorically.

"Yeah," said his ally. "The Jews."

"And the Jews," Saif launched into his diatribe. "They are America. America itself is full of Jews."

"Full of Jews."

"What I mean, the Jews who talk in America whom we are fighting. By God. Their mother. They run this country."

In addition to this, part of which he said in English, Saif swore in English to the FBI agents he was certain were listening in.

By Valentine's Day, Luie Nijmeh was despondent. Before Thanksgiving he had told Tawfiq Musa he could not sleep for a week. It was not the murder of the girl that grieved him but the orgy of purges within ANO itself. "I don't believe in them anymore," Luie said as he waited on a customer in his grocery store.

"All our work was for nothing," Luie told Zein when the latter called collect from his jail cell on Valentine's Day.

Zein understood. "The guy in New York has been incarcerated for four years [sic, three] . . . and no one asks."

"This whole business is a business about money," Luie said. "A person wears himself out and exerts his utmost effort and . . . in the end it's a question of money. All this work is for nothing. . . . The problems are caused by the top leadership."

Zein agreed. "Money and betrayals, empty talk and phony leadership."

*   *   *

Although he had been transferred to head up Internal Affairs, Lieutenant Hegger continued to work on the Isa case. At least once a week for more than a year, he would replay his copy of the murder tape, listening carefully for nuances. Hegger could hear Zein and Maria sitting silently,* rocking back and forth on the sofa and chair as they waited for Tina to return home. He heard the meleé as Tina fought to escape her father's butcher knife, the furniture being pushed around, the wiretapped telephone knocked over. The receiver thudded as it bounced on the living room floor and came to rest so close to Tina that it recorded her heart fibrillating, slower and slower and slower. What struck Hegger was how Tina's voice changed. Initially, her crying sounded like that of a teenage girl. As she lay dying, her voice regressed back to that of a youngster, and finally, as she was gasping for air, she sounded like a small child, pleading for life. He heard barefoot Zein pad down the hall to the bathroom, urinate, and without washing the blood from his hands and body, return to sit on the sofa as Maria called the police. There was never any sound of crying or wailing for the dead daughter. Hegger wondered whether Zein was capable of being so callous because this was not the first time he had killed a human being.

Hegger could not help but think of his own daughter, a few years behind Tina in high school. He remembered how amazed he had been at her birth—how tiny and fragile she was. He had been around infants before, feeding and changing his baby sister. But this one was different—she was his.

He named her after his mother, Carol,† whose courage had overcome a wretched childhood out of Dickens. Carol's mother had died when she was born, her father abandoned his children, and she grew up in an orphanage, brutalized by sadistic nuns. Her fingers became arthritic from all the times the nuns broke them hitting her with rulers. But Carol was spunky. "My mother ran away so many times, they classified her as incorrigible and gave up," Hegger laughed. Carol won her freedom when she was fifteen, and made her way in the world. Her son hoped his daughter would be as spirited. Indeed, over his desk the lieutenant pinned up a cartoon of a frog half-swallowed by a seagull

---

*The Isas told Qualls they had been watching T.V. but the tape does not reflect this.

†The girl's name has been changed at her father's request.

and struggling to break free, with the words, "Never ever ever give up."[*] It was apparent to others that Harry Hegger had more than inherited his mother's valor. And some noted how similar in mettle Tina Isa was to Carol as a girl.

Hegger and his wife separated before their baby's first birthday. He would pick up his daughter at the sitter's every day—where his ex had dropped her off early in the morning—and keep her until two P.M., before he went in to work. He was with Carol as much as he could, also to compensate for the holidays he had to work as a rookie police officer. He intended to give her a better childhood than the one his mother had to endure.

Hegger strongly believed a part-time parent still had full-time responsibility. "I had to make certain she grew up into a decent human being. But because I was the other parent, I didn't want Carol to take home her last memory of Daddy as the archdisciplinarian who spanks me." So Harry invented "Suzy Q." When Carol was three or four and acted like a brat, he would tell her, "My other daughter, Suzy Q, doesn't act that way." "She got the point. I said Suzy Q was make-believe but she showed how a little girl should behave. I never had to spank her." Suzy Q became their private joke.

When Carol was thirteen, she went to live with her father permanently. "She was doing poorly in school and was beginning to run with the wrong crowd. My ex-wife had her hands full with other things, so we thought about creating a new environment. Her grades were 1.3 in seventh grade. Each year, she progressed; she graduated high school as an honor student, a three-plus average. I was very proud of her.

"I'd been concerned about my daughter getting pregnant in high school, it's been so prevalent—every father's nightmare. I talked with her about respect."

"Carol's real responsible now." Away at college, she still complains how strict her father is. He laughed. "I control her by phone. But I'm really trying to get her to be on her own. That's why I wanted her to go away to school so she could learn to think for herself, to survive on her own, to grow into independence."

*   *   *

[*]Winston Churchill originated this with, "Never give up, never give up, never ever give up."

While Hegger was taking notes on the murder tape in his office down-town, in his Clayton apartment Mohammad Masad replayed the taped conversations between Zein and his daughters. He was fascinated by the Isa tale, beginning with the fact that Maria was a second wife. That was such a rarity these days. In Masad's whole village of thousands, there were few second wives.

His own wife wandered in, picking up after their toddler son. Masad liked working at home, where he could be with his family. As a grad student, he spent too much time away from them in the library carrels.

He could not understand any of the Isa family. The sisters lived sep-arate lives from their husbands, who were away working long days in their grocery stores. Indeed, in conversation the women rarely even mentioned their husbands. How could family honor be so important to these people when they lacked a family life?

The lives of the Isa daughters in general seemed pathetic. They were in a self-imposed social isolation from their American neighbors. Their minds were so restricted. "That kind of existence is a breeding ground for resentment," Masad explained to his wife. "You don't have to be educated and open-minded to get out of the house," she pointed out.

Masad returned to the tapes, carefully noting phrases Zein's daugh-ters used. He frowned as he listened. He was shocked by the family's vulgarity. "Such coarseness is definitely not something you hear," he said. "Calling a relative a whore was extreme, something never, never used." In anger or anguish a man might use such phrases, but never that graphically, never to a woman, and never, never to a daughter. (Everyone with experience in the Middle East reacted the same way to the Isas' conversations.)

Masad was embarrassed, he did not want Americans to think all the Palestinians were so monstrous. His parents had been poor villagers and all their children were at minimum college graduates. And his family had embraced his American wife.

What did impress Masad favorably was Zein's love for all his chil-dren. "[While] sons are still preferable in the West Bank I never had any sense that Zein was upset about having six girls, although six is no cause for celebration. On the tapes he usually spoke very lovingly, very highly of his girls."

Zein's feelings about Tina fluctuated widely, Masad noted. He loved her so, yet felt she deliberately refused to acknowledge "his gifts of nurture." This was not unusual in honor killings. A father who kills his daughter because she besmirched the family honor does not mean he did not love her, an eminent professor of psychology at Bethlehem University said. "One feeling does not preclude the other." But another academic added ominously, "Zein doted on Tina as long as she fit his ideal and did not deviate from that."

The next day, as he went over his translations, Masad pointed out to Professor Heath that the dialect in the Isa conversations was often archaic. "They were so isolated from moving around so much, they didn't keep up with the language," Masad said. Gutter Arabic, other experts called it.

Estranged from his old land and his new country, Zein Isa had clung to an atavistic version of honor. Masad did not think Tina's virginity was as important with the Isas as Tina's defiance of her father. Zein was desperate to maintain status/honor in his community which was difficult to do when he was being challenged by a sixteen-year-old schoolgirl. Heath added, "When you're poor, all you have is saving face." "What is most problematic here is, what is tradition today?" Masad later said. It varies from Jerusalem to Nablus to Hebron. A family who five years ago did not have indoor plumbing now watches CNN in a real global village. A barefoot, illiterate, wrinkled mother of forty who looks sixty, leading her donkey laden with sacks of flour, hurries home to call her daughter, who is studying for a Ph.D. at Harvard.

"Change is never systematically even," Masad explained. "Intellectual progress [often] fails to match social progress. One could be the most conservative Muslim yet be a graduate of Princeton and a computer expert, and treat one's wife like a heifer. Part of the Islamic revival is theological and part is sociopolitical." To differentiate themselves from the West, the Arabs return to their traditional ways (akin to African-Americans celebrating Kwanza and Irish nationalists speaking Gaelic).

"And predictably, there is a backlash at feminism and liberalism." The Hegelian reaction: two steps forward, one step back.

Zein was like a member of a street gang who kills an innocent person who "dissed" him.

Zein used honor as an excuse for violence, Heath explained to Hegger. Arabs have a system to deal with rebellious daughters. She could be encouraged to marry someone suitable, she could go live with a relative until the gossip died down, and family mediators could be brought in. Tawfiq's last-minute pitch to Tina was, obviously to her, not a mediation per se but a way to protect the Abu Nidal cell. And Tina was justly afraid to live with relatives.

Tina might have been spared had Zein's first wife been her mother rather than Brazilian-born Maria. An Arab mother's role is to play intercessor between her children and her husband, ameliorating the father's wrath. She allows him to save face and he can tell his male relatives that he would like to punish his rebellious daughter but his wife won't let him.

"Turn it around," Heath said. "To Maria, it was either sacrifice her child to family harmony or sacrifice the family breadwinner."

Masad summarized the case: "Murder is not a logical option in my culture."

Hegger thought crimes of honor are analogous to lynchings in the pre-civil rights South. The basic problem was the philosophy that covertly sanctioned such murders: that blacks before the civil rights movement or women in the Middle East were subhumans. While most people condemned such practices, they did so in private; not enough of them publicly fought to stop such murder.

Ironically, the year that Tina was brutally murdered was the year that a group of Israeli Arab women began marching in the streets of Israel and the West Bank to protest honor killings.

CHAPTER EIGHTEEN

How to Build a Bomb

OCTOBER 18, 1990   WEBSTER GROVES, MISSOURI

It had been a clear morning of sixty-eight degrees in Webster Groves, a quaint old city, now a suburb of St. Louis, filled with antebellum red-brick homes, Victorian turreted frame mansions, and century-old farmhouses. Real Americana replete with a traditional Fourth of July parade.

About ten that morning, fire engines raced to a contemporary frame house at 1651 Grand Road. The house burned quickly, becoming engulfed by flames so strong two suburban fire departments responded. A Cadillac parked nearby was destroyed from the high heat. Fortunately, no one was injured—none of the firefighters and none of the eight to ten residents of the tiny five-room house. The inhabitants spoke in such vague terms and in such poor English that the police were not certain how many people lived there. All the police knew was that this was a definite housing code violation.

Fire investigators ruled out arson, but what they found as they sifted through the debris triggered a bigger investigation. First the detectives found a cache of foreign currency, gold jewelry, documents, and newspaper clippings. From reading them, the police realized the goods belonged to Zein Isa. His daughter Leilah was one of the residents of the rented house.

Next they found what appeared to be the tools of terrorists: A packet mailed from the Middle East. Inside was a manual in Arabic, its cover featuring a photograph of a plane within gunsights. Nearby, investigators seized a sketch of the Jewish Community Center Association in West St. Louis County.

The next day Webster Groves detectives and an FBI agent who spoke Arabic went to the hotel where he had moved since the fire and questioned Rabih "Ricky" Hamed, Leilah Isa's husband's relative.

183

Hamed was the official head of the Webster Groves household and manager of Rickey's Nightclub, in the 11000 block of West Florissant Road. He calmly explained that a year earlier, he and other members of his community had planned to demonstrate at the JCCA over a speech there. The map was merely a crude drawing of how to get there.

Ricky's body tensed and his eyes stared when the FBI agent asked him about a hand-drawn diagram with a letter in Arabic, both showing how to make a bomb. Why do you have instructions on how to make and trigger various bombs? the agent asked over and over. Ricky maintained there was no earthly reason why anyone in his house should have such a thing.

The police also questioned Ricky about travel papers showing how he and a relative had traveled through Yugoslavia recently, the agent knowing that Belgrade happened to be the center of the Abu Nidal operations in Europe. But Ricky's answer was they were en route to a wedding in the homeland, and one always had to go through Yugoslavia if one flew Yugoslav Airlines.

Ricky refused to let police search his motel room. But the police had enough. Ricky was not formally charged with a crime. Ricky had spent a year in Israeli jail for associating with terrorist groups (it should be noted, the Israelis also imprisoned numerous PLO members who were not terrorists, on charges of political association). Ricky had been arrested three times in Chicago for gun violations. He was known to associate with a Palestinian-American nicknamed "George." George was rumored to be a "help" if "a fortunate fire" was ever needed, according to Police Intelligence. George's real name was Fawaz Mohammed Hamdan.

The FBI was most fascinated with the panoply of documents found in Zein's briefcase. They had believed he kept a code book in it; they took it away, and the local police never saw it again. This may have been the book of "true names" and addresses that Atta gave him two years earlier in Mexico City.

The Bureau did tell the local police that Zein Isa was a senior member of "an established international Palestinian organization." And that, since Lieutenant Hegger had arrested Zein Isa for Tina's murder on November 7, 1989, the FBI taps and bugs became extremely quiet, not only in St. Louis but nationwide. "They short-circuited our investigation. We'd have gone on longer," Hegger's friend in the FBI, Tom

Newman, later told him. The police also learned that the FBI analysis determined that the map to the JCCA was crudely drawn, similar to directions sent with party invitations, and that while there had been a Palestinian rally at the Jewish community headquarters, it had been "uneventful." The JCCA was made aware of what the authorities found.

What did Tawfiq, Saif, Luie, and the others say privately about the FBI seizing Atta's little black book? Why hadn't one of them taken it after Zein was arrested? Didn't they realize that American authorities could have dozens of spin-off investigations into more nefarious schemes?

The next time Hegger heard about this particular group was three and a half years later, when a St. Louis County Police Evidence sergeant told him about a case that sickened both of them.

CHAPTER NINETEEN

"As Organized as the Mafia"

Detectives from Intelligence were telling Lieutenant Hegger a fascinating story about the Isa family. Hegger had been aware of undercover investigations within the Palestinian community, but now Detective Sam Jackson* was telling him there was a real crime ring—one including members from the Isa tribe.

"They're as organized as the Mafia but not nearly as lovable," Jackson told Hegger. "The Mafia has more respect for human life. The mob only offs members and those who've crossed them. This group is far more violent, far more dangerous. You'll see."

"Jesus," Hegger laughed. "Guys who make Gotti look good."

On January 28, 1991, Detective Jackson along with 107 police officers and federal agents burst into eight corner grocery stores in St. Louis City and County (Alliance Market was not among them.) They arrested ten Palestinian-Americans with warrants for running a network of stolen goods—food stamps, baby formula, cigarettes, and other merchandise—and coupon fraud. The sting had followed a six-month multiagency investigation. The various Intelligence units had thick files on a number of people from Beitin.

One part of Jackson's work consisted of seventy-two separate illegal sales. As an undercover, he found a whole new society of criminals, one that, when all the other police agencies pieced together what they knew, was the most organized crime network in St. Louis (where there is no large Mafia ring).

The sting began a year earlier, in 1990, when two heroin addicts told Jackson that Palestinian grocery owners were buying up large amounts

---

*The undercover detective's name and identifying features altered at his request for protection. The facts of his work are unchanged.

of stolen goods from drug users and reselling them. The owners were recruiting black junkies to stand outside ghetto stores and lure addicted welfare mothers into selling their food stamp coupons for cash or drugs. The profits were high; the owner could buy $60 worth of food stamps for $20. Police found the hardworking blacks in the neighborhoods resentful about the rip-offs.

Jackson went to his supervisor about the racket, and together they interested several state and federal agencies (the USDA, which handles food stamps, the FBI, U.S. Customs, Immigration and Naturalization, and ATF) in a joint undercover investigation.

Jackson began posing as a heroin addict, creating track marks on his arms with a pin. He would go into a shop and offer a case of Similac for $20 that the owner could sell for $48. Or he would sell $5,000 in food stamps for $2,500 in cash, which the owner would redeem for the full $5,000 the next day.

One day a colleague of Zein Isa's asked the undercover, "What do you do for a living? You're not a cop or an FBI man, are you, man?"

Jackson swallowed and said, "I'm an addict and I steal for a living."

During the sting operation, Jackson went into deep cover, living his new identity around the clock. He rented and lived in a special apartment, a home base for his apparently addictive activities. From there he made his phone calls and met with his informants. His main objective, as he said, was not to compromise them but to keep them alive. "The Palestinians were desperate to know I wasn't a cop, which is why we rented the apartment, so they could call there and place their baby formula and cigarette orders." But they still sent their countersurveillance to tag him several times: Like when Jackson drove through the circle in Tower Grove Park twice, with another car right behind him.

Because Jackson was clearly Irish-American, with his vestigial nose, ocean blue eyes, ruddy skin, and curly carrot-colored hair, the Palestinians assumed he did not know Arabic. That was true, but stupid. As they spoke freely in their dialect, Jackson's body wire picked it all up and a police interpreter translated their every word into English.

By October 1990 Jackson was becoming a regular supplier to these Palestinian grocery store owners. During one transaction, as he was selling thirty cartons of cigarettes and $300 worth of food stamps, the owner ran out of cash to pay him. But Zein's son-in-law Nai'el, Mona's husband, gave Jackson $655 and walked him outside.

"Come to my store in Hanley Hills," he said. "It's bigger and I can buy more stolen goods."

When he went up to Nai'el's place, in the backroom, Jackson saw photographs of Israeli soldiers superimposed in the crosshairs of a gun. He deliberately kept his face expressionless when, during the advent of the Gulf war, Nai'el said he had named his new son Saddam. (His wife preferred another name and wrote it on the birth certificate, for fear "Saddam" would lead to fistfights in school. A relative had named his son Hitler, and the boy was chronically beaten by the other boys.)

Jackson had thought Nai'el vicious after he asked Nai'el if he had any children.

"Yeh, they're in Israel with their mother," he said.

"Oh," Jackson asked. "What're they doing there?"

"Throwing rocks at the Jews," Nai'el said. "If I could get 'em rifles, I would."

In the process of working deep cover, Jackson found several types of crime as everyday activities: The store owners' wives would get together for a day of coupon fraud, sitting around a kitchen table and clipping all the food coupons from a stack of old newspapers. Their husbands would mail the coupons to the manufacturers for reimbursement. When the authorities were tipped off by Jackson, they discovered there was no way a small corner market could have the sales volume to redeem $1,000 worth of coupons every two weeks, as a large chain supermarket would.

Jackson also found most, if not all, of these Palestinian stores seemed interrelated. The owners were all connected by blood, marriage, or business. They bought and sold stores on a handshake, not bothering to change the titles. Ownership became a quagmire for government auditors. For example, Zein actually bought Alliance Market from Nai'el's brother Mamdouh ("Mike"), who was married to Fayrouz, although the deed of sale was from a man named Flowers. The accounting systems of borrowing and lending within the stores were Gordian knots that no revenue agent could unravel.

Worse yet, Jackson told a colleague, "They change their names and addresses without updating their driver's licenses, so then when I arrest them, I have to fingerprint them to know who is who. And then they all tell me, 'I don't have any money. I make only $11,000 to

$15,000 a year gross, and I have a big family and do extensive traveling to the homeland.' "

But the investigators discovered these owners had secret caches of money tucked away in their store safes and safe-deposit boxes. Nai'el stashed away more than $40,000, which his wife knew nothing about. (Nai'el later claimed he had set aside the money for his girlfriend.) Another man held $100,000 in cash and a treasure trove of gold jewelry in his four safe-deposit boxes "that we knew of," Jackson commented dryly. One bank account, interestingly enough, had three withdrawals totaling $9,000 in a single day going from a St. Louis bank to a New York bank to a Swiss bank. By law, if withdrawals from one account total more than $10,000, the bank has to notify the IRS. "This group hates banks," prosecutor Bob Craddick told Jackson. "Because that way the feds can track their money."

But informants told Jackson that some group members or their relatives had been ordered to funnel certain sums of money each year to terrorist organizations. And that went through New York and Swiss banks. According to the FBI tapes, other members would launder their money for Abu Nidal by sending it from St. Louis to South America, and then on to the West Bank.

The IRS had been unaware of these accounts. During questioning, several grocers told auditors that they had been saving money for poor relatives in the homeland, that they were saving for their children's education, that they did not believe in drawing interest on bank accounts. And it was very difficult for the IRS to prove that any of the monies was ill-gotten. But ultimately the government found other red flags: One man filed $30,000 in gross receipts to the state revenue department, but turned in $80,000 worth of food stamps to state welfare. He claimed it was a computer error.

Jackson learned there were three criminal Palestinian-American factions in the St. Louis area. Any other Arab needed their permission to open a store. One faction funnelled stolen property. One had a compound out in Pacific, Missouri, where they beamed high-tech surveillance on anyone driving in or out of their area. And one group involved Zein Isa.

Zein was very important. He was well connected with other shop owners around the country. Jackson was convinced Zein had an interest in a number of stores, including Regal Meat Market, which his sons-in-law owned.

Nai'el pleaded guilty to receiving stolen property and unlawful conversion of food stamps in the fall of 1991, just before his in-laws went to trial for Tina's murder. After he paid restitution his sentence was suspended, which infuriated Jackson. "Most of the officials were interested in our cases, but thought the stores would be too hard to penetrate. In four days' time, I got into five stores that the feds couldn't get, and what did George Peach, [then circuit attorney] do? He promised 'vigorous prosecution' and then gave everyone who pled out two years SIS* (suspended imposition of sentence) like Nai'el."

One of the other shop owners whose sentence was suspended was Harbi Hamdan, owner with his wife of Sam and Linda's market. By 1994 Harbi was in the state pentitentiary for parole violations and awaiting sentencing in federal court for food stamp fraud convictions. And his brother "George" faced worse charges.

The sting did lead various federal and state agencies into initiating their own investigations. One told Jackson, "We knew we had this problem. We just were not sure how to attack it." The sting also compromised many of ANO's sleeper cell members, because one needs a clean record to legally buy weapons.

The three Palestinian-American crime groups presented other headaches to law enforcement. One was arson. Some inner-city Arab grocery store owners in St. Louis, Chicago, Cleveland, and Brooklyn are notorious for torching buildings. Solving such crimes was difficult; whenever there were too many arsons, the culprits would lie low for a while. They would be at war with each other one day and buddies the next, allied against the cops.

"They see the heat as being on all of them," Sergeant Steve Sorocko of St. Louis Police Bomb and Arson told Jackson. "This is a very well organized, very tight group," Sorocko added.

Sergeant Sorocko found the Arab arson cases erupted in spurts. There were two types. One is arson for profit, in which the alleged victim owns several stores. Say one shop has money problems, or has lost

---

*First-time offenders in Missouri who are nonviolent usually have their sentences suspended because of prison overcrowding. They are put on parole and if they violate those conditions, then they are sentenced to jail.

its liquor license, or has a bad manager. To cut his losses and make a little insurance money, the owner has the place torched.

"Miraculously," Sorocko quipped, "the place that has the fortunate
fire is always the one that's well insured."

Then there are territorial, eliminate the competition fires: Starting
in 1985 Sorocko investigated fires at twenty of the city's 500 corner
markets; all were new stores that had not been approved by one of the
factions.

There was the case where a man had refurbished a mom-and-pop
shop that had been closed for ten years. He was outside sweeping one
morning when another Palestinian told him not to open. He did anyway, and that night took a call at home that his new store was engulfed
in flames. The suspect was a cousin. While the victim was anxious for
law enforcement to prosecute, because he was uninsured, ultimately he
did not want to testify against his tribe. For dropping the charges, his
relatives paid his losses.

Territoriality is so important that some store owners have civil attorneys draw up noncompete clauses. (The owners often pay their legal
fees in gold, not trusting paper money.)

Detective Jackson felt sorry for the other Palestinian-Americans, the
honest ones, embarrassed as all minority members are by unsavory
countrymen. "Some come here to hide out, and stay because it's so
easy to beat the system and fleece Americans. But most come here to
live normally and are opposed to these criminals," he said. "Most are
not lawless."

The crime groups mostly stuck with medium- to low-level hoodlum
activity. These immigrants focused on what they thought was fair—
ripping off the American system. They posed no threat to human life.

That changed in 1994 one Sunday in May. That was the story that
upset Harry Hegger.

On a perfect, sunny afternoon, Nancy Nolle was planting flowers in
the front of her house, in a pleasant middle-class neighborhood. Her
husband, James, was nearby patting seedlings into the ground when
the twelve-year-old girl down the street road her bicycle over their
lawn. Having repeatedly asked her not to ride over the grass, the
Nolles yelled, "Bug off, kid."

"Mama," the girl screamed, and Ibtisam "Sue" Hamdan, wife of

Fawaz "George" Hamdan, came running. During a heated exchange of words, Ibtisam Hamdan slapped Nancy Nolle. James Nolle separated the two women just before George tried to hit him. James knocked down George, who, at five-foot-seven and nearly 200 pounds, was built like a fireplug.

Having lost face publicly, George returned home. James ran inside his house to call the police. A few minutes later, one of his children flew in crying hysterically.

"Daddy, Daddy," the child sobbed.

James rushed to the front yard, where his nine-year-old stood petrified. Neighbors were running over to help. His wife lay on the ground bleeding. She was dead, having been stabbed three times. George stood nearby with a butcher knife, then turned and charged James, stabbing him in the chest and arms and on his hands.

George was charged with first-degree murder and jailed without bond. His wife, Ibtisam, was charged with striking James and another neighbor with a stick when they tried to restrain her husband.

"It could have been anybody," the county cop told Hegger. "Any one of us could have been Nancy Nolle asking a neighbor kid to stay off the grass."

CHAPTER TWENTY

Brain Sandwiches

Whenever they could, Tom Murphy and Mike Tully drove to Dickmeyer's for clam chowder. The southside restaurant had other things on the menu, but Murphy liked the chowder, not the famous fried brain sandwiches for which the German descendents, called Southside Dutch, would drive from miles around and heap with onions and mustard. The fried beef brains are light and fluffy, like thick scrambled eggs, and they taste like chicken. "Everything fried here tasted like chicken," Murphy commented gruffly. "You'd think we had no other flavors here in St. Louis."

Murphy was a tall, lean, black Irishman with the map of County Cork engraved on his face. Tully was a younger, thin redheaded Irish-American. As chief investigator for the circuit attorney, Murphy oversaw twenty-five other investigators, who helped the prosecutors prepare for trial by rounding up and weeding out witnesses and information. Tully was his deputy. Both dressed in Brooks Brothers-style, far better than some of the prosecutors they worked with. The two investigators were so well connected they knew the goings-on in and out of the circuit attorney's office, the city and county police departments, many federal alphabet agencies, and elsewhere. (In the city of St. Louis, which is its own county, what would be called the district attorney is the circuit attorney.)

Murphy was the virtuoso of the telephone; he could find anybody and get him to talk. He was like thirty-year-old, single-malt scotch: he was smooth, soothing, and could loosen tongues.

Not that his job did not require physical work. Along with the typical stakeouts shown in the movies were even less savory routines. Like the time Murphy and Tully tracked down an acquaintance of the Isas' in a rickety two-story building that had been built just after the Civil War and forgotten by time and the Land Clearance Authority. The one-room flat was drab, dark, and dank, thick with a ferocious stench of indeterminate origin. The pair of investigators breathed through their mouths.

"No thanks, ma'am," smiled Murphy when offered a seat on the sofa festooned with various stains and sprawling springs.

"Me too," Tully said, bobbing his head.

Both men squinted at the furniture to see "anything with lots of legs moving." Murphy had learned from experience; he had retired after thirty years with the St. Louis PD and joined the circuit attorney's office. As a young detective, he had interviewed a man whose sofa was stuffed with lice. "On the way home I felt something crawling," Murphy recalled. "By the time I was stopped by another officer, 'bout a block away, I was buck naked. All my clothes in a pile on the floor. Had to have 'em fumigated and dry-cleaned."

Such initiation into detective work proved to be metaphorical. Sometimes Murphy and Tully spent their days crawling around the underbelly of society. Now it was foreign intrigue, for both Murphy and Tully were on the phone constantly with Lieutenant Hegger.

Hegger wanted to know who Zein's cronies were. The investigators picked up the visitors' lists at the city jails where Maria and Zein were kept pending trial. Along with the signatures of the Isa daughters—each spelled a variety of ways—were that of Zein's brother, Zein's Chicago son-in-law, and friends from Wisconsin and Colorado. Her stepdaughter Fayrouz seemed to visit Maria more than her own girls, a bit of news that made Maria's defense lawyer unhappy.

Fayrouz was a bit of an anomaly. Schmoozing with various Palestinian shopkeepers, Murphy learned that the family was not one of solidarity: Fayrouz and her husband, Mamdouh ("Mike") Abdel-jabber, had opposed Tina's slaying before and after. Fayrouz quite vehemently thought the murder was wrong, but would not publicly attack her father. The prosecutors felt she would be a good government witness. If she were reluctant, they could subpoena her. But Fayrouz outwitted them.

Familial and tribal ties were stronger than justice. Fayrouz packed up herself and her children and fled to Beitin. "We'd have paid the air-fare for her and her four kids if she'd fly back to testify," Murphy told Hegger. "But she won't." "You can't extradite a witness from the West Bank," Hegger pointed out.

When he was not tracking down people, Murphy sniffed out tips, and passed them along. In return, he received sub rosa information: that each FBI office's counterterrorism squad was looking for derelict Palestinians hiding out from Israel, "like Nazis in South America," Murphy quipped.

"So why does Immigration let them in?" Tully asked.

"If they naturalize them, INS thinks it's easier to keep track of them," Murphy answered.

And if the feds could not find them, these Arabs would turn each other in: "They'd rat on their own mother to avoid going to jail," Murphy remarked. "Like they did in the food-stamp sting case." Before that, police investigators had been using a Palestinian informant on their other cases.

Murphy also heard that Zein had been a terrorist for three decades, possibly with various factions, as switching around is not uncommon. Zein now belonged to the most violent terrorist organization in the world. "That fits," Murphy said to Tully. "If you're a terrorist who can take out a whole planeload of innocent people, including babies, how hard is it to kill your own flesh and blood?" He flashed a newsletter called *Crime Control Digest*, dated February 4, 1991: "The FBI head of counterterrorism says the FBI has under surveillance supporters in America of Abu Nidal Organization, Hezbollah, the Palestine Liberation Front, and the Democratic Front for the Liberation of Palestine."

With all his contacts, Murphy liked to help people out. He told Helena Mylanos where to get her car transmission rebuilt cheaply. He found Cliff Walker a job at a large supermarket. And he warned him about the Isa family at the trial. "They might try to hurt you for testifying. We'll be glad to give you protection during the trial," he offered, but Cliff shook his head. Murphy was concerned, "Look, had you gone up with Tina that night, they'd have killed you, too." But Cliff was impassive.

And passive—at least to Murphy and Tully, who discussed how different he was from bouncy Tina: slender, delicately drawn, refined features; soft-spoken, sensitive, romantic, artistic, quiet, patient. And he absolutely adored her, even in death. He had waited on her and for her. He did not push sexually. He wrote poetry about her and drew her portrait. "Cliff must have been a welcome relief to Tina after the violent emotions of her family," Murphy told Tully. "Cliff has no police record, no history of drugs."

"Hell, Murph," Tully said, "he doesn't even smoke."

*   *   *

First Assistant Circuit Attorney Dee (Dreama) Joyce-Hayes had thought it was going to be a routine pretrial visit: She and an artist were meeting at the Isas' apartment so he could draw the layout of the crime scene for the trial. A piece of mail in the apartment caught Hayes's eye and she read it. The University of Missouri at Columbia had written Tina that they had received her transcript and were eagerly awaiting her application for admission.

Back in her office, Hayes typed up the translators' version of the tapes so that she could familiarize herself with the details. Hayes was efficient, with everything in its proper file folder. Years earlier, Hayes had been married to an up and coming state representative. After she put him through law school, she went there, too, and then into the circuit attorney's office. During an office shake-up, she emerged as the new first assistant. Her marriage had ended and she remarried her investigator, Gary Hayes, who was now a private eye. Dee Hayes, who looked as though she could be Annette Bening's aunt, was so charming and poised that within two years she would run for office and become a far more adroit politician than her ex-husband. Talking to juries proved good training for a ham like her, she joked. But she went further than anyone expected—even herself. Her only regret was that her father, who had always listened to and encouraged his eldest child, did not live to see her accomplishments.

Hayes was going to try the Isa case, although more experienced prosecutors coveted it. Usually the Homicide detectives tip off the big-gun prosecutors who come over during suspect interrogations. Later, Homicide can usually request one of these prosecutors, saying he's been in on it since the beginning. Until the advent of the FBI tapes, these prosecutors had wrinkled their noses at what appeared to be a routine domestic murder. Hayes, who had worked with Lieutenant Hegger on the arrest warrants, was licensed in federal court, where the legality of the tapes would be fought. Those factors led her boss to decide to allow Hayes to continue on the case.

When Hayes had read the autopsy report, she realized she and Craddick had been too conservative in their original estimate of the murder. "You don't stab your daughter multiple times through the heart and lungs in self-defense," she said. In fact, when she read the medical examiner's report, she was sickened. "Stabbing is so personal and so cold-blooded. It's not like a gunshot—you have to stab at close range. And to stab your own child thirteen times. She clearly had to have been held down." Then there was an oddity: "To fatally stab someone, one knifes the person in the back, where it's easier to get to the heart."

Bob Craddick, a genial fellow and a rising star, wanted to second-chair Hayes. After he heard the murder tape, he wanted to send Zein and Maria to death row. That was fine with Hayes, who said she was "on the fence morally and theoretically about the death penalty." The pair amicably divided up the trial: She would present the first half, the guilt phase; he would argue the punishment phase and handle all the tapes. Listening to the murder tape repeatedly, Craddick kept thinking, When will she die? When will she be out of her pain?

This was Craddick's first death penalty trial, and the first in St. Louis in which two defendants would be tried jointly for capital punishment. There was a possible scenario in which both Zein and Maria could avoid the death penalty: The state had offered Zein life without parole if he pleaded to first-degree murder. If he accepted that, Zein could testify at Maria's trial, crying, "I'm old, I'm sick, I lost control, I'm so sorry, my life is ruined, please spare my wife she had nothing to do with it, I knocked her out just before I killed our daughter." Maria could then take the stand and cry, "I should have done more to protect my girl, I'm a lousy mother, but he beat me and I'm a battered wife."

Craddick said, "What juror wants to put a mom to death? All Maria needs is one juror who identifies with her."

But Zein refused to plead guilty. He held out, saying that he had stabbed his daughter in self-defense, and that she had so shamed him, he had to commit a crime to restore his honor.

Hayes raised her voice at the mere mention of the honor killings. "Where in the Qu'ran does it say it's okay to kill your daughter? I make no excuse for these people or their culture. They lived *here*, they benefited from our prosperity." Why here? She and Craddick did not ask the U.S. Attorney's Office nor the FBI many questions, because the feds made it clear they could not answer, top secret, you know.

Hayes and Craddick worked well together. "We have so little in the way of evidence and so little discovery," Craddick commented to Hayes, "that we sure don't need the [grocery] cart we normally use to haul the exhibits down to the courtroom."

"We have the tapes," Hayes replied.

CHAPTER TWENTY-ONE

The Heart as Judge

Charlie Shaw sprang from his Mooney four-seater airplane as gracefully as he had vaulted from a B-17 bomber half a century earlier. Back then, one of the men in his squad had been a mustached actor with huge, jutting ears. Older guy by the name of Gable. During World War II, Shaw had flown twenty-four successful missions as a navigator for the air force. The twenty-fifth was not so lucky. He was shot down by the Nazis over Berlin in 1943, and at age twenty-two was imprisoned in Dachau and then in Stalag III, near Breslau, Germany.

Shaw was irrepressible. Five times he escaped prison camp and five times they hauled him back. The sixth time, before Christmas 1944, he got lucky. "I dressed like a Frenchman while I was in eastern Germany near the Polish border, where they can't speak much French, and I dressed like a Pole in western Germany near the French border, where they can't speak much Polish." It didn't hurt his cause that Shaw was as handsome as Gable, as charming as Errol Flynn, and that his eyes always twinkled like Spencer Tracy's.

Shaw vowed that prison camp was the last time he would be confined. The concept of liberty was so precious, he flew home, raced through law school in two years, and bypassing the silk-stocking law firms he had entrée to, practiced keeping the accused out of jail. No matter how vile the defendant, Shaw empathized with his fears of incarceration.

Or her fears. In 1952, five years out of law school, Shaw established himself with the murder trial of an Ozark Airlines stewardess. She was a small-town southern beauty queen, all of twenty, who had followed her lover, a dashing airline executive in his forties, to St. Louis where they planned to marry. As soon as he left his wife. Guess what? "He went back on his word," Shaw told the jury. "He *promised* to marry her, he *promised* to make her respectable. He did not." Hurt and humiliated, the scorned woman did not know where to turn or what to do, or how she came to empty that automatic into her boyfriend. By making the jurors see past the sordid crime to a helpless human being worthy of compassion, Shaw walked her out of the courtroom.

"Charlie Shaw always walks 'em. Hell, I'd call him if the cops picked me up," a prosecutor chuckled before launching into his favorite Charlie Shaw story: A *Post-Dispatch* fashion writer was on trial in the late sixties for shoplifting a designer dress from Stix, Baer and Fuller, the then nicest department store in St. Louis. Shaw argued she had "borrowed" the clothes to take back to the newspaper to write a fashion spread. "Ladies and gentlemen of the jury," Shaw said, "this little nothing of a dress cost two hundred dollars. *Two hundred dollars*. It cost Stix only half that. And I ask you, ladies and gentlemen, who was trying to steal from whom?"

The reporter was acquitted.

Shaw performed with such grace and humor, there was a contingent of courthouse groupies who followed him from trial to trial. The cops liked him, even after he had shattered their cases based on identification. "Charlie gets you so confused on the stand that you couldn't pick your own mother out of a lineup," Sergeant Guzy laughed. "He's larger than life."

Actually, Shaw was merely average tall, six one, but court watchers and jurors, especially women, were convinced he was six five at least. He looked and moved like a man twenty years younger. Some of that exuberance came from not being weighted down by pomposity, an occupational hazard of some big-time attorneys. He was the last of the old-time trial lawyers trained to try cases by his wits, decades before the rules of evidence and discovery changed the court game into a nit-picking contest. Not that he couldn't master the new rules; Shaw just liked the old-fashioned style of appealing to emotion. He liked to say, "The heart is the best judge."

Shaw's lack of pretension stemmed from his background and his Good Ol' Boyhood. Back before people appraised a person's value by a person's net worth, or how useful that person might be, St. Louisans were brought up to treat everybody with the same set of good manners. Everybody. Charles Major Shaw was securely rooted in Clayton, a quietly well-to-do suburb where his father was a four-term mayor. Everybody there knew who you were. And Shaw never thought he was any better than anybody else. "Hell, my father wasn't rich when I

was growing up." He was in real estate, and he and his partner, the
father of the FBI supervisor, Tom Newman, built their stucco houses
side by side on Wydown, a beautiful shaded boulevard of six-story
oaks with dogwood and redbud trees flowering down the greensward
of the divided street.

Charlie Shaw liked to play jus' folks in court. Once he actually told a
jury, "I wasn't born with a silver spoon in my mouth like this fella,"
referring to the prosecutor, who had to work his way through school
and who promptly turned red before he exploded at Shaw. That out-
burst cost him points with the jury which is what Shaw intended. "It is
not enough to make the jurors like the accused, Shaw said, "they also
have to warm toward me to acquit my client." In the Isa case, he would
ask prospective jurors, "Is there anyone here who feels . . . he might be
persuaded to change whatever opinion he may [have] . . . because
someone else on the panel may have more formal education? Your
opinion . . . is considered just as good and just as valuable . . ."

So how does a rich lawyer, the grandson of Italian immigrants,
become a Good Ol' Boy? Growing up, Shaw was enthralled by Tom
Mix and John Wayne cowboy movies, interspersed with newsreels of
the Lindbergh kidnapping/murder trial and Bruno Hauptmann's
defense lawyer, Edward J. Riley. Eons before it was fashionable, Shaw
collected Native American jewelry and southwestern art. He sallied
forth into federal court in cowboy hats and into country club weddings
in Navajo turquoise rings. After a client gave him a horse, Shaw and
his wife began raising them on their 600-acre farm and taking their
four children to horse shows around the country. Until their youngest
child was killed, the Shaws spent weekdays in their turn-of-the-cen-
tury mansion in the city's Central West End so that their boy could
attend private school in St. Louis. Back home on the range, Shaw was
known to answer the door with a shotgun, a reasonable thing to do
considering his line of work.

Pro-NRA, pro law-and-order, and pro Republican, Shaw was an
old-fashioned conservative that liberals loved to love, especially
women. "He has that invisible arm," said former *Globe Democrat* courthouse reporter Mary Scarpinato, "that when he takes on a client, he or
she feels protected." In the Age of the Indecisive Male, Charlie Shaw
was a Real Man (which is related to Good Ol' Boy) which meant: He
wasn't "into" "sharing and caring," he liked spunky women, he

wouldn't be caught dead wearing a baseball cap backwards, he had a playful sense of humor, he was unfettered by political correctness, and his word was good which was paramount in St. Louis, a big city that thinks like a small town.

After four decades worth of clippings in the newspaper morgues, Shaw hated news conferences. "Whenever a lawyer goes looking for publicity, one day it will come looking for you when you don't want it," he said. "Publicity seeking demeans the client. The client wins the acquittal, not me."

After more than a hundred capital murder cases, Shaw had yet to visit a client on death row. He flew his Mooney around the state to file motions and to see clients.

Whenever they were both free, Shaw lunched at the quietly chic Daniele Hotel in Clayton with another former Clayton boy, Daniel Reardon. The two had become friends more than thirty years earlier when Reardon, then an assistant circuit attorney, had prosecuted one of Shaw's clients. Reardon went on to become the circuit attorney of St. Louis (after his boss, Tom Eagleton, became a Missouri attorney general and ultimately, a U.S. senator.)

Reardon had been born and bred in a lovely, large home with plenty of servants and was educated at private Catholic schools. At sixty-one he was tall and thin with a full head of silver hair. In a courtroom, his face flushed; Dan Reardon was as emotional as Shaw. The father of five daughters and a son, Reardon had lived through every form of teenage rebellion. It would be difficult for a man who had never spanked his own children to comprehend Zein Isa. Initially, it seemed a straightforward case of self-defense.

Following the recommendation of a bail bondsman, the men of the Beitin Association asked Reardon to represent Zein shortly after his arrest. The group had raised $17,000 at their mosque; more would be forthcoming. After visiting Zein in jail, Reardon thought he could get his client released on reduced bail. But the judge refused to lower the $1 million bond, saying there was evidence Zein would flee to Brazil. Reardon heard from an undisclosed source that the FBI had a Palestinian informant whom the Isa family had long trusted.

Yet, when Tawfiq Musa learned that from Reardon, he was shocked that a *fedyaheen* had betrayed his Arab brothers. Is there any man that bad in St. Louis? he asked Saif Nijmeh. Many, more than you can believe, Saif replied. The feds are monitoring your telephones, Tawfiq warned. And what about Alliance Market, who would run it now with Zein in jail? he asked. They don't want to give it to me, Saif wailed. Tina must have gone to the authorities before she died, Saif's brother, Luie, surmised.

Reardon still thought Zein had a chance. "According to his version, it was self-defense. I thought he had a triable case. Until the tape of Tina's murder was released.

"Our translation—by Fayrouz—was so damned bad from a defense point, that there was no quibble over semantics," Reardon said. When the news leaked out that there was a recorded murder, the Turks and other nationalities at the mosque were furious and disgusted, saying that Zein was the "scum of the earth for what he did." Police undercovers discovered, however, that many of the Palestinians supported Zein privately. Public support would have cost these businessmen their positions in the neighborhood. "They tell Americans what you want to hear," Detective Jackson explained to Lieutenant Hegger. "You never know where they really stand. They lie."

The defense fund dried up. That was only a fraction of Reardon's problem.

Communications between attorney and client became strained beyond the difficulties of the language. Listening to the tape, Reardon was shocked that Zein and Maria had waited half an hour before they called an ambulance for their child. "I could never fully understand what Zein did or why he did it." Then Reardon went through the recording with him—there was no mention of Tina having a knife. Zein did not care; he was contemptuous of American justice. The prospect of a murder trial did not faze him; he was undaunted. Even his son-in-law, Amir Darwish, admitted that the family knew an honor killing was a crime in the United States.

"He kept telling me the same story—self-defense. He isn't stupid, he's average and he's literate. And he wasn't crazy then or when it had happened. He wasn't any worse than other psychopaths; he just had made up his mind," Reardon said. His lawyer begged him to plead guilty to spare his wife. But he wouldn't listen to anyone.

When the FBI released the rest of the tapes and Zein heard them, he said he would accept all responsibility. He would even take the long walk to the death chamber. There was legal precedent, in *Missouri* v. *Hunter:* A criminal can plead guilty to first-degree murder and be sentenced to death. "But the catch is he wants his wife set free," Reardon told Craddick. The circuit attorney's office would not and could not do that when they had Maria's complicity recorded on tape.

When Maria was arrested, Reardon asked his good friend, Shaw, to represent her. They both wanted the Isas tried separately for legal reasons and for appearances: "The jury thinks if you have two lawyers at the counsel table that you'd paid a lot of money, and the jury doesn't want to be bamboozled by some slick lawyer. You always want to look like the underdog," Shaw explained. Shaw felt sorry for Maria, whereas Reardon loathed his client. His disgust went beyond Tina's crying on the tapes.

Reardon did some research into the tenets of Islam. Nowhere in the Qu'ran did Allah demand that a father sacrifice his daughter to honor. Nowhere in the Hadith did Mohammed exhort his followers to kill a shameful girl. Reardon tried desperately to find some palatable image of his client acceptable to a jury, but Zein would not cooperate: Zein maintained that *his* way was the right way.

Reardon railed against the admissibility of the tapes, calling the secret court that authorized the bugging, "a star chamber." (The Star Chamber was a secret English court of law held without a jury. Parliament abolished it in 1641 because of its notorious abuses, e.g., no defense lawyers were allowed.) In traditional electronic eavesdropping, under U.S. Criminal Code, Title III, if the prosecutors or police have information that there is probable cause of a crime, they can apply for permission to use intrusive surveillance. A federal district judge may grant the search warrant for one to three months, which is renewable. The defense is entitled to all taped conversations to see if there is anything on the tapes that is exculpatory. The lawyer is also permitted to know how long and for what reason his client was wiretapped and bugged and in which buildings the surveillance was installed. If any other person's conversation has been recorded under Title III, the federal government must notify that person by letter.

The Isas were being monitored under a different statute, one for domestic spying: The Foreign Intelligence Surveillance Act (FISA) of 1978, Title 50(L). Tapes from such surveillance are classified—so classified that even the prosecutors working on the case must have top clearance. And to obtain it, they sign papers abrogating free speech, meaning it's illegal to discuss the case.

FISA surveillance is requested only by federal agencies, whereas a state attorney general and the local police can ask for permission to install a Title III wiretap or a bug. (A wiretap goes over telephone wires, while a bug is installed on walls, lamps, radios, cars, or even on a pet's collar.)

Reardon asked the federal district court to suppress the tapes, saying they were unlawfully obtained. The first hearing was held in chambers before then Chief District Judge John F. Nangle with only the lawyers present. Reardon argued he and Shaw should be allowed to read the warrant applications authorizing the surveillance of his client. He only knew from the few declassified papers he had seen that the request did not come from either the FBI or the U.S. Attorney's Office in St. Louis.

The case had been generated from Washington, D.C. and was signed by U.S. Attorney General Richard Thornburgh.

"How many of these poor bastards are you bugging?" Reardon rhetorically asked Terry Adelman, the brilliant first assistant U.S. attorney handling the FISA admissibility. Adelman, who shortly thereafter became a federal magistrate, could not answer because the information was so secret. And even he didn't know about all of them.

"Why can't we have all the tapes like we would in a Title III case?" the defense lawyers asked the judge. "John Gotti and the Mafia chieftains get all their tapes. Where are all the phone conversations between Tina and her friends in which she says how she kicked her father?" Reardon asked. "What about all the fights between Tina and Zein?"

"Your honor," Adelman protested, "these people are terrorists."

The court ruled the tapes were admissible. The decision was upheld by the Eighth Circuit Federal Court of Appeals and the U.S. Supreme Court refused certiorari (meaning, they would not review it.) But the judge did order Assistant U.S. Attorney Jim Steitz, who had top clearance, to do a Brady Sweep—check the logs for any evidence that Zein and Maria could use in their defense. Between digging for exculpatory* tapes and the appeals, it took nearly two years for the Isas to

---

*Exculpatory material is called Brady material, after the U.S. Supreme Court case *Brady v. Maryland*, in which the justices ruled that the government must declassify any material which can be used by the defense to prove their case.

come to trial. There was a third reason for not complying with the Isas' constitutional right to a speedy trial: The Gulf War. Their trial originally was set for February, 1991.

For all their work, Reardon and Shaw were paid a minute fraction of the total bill; their clients' family never finished the payment schedule. Worse yet, the clan discussed on the tapes how they intended to "stiff" the lawyers. The taping continued at least until July 25, 1990, the last released tape being a telephone conversation between Saif Nijmeh and Tawfiq Musa. The federal government either discontinued surveillance after that, or what they discovered is still classified information.

It was not only the tapes that had brought Zein and Maria to court. At least one of their inner circle was a snitch.

CHAPTER TWENTY-TWO

"Extra Love"

APRIL 1991

Harry Hegger's big, deep, brown eyes were those of a bewildered child. "You're a woman, you tell me," he said to a reporter, "how can you carry a baby for nine months, nurse it through chicken pox and measles, help her with homework and teach her to drive, then, when she's on the threshold of adulthood, hold her down to be murdered?"

This was becoming a late-afternoon ritual. A reporter would go into Hegger's office about the latest homicides du jour and the lieutenant would close his door, a rarity, and begin: "And as far as teenage rebellion went, what was there to complain about?" He counted off Tina's accomplishments. "An honor student. With a scholarship. With a job. Didn't smoke. Didn't drink. Didn't do drugs. So she had a boyfriend her parents weren't crazy about. So what? It wasn't like she was going to run off and marry him. Jesus Christ. Here's a girl anyone would be proud to have as a daughter.

"What interests me most is the motive here," Hegger said, pointing his hand to his heart.

In Hegger's mind, the fundamental conflict in the Isa household arose upon expectations of life. "Remember in college psych, about Maslow's hierarchy of needs? Zein and Maria never got beyond the bottom—the safety level of food and shelter. That was enough for them. But Tina wanted more—all the way to the top of the pyramid. The Isas thought the world was great if they had meat for dinner, whereas Tina wanted to fulfill her personal dreams."

Maybe Maria too once had dreams. She clearly wished to be educated. Alone, awaiting trial, she took advantage of a literacy program for inmates and, as she had studied Arabic in East Jerusalem and Spanish in Puerto Rico, she practiced reading and writing in English. Her tutor,

Barbara Horlick, marveled at how bright and quick Maria was, despite her lack of schooling.

Horlick also saw her sorrow, for Maria would cry and say how she had not wanted to kill her daughter and how sorely she missed her. Her impression was Maria was afraid of her husband, that she would do what he expected. "But her heart wasn't in it. I think she feared for her life. She was so sad. Such a warm individual and he mistrusted her for that. She felt warmly toward anyone who treated her decently. Like a puppy dog." Maria would hug and thank her teacher for each session.

As they came to know each other, Maria confided in Horlick. How she had lived with Zein's first wife. How she worried who was running their store now, but told Horlick they had many friends who would take care of everything. She still felt loyal to her husband despite what had happened, fretting about his infected leg, worrying whether it would have to be amputated, brooding how he had no one to care for him, to make certain he bathed and had clean clothes. But Horlick believed she was very much afraid of him.

In jail Zein wrote an affidavit to be used in his appeal for bond. He swore that between 1984 and 1989, he went home to the West Bank "perhaps three times." He said he paid for the visits himself to see his family, including "wife Foiziya." He wrote that he had never belonged to nor sympathized with the PLO; that he was loyal to the United States, and had never done anything to hurt it or its residents; he had even become a naturalized citizen in 1980. He said he had received calls infrequently from the West Bank, in Arabic, which concerned personal matters.

Listen to the tapes, he wrote, they proved he had no connection with any terrorist group.

Zein also wrote a rambling nineteen-page letter portraying himself as a good father but a helpless one. He blamed outside causes for his problems. In Israel everything had been the fault of the Jews. Now, the source of his problems was a Satanic cult.

Zein genuinely loved the youngest of his seven children, his pet, his *chica*, his Tina. It began when she was a baby and because he spent more time with her—her older sisters being in school—that created "an extra love." Despite being isolated by language and penury, Zein described the family as happy. Whenever Tina went to visit relatives, Zein said he became lonely and missed his daughter.

Abruptly Tina changed, beginning in January 1989. She no longer told him where she was going, what she was doing. When he asked, she answered him rudely. He told her how he loved her and worried about her, but that irritated her into more insolence. She no longer said good morning when she got up, no longer said good-bye when he dropped her off at school, no longer would bring him a cup of coffee. Grabbing the phone, she would lock herself in the bathroom and chat with her friends for hours. When her mother asked who she was talking with, she would answer, "The Devil." She began lying.

Zein fretted, yet did not want to discuss the problem with anyone. He was embarrassed how his daughter was treating him. Zein worried that Tina's rude manners had threatened Soraia's future, since her fiancé witnessed Tina's behavior. Three days after the prom fight, Zein took Tina for a drive and calmly asked her why she acted so hateful. "I hate you," she told him. "I hate both Christianity and Islam. . . . I worship the Devil."

At last Zein asked Leilah to find out why Tina was behaving so oddly. Leilah reported back with a warning: Tina belongs to "the Satan Cult"; be careful, she wants to kill you. Zein begged Mona and Soraia to talk to Tina. They came back with similar stories.

One day in August, at Alliance, Maria asked Tina to help her father fill the cooler. Tina continued standing at the cash register listening to her earphones. As Maria took off an earphone, Tina shouted, "Fuck you, fuck you," and stormed out of the store. When her parents returned home, she was not there.

For four days they had no idea where she was. When she came home, Zein pleaded, What do you want? To join the tennis and soccer teams, to go shopping, to go to college, she said, and I'll promise to be good. Agreeing to her demands, her father hugged and kissed her. The next morning she was so cheerful, he thought everything was back to the way it was. Tina went back to school and played tennis afterward; Zein picked her up at the courts. But after three days Mona warned Zein that Tina's tennis coach had tipped her off that the girl might commit some crime.

Zein's friends counseled him to ignore Tina. He could not; he loved her too much. He beseeched his other daughters to "convince Tina to treat us right." That failed. He turned to his cousin Tawfiq in Milwaukee to talk to Tina. But instead of meeting with Tawfiq, Tina locked herself in her room.

Zein was undeterred. He offered to pay her expenses for college, which could cost a minimum of $10,000 a year. Tina rejected his generosity with "I have friends, powerful friends, who can get anything they want." He thought Tina was stealing money from the store safe for her cult group.

Mona warned him again, Tina wants to be free and will kill you. Here he was, middle-aged, ill, a law-abiding citizen of the United States who had no criminal record, not even a traffic ticket, who had never even bought a gun, and the Satan worshippers were going to kill him, using the child he loved most as their weapon.

Zein prayed for God to help the State of Missouri track down the Devil worshippers and stamp out their evil. Zein wrote that he belatedly realized that there had been nothing emotional nor physical between Tina and Cliff. Their only bond was belonging to the "Satanic Klan."

CHAPTER TWENTY-THREE

"An Enemy in Your Own House"

MONDAY, OCTOBER 21, 1991

Buster the German shepherd lay sleeping in a patch of sunlight on the cool inlaid tile of the courthouse hall. "He's tuckered out, said his handler, after sniffing for explosives since four A.M. The dog was a new fixture, an antiterrorist precaution stationed outside the courtroom.

Dee Joyce-Hayes and Bob Craddick were already inside, having traversed the corridors connecting the circuit attorney's office with the judges' chambers and courtrooms. The pair of prosecutors wore their "lucky suits"—grey glen plaid for him, and navy, Chanel-style with gold-tone buttons and jewelry for her.

"This is the trial of your career, a really big case," a reporter told Hayes. "Yeah, and if I screw it up, and with those tapes as evidence," Hayes joked, "they might take my law license away." While she was worried about working late during the trial, with a three-year-old at home, Hayes was excited about trying a big case against Charlie Shaw and Dan Reardon. "They're both honest, bullshit free," she said. "They don't play tricks in the courtroom."

She picked up several large, quilted brown paper sacks, evidence bags marked Exhibit 10-A, Exhibit 10-B, etc., and took them over to the balustrade separating the courtroom participants from the courtroom watchers. She neatly opened them and draped pieces of clothing over the handrailing as if she were laying out a child's outfit to wear to school the next day. But each garment was stiffened and stained with blood that had turned greenish over time, including Tina's blue denim jacket which she never was given the chance to take off.

As Hayes finished her grisly task, the jurors filed in. "All rise for the judge," the bailiff announced.

Back in his chambers, Judge Charles A. Shaw (no relation to Maria's defense lawyer, Charlie Shaw) drew on his black robe and walked onto the bench. During a dull docket call, he had once come twirling out in his robes as his bailiff singsonged, "Hea' come da judge, hea' come da judge." Such a lighthearted demeanor belied a hard core of ambition, brains, and depth. He had spent eight years as an assistant U.S. attorney, where he was known to be an exceptionally bright and able trial lawyer, one who cared about justice. Seeking a fresh challenge, Shaw had applied twelve times for circuit and appellate judgeships before he was appointed to the state bench. What he lusted for now was the federal bench. Three times Shaw threw in his name and made the semifinals, and three times he was not anointed. He never despaired: "The process is more like jumping hurdles than winning a race. I don't take it personally if there has to be another round." And considering his dozen applications for state jobs, the judge laughed, "Probably my strong suit is persistence."

Fascinated with the Isa case, Judge Shaw also worried about the responsibility of a murder trial with two defendants. Despite her lawyer's arguments, the judge had ruled that Maria could be tried with her husband. "Why sever their trials? The same set of facts will be presented in each case, the same evidence, the same tapes. You sever a trial when evidence against one cannot be used against the other. And with the Isas, we have a conspiracy—they acted together, although Charlie Shaw feels Maria was influenced by her husband."

Severance would double the cost, the judge pointed out: The hotel and meal bills alone, for sequestering the jury for the nearly two-week trial, would be $20,000. The taxpayers would pay an additional $8,000 for the tag team of interpreters for the Isas.

The jury was already seated, waiting for the judge. They had been chosen with great care over five days. Almost all the citizens called had been more creative on why they could not perform their civic duty than a pack of ten-year-olds on where they had left their sweaters. The judge had to constantly point out that no one volunteers to be on a jury.

Hayes glanced at her notes, walked over to the jury box, and in a low voice with a slightly Southern lilt presented her opening statement—the summary of the state's evidence and testimony. She was at her best talking to juries, reducing a tangle of emotions and facts to a simple narrative with what English composition teachers emphasize—

plot, theme, and characters. Palestina Isa, not yet seventeen, had been an honor student a year ahead of herself. Fluent in four languages, she was mastering her fifth, French. Not just a bookworm, she played on two sports teams and in the school band, and worked on the yearbook. Tina was popular with the other students, who still grieved for her short life and missed her laughter and enthusiasm.

Despite her accomplishments, Tina spent the last year of her life miserably fighting with her family. They denied her the perks of any American high school student—field trips, proms, special summer programs, and dating. But Tina persisted in seeing her boyfriend. He was black, which infuriated her parents, and they beat her severely. Tina ran away. And when she returned, they became more punitive, taking her out of school temporarily. In early November Tina committed the ultimate disobedience: She took a job outside the family store. Her wages would make her independent of her parents. That her father could not and would not bear.

Hayes promised the jurors "you will hear" Zein plotting Tina's murder and, with his wife, "you will hear" them slaying their child and "you will hear" them lying to the police. It was all on tape.

The jurors were spellbound.

Following that speech was harrowing for Dan Reardon. What was there to say about a father who murdered a popular honor student? As other trial lawyers said later, Reardon acquitted himself very well. He began his opening statement by implanting doubt about the tapes. "When Mrs. Hayes said repeatedly, 'You will hear, you will hear,' what you will hear will be . . . the language barrier. . . . *Translators* will tell you what occurred."

Reardon offered up a forlorn tale of woe, of a poor immigrant patriarch who slaved fourteen hours a day and more to feed and educate his children. Instead of returning his favors with gratitude, his youngest child disobeyed him. She laughed at the traditions her father held dear, traditions his other children had embraced. What most humiliated her father took place at a party of family and friends from Palestine, where all wore their native dress. All but Tina, who wore black—all black— which she did so often, her family believed she had joined some cult.

His daughter's teenage rebellion was exacerbated by the repressive mores of her father. "This is a tragedy," Reardon said. "This is not murder in the first degree."

*   *   *

Rubbing his old Devil's Dance Zuni bracelet, Charlie Shaw picked up the theme of culture clash. Maria, he reminded the court, was not an American citizen; she was a Brazilian who spoke Portuguese. She became involved with Arabic customs only when she married *Zein*. Her culpability hinged on the low status of women in *his* oppressive and punitive culture. Shaw's deep, rich baritone took on aggrieved tones: his client was being tried for a crime *her husband* had instigated.

Shaw frequently patted Maria's broad shoulders as if to prove to jurors that she was really a warm, likable person. Maria was a loving mother who had fought her husband over privileges for Tina, he said, while Tina's mean-spirited sisters sided with their father. When "Maria began to stand up on her own two feet . . . [it was] the worst thing an Islamic woman can ever do to [her] husband.

"Now, jurors, on the evening in question . . . you will hear that Maria had absolutely nothing to do with the holocaust that followed"—Shaw's voice deepened over the next phrase as if he were telling a deep, dark secret—"it was *strictly* between Zein and Palestina."

Nobody in the courtroom except Reardon knew the emotional strain that talk of a dead child was making on Charlie Shaw. In 1973, Shaw and his wife had given their son Randy a new car for his sixteenth birthday. The youngest of his four children, the youth looked like a blond version of his father, who was intensely proud of him. Shaw had to be called back from a business trip within days, after Randy's new car flipped over and rescuers had to cut it open to remove the boy's mangled corpse. Only once during the trial did Shaw allude to his loss.

Maria and Zein gazed at their lawyers with rapt attention. Zein, in his worn blue suit and maroon tie, with his mustache, short beard, and aviator glasses, looked like some seedy instructor at a shabby fourth-rate college. Maria looked odd and out of place in a St. Louis court-house, neither Middle Eastern, neither North nor South American. Her hair hung in a single braid down to her waist. She wore a long-sleeved white blouse tucked into a homemade snow-white polyester satin skirt that brushed her ankles.

Neither Zein nor Maria flinched at any evidence or testimony. As the expensive team of interpreters translated the witnesses' words into

Arabic and Portuguese, several witnesses portrayed the Isas as liars who understood English, having spoken it for years. The police testimony was frightening.

Sergeant Michael Guzy testified that Maria told him she had grabbed Tina's long hair to pull her away from her father whom she was trying to stab with a knife.

As he began his cross-examination, Shaw handed Guzy the first draft of Guzy's police report and asked him to read it aloud. Guzy had first written that Maria told him she had walked behind Tina and grabbed her daughter's long hair to separate her from her father. Guzy also read how Maria emphasized to him that she had never stabbed the girl.

Shaw repeated that for emphasis; Maria did not stab Tina?

Guzy agreed.

Shaw again repeated that his client had "grabbed" the hair in order to break up the fight. Repetition is necessary when arguing orally. As a Southern Baptist minister known for his sermons once said, "You tell 'em you're gonna tell 'em, you tell 'em, and then you tell 'em you told 'em."

Yes, Sergeant Guzy agreed.

"So, when you, when you changed one word from *grabbed* her hair from behind, and you say she *held* her from behind, that's a big difference, isn't it?" Shaw asked Guzy.

"If you say so," Guzy said sarcastically. "It's not significant."

Shaw deliberately looked astonished. "You don't feel that holding somebody while somebody's stabbing her is different than trying to separate them?"

Shaw turned to the image of Maria he wanted the jurors to see. The submissive wife. He asked the sergeant wasn't his client reluctant to tell him *her husband did it?*

"Yes," the cop said. "She was."

Shaw's strategy was wasted on the Palestinian men—family and friends of the defendants—in the courtroom. They behaved as though they were watching a soccer match on TV in a bar. American law was so much gibberish to them. Even when Hayes brandished the two large knives during testimony, they were nonchalant. Hirsute, with shirts open to midchest, they clipped their nails, jingled their keys, and jiggled their legs stretched out into the aisles. Deputy sheriffs constantly reminded them of proper deportment throughout the trial.

Maria's mother, who had journeyed all the way from Brazil, under-stood the gravity of a death penalty case. But Maria seemed uncon-cerned. When Maria returned from the recess, she turned around and smiled at her mother, her daughters, and a niece. As the girls cheered her with, "Yeah, Maria," she raised her fist high in salutation, like some six-ties revolutionary. During the shorter breaks, she and her husband made no move to chat nor touch. Instead, they chatted with their interpreters.

By afternoon Hayes and Shaw were sparring so frequently, continu-ously objecting to each other's points, that the judge jokingly would say, "C'mon, c'mon up here." By the next day, he would no longer smile when he said it. Telling a reporter the third day, "This is now a serious fight. They won't be so friendly for a while." Charlie Shaw seemed to be able to pinpoint exactly when to jump up, interrupt Hayes, and object so that she would lose her normal aplomb and shriek at him.

Finally, when he looked down at her and gravely said, "Calm down, calm down, or you won't live to my age," the judge intervened. Even for lawyers arguing during trial, this was exceptional. The judge defused the tension by telling Hayes, "That's what Charlie told me eight years ago when I was trying cases against him," but the bickering continued up at the judge's bench and into his chambers.

For example, the defense wanted to call Kent Dickens, the case-worker who investigated Tina's call to the Child Abuse Hotline. Shaw wanted Dickens to testify there had been no bruises on Tina, no signs of abuse. "Your honor, that's rank hearsay," Hayes told the judge dur-ing a hearing while the jury was recessed. "Tina told him [Dickens] that before her parents."

The next day Hayes emphasized Tina's ample size. Tina was five-foot-four-inches and weighed 174 pounds, the assistant medical exam-iner testified. Stocky with well-developed muscles. The dead child weighed about the same as her slightly built, five-foot-nine father. If Maria, who police said weighed in at 224 pounds and at barely five feet, had not held her back, Tina would be alive. It was clear from the autopsy that Zein could not have acted alone.

Hayes asked the pathologist to describe the magnitude of the wounds: There were six fatal wounds directly over the bottom of the sternum. All were inflicted by a knife going upward through the body,

front to back, right to left. The topmost wound went four inches into
the body, tearing the heart. The leftmost wound punctured her left
lung. Tina lost a quart of blood from these two slashes. The four lower
wounds penetrated the liver where Tina lost only half a cup of blood.
That proved that she was dying or dead by the time her father stabbed
her there during his frenzy.

Hayes emphasized the heart wound, asking, "All the way through
that bone? Do you have any medical opinion as to the degree of force
required for a knife to actually penetrate through the bone into the
heart?"

Only powerful pressure and a sharp knife could inflict such a blow,
the assistant medical examiner testified.

Any significance to the wounds all going upward in the same general direction?

Yes, it's rather unusual, said the pathologist.

Any significance? Hayes asked again.

Yes, he repeated.

What? Hayes asked for a third time.

"The subject may have not been moving much when she was
stabbed."

Any conclusion from the seven puncture wounds on her left breast,
six on the lower half and one above the nipple?

The clustering showed Tina was either unconscious or unable to
move when they were inflicted. As Tina tried to ward off her father's
knife, she received numerous small defensive wounds on her hands.
Overall, the wounds could not have been inflicted during a free fight.

Zein could have received the cut on his hand as he tried to grab the
knife, the doctor said. Or, as he stabbed Tina's sternum with such force
to break it, that the knife slipped in his hand, wet with his daughter's
blood.

Before he stepped down, Hayes asked the pathologist about Zein's
allegation that Tina used drugs: Preliminary examination showed no
blood alcohol nor illegal drug use, the physician said. There had been
no further toxicology tests.

Tina was not the type to use drugs, said her guidance counselor,
Pamela Fournier, in a low, husky voice. Already accepted at St. Louis
University and nominated for the assistance program for minorities,

Tina was seeking other scholarships as well. Until her mother tore up the application forms.

But Maria was the Good Mother, Shaw pointed out during cross-examination. Yes, Fournier admitted, Maria attended report card nights, parent-teacher meetings and the like, without Zein. Yes, Fournier admitted, Maria needed Zein's approval before Tina could return to school.

Tina's friends were next. Clifford Cortez Walker was frightened. When Hayes handed him Tina's blood-encrusted clothes and winter coat to identify, he looked stricken. He had not wanted to come; indeed, Tom Murphy, the chief investigator, had driven Cliff in to ensure his appearance. Cliff had reason to fear Tina's family. They wondered how much Tina had told him about her father's political intrigues. As Cliff ran down the courthouse steps after testifying, the Palestinian men standing around outside during the recess made cat-calls and harassed him, as they had other witnesses.

Helena Mylanos was even more soft-spoken than Cliff, but steadfast in her testimony, a good witness. As soon as she finished, Hayes and Craddick looked at each other: Helena had arranged her hair in a new style, copying the one Tina wore in her class portrait. As Helena walked out, she was surprised to see Tina's sisters with head scarves on. "I never saw any of them wearing a *hijab* before," she said.

Of the fifteen witnesses for the prosecution, not one member of Tina's family had testified.

The star witness in the Isa trial would be the murder tape. That was devastating for the defense. If it became known why the Isas had been under electronic surveillance, it would hasten Zein's and Maria's journey to the death chamber. It would not do to announce the truth: Ladies and gentlemen, what you are about to hear are tapes the FBI secretly recorded in the Isa home and elsewhere. This was authorized under the Foreign Intelligence Surveillance Act, for Zein Isa and his friends are suspected terrorists, members of a group that hates Americans, Westerners, Jews, and Israelis. One whose great patrons are Saddam Hussein and Mu'ammar Qadaffi. One with numerous international cells.

At the request of the defense, Judge Shaw merely announced that "the tapes were lawfully obtained." Craddick, who had organized the twenty-five conversations and determined which selections to play, began with five excerpts about planning the murder. For two and a half months, Zein had discussed and been goaded into killing Tina:

- August 16, 1989. Zein tells Fayrouz, "This one is burned forever. . . . The glass when it becomes dirty and gets broken, is there any way to repair it? . . . Is there a way to cleanse my name . . . after she left home? . . . this one has become a burned woman, a black's whore. There's no way to cleanse her, except the red color that cleanses."
- August 18. Zein argues with his son, Faisal: "Teaching her, I think, must take place in the hotel that is under the ground."
- Also August 18. Zein tells his future son-in-law, Amjad Salem, " . . . the world does not lack guns."
- October 13. Zein promises Mona, "If God makes my wish, I will put her in the grave."
- October 14. Zein deliberates how to kill Tina, during a protracted long-distance discussion with Soraia. "I should buy myself a gun; a person like her has no more life left for her." Soraia suggests hiring a black convict to kill Tina. "No," Zein cries. "It is necessary that I do the story. It is not possible that the shame would be erased from me, that some stranger killed his daughter."

  "This one, this one doesn't deserve to live one year on the face of the earth," Soraia agrees. "A whore. . . . She doesn't deserve dog shit." Returning to her plan, Soraia tells him, "As you have said, 'She threatened me and I killed her.' "

  "She threatened me," Zein echoes. "And I'll put the knife in her hand after she falls. Leave the story to me."

Maria wiped her eyes, while on the tape Soraia was describing how horrible Tina was. Was Maria tearful because she missed her child or because she remembered Tina's contrariness?

Charlie Shaw pointed out the conversations proved Maria's lack of culpability. Did Zein not say that his wife was "overlenient"? Was he not angry with Maria for allowing Tina to continue in school sports? Maria still believed Tina could be redeemed, wanted her saved. Zein complained to Soraia that his own wife had threatened to leave him and rent an apartment for herself and her youngest daughter if he did not stop harassing the girl.

*   *   *

Peter Heath, the professor of Arabic literature from Washington University, was the expert witness on the Arabic translations of the tapes (there was a Portuguese expert, too). Heath had thought he had been fair. To avoid inflaming the jury, which included nine blacks, with the direct translation of Zein's derogatory terms for African-Americans—*black slave* or *nigger slave*—Heath had substituted the word *black*.

He was surprised when he left the courthouse that evening and was stopped by a Palestinian youth. The man argued, "You taught at Bir Zeit. You know why he did it."

"I don't approve of people killing their children," Heath replied, and kept walking to his car.

The man retorted: "He had to do it. He was losing face in front of the men of the community."

Heath sensed this man was being pressured. But he thought this case was less about honor killing and more about a struggle for power within the family. Heath had worked with families of runaways and understood the dynamics. "Control of Tina was the primary issue," Heath later said, adding, "death is the ultimate form of control."

The third day of testimony began as a beautiful Indian summer day, the brilliantly colored leaves set against a bright blue sky. Hot and sunny, 81 degrees, but so far, low humidity. It quickly became too warm in the overcrowded old courtroom, so heated the judge had a fan set in the window ledge and turned on high. Later this morning, the audiotape of a murder would be broadcast. First would be the evening conversations preceding the murder at midnight.

There are two interesting themes in these conversations. The family begins to reduce Tina to an object, referring to her as a "little girl," "she," and "her." Second, Zein's older daughters admonish him to "take charge." Zein's floundering about, discussing Tina with everyone, even outsiders, reveals him as incapable of properly handling his daughter. His children do not respect him and speak to him disdainfully. (Note, "By God" is an oath in Arabic; it is not swearing.)

7:09 P.M. PHONE CALL BETWEEN ZEIN AND FAYROUZ

Zein complained, "One can fight the whole world, but who wants to fight an enemy in your own house?"

Fayrouz's rejoinder was, " . . . when the news comes to me, I will put on my best dress and go out. My worries will be gone forever."

7:14 P.M. PHONE CALL BETWEEN ZEIN AND MONA

Mona sprightly announced to her father that Leilah told her that Maria was going to kill Tina that night.

What? Zein exclaimed.

"That Mother is going to kill her!" Mona replied.

"By God! Tell her [Leilah] to put shit in her mouth!" Zein answered. "Your mother is nervous. (Unclear) . . . Mother does not want to do anything, see?"

Maria picked up the receiver, "I am very upset with my nerves. I am finished . . . " she said.

9:23 P.M. PHONE CALL BETWEEN MARIA AND LEILAH, AND BETWEEN ZEIN AND LEILAH

Maria told Leilah Mona had called to repeat the news that Tina would be killed later that night. "Your father says to shut your mouth."

"It's for him to close his mouth," Leilah snapped back. "Since when has he learned how to shut his mouth?" she added as her father ranted on unintelligibly in the background. "He's always talking. Now you can tell him for me . . . 'It's for you to shut your mouth! You who haven't learned to shut your mouth yet! . . . ' "

Zein grabbed the phone. "Mother is not going to do nothing, nor am I. Let's say that a nigger killed her. The bitch is going to give him her blood."

Leilah replied that she no longer cared. Whatever they decided to do, do not call her about it. If you kill Tina, she said, don't call me!

9:30 P.M. PHONE CALL BETWEEN ZEIN AND MONA

Mona told Zein that Leilah said Maria was so distraught that when Tina came home, Maria was going to murder her. Zein responded that while no one knew when Tina was going to be killed, it would be very soon. Interestingly, he constantly used the word die, as if the robust athlete would expire from natural causes.

Mona interrupted, with what were her parents waiting for?

"To fix her!" Zein cried. "What do you think?"

9:39 P.M. PHONE CALL BETWEEN ZEIN AND SORAIA

The first part of this conversation, while declassified, was neither played nor read aloud in translation, for the trial was only months after the Gulf war and the reference to Iraq could inflame the jurors. Soraia, who had called long-distance, asked Zein, "Those guys from Iraq that you told me about, Leilah says that they didn't come back, no?"

"After that guy called here," Zein said. "Do you understand? We brought her back to the house because we had that problem with that nigger. . . . she left a piece of paper on the TV. She says, "I'll have to work until eleven-thirty.""

Zein began to say something else, but Soraia interrupted with, "This coming month she will be seventeen. May God keep her from making it!"

"I don't think she will make it," Zein promised.

Soraia went on with her ideas: While "she" is gone, lock the doors, the windows, and throw her clothes into the trash.

That won't solve anything, her father said. No, no, "we will rest from her" (A Portuguese idiom for "We will get rid of her.")

Soraia goaded her father with, "But what is it we are waiting for to relieve us from her?"

"Give me time!"

"Time, what time? She has only twenty-five days before she becomes seventeen."

10:50 P.M. PHONE CALL BETWEEN ZEIN AND FAYROUZ

Fayrouz called, asking had "the girl" come home yet. Zein said "she" had left a note not until 11:30. Fayrouz was horrified and said she would call Helena Mylanos to see where "she" was. Call me back? Zein wailed.

10:55 P.M. ZEIN AND FAYROUZ

Fayrouz reported back that "the girl" had taken a job. How could a job last until nearly midnight? she asked. She's a whore, Zein replied.

Fayrouz asked Zein why he couldn't take charge and tell his daughter she had to call home. What had happened in their household that Zein was no longer in control?

I'm waiting to tell her, Zein said, then asked whether he should let Tina in or not.

You have to, Fayrouz said. Where would she go? Besides, you're responsible, she's a minor.

But instead of planning what to do, Zein bemoaned his fate. "By God, I've lived in Europe, in Brazil, in Puerto Rico. I've never seen anything like this. . . . I don't believe even black people do this!"

Again, his daughter urged him to take responsibility. Issue rules, she said, tell Tina what time she must be home, tell Tina she was not allowed to work. And tape record this sermon.

I don't have a recorder, Zein said.

Get one, get one, Fayrouz said. You have to prove your case against her.

Leave it to me, Zein said.

The murder tape was next. It was fifteen minutes long, with two parts, about seven minutes of conversation between Tina and her parents. What the state was calling "the assault" lasted about eight minutes.

The bailiff locked the old, heavy, wooden double doors. The wrap-around sound stereo system was checked. It was 11:52 A.M. Craddick asked Tom Murphy to play what he called The Tape, what Hayes had labeled as State's Exhibit Number 1-A, and what Charlie Shaw and the media came to refer to as The Halloween Tape.

CHAPTER TWENTY-FOUR

State's Exhibit 1-A

11:59 P.M., SUNDAY, NOVEMBER 6, 1989
3759 DELOR STREET

The door opened and Tina walked into the living room closing the door loudly. As soon as she crossed the threshold, before she even took off her coat, her parents began firing questions at her, often overlapping, as it happens in arguments.

"Where were you, bitch?" Maria demanded.

Working, Tina answered.

You have five sisters, none of whom ever worked outside the store, Maria snapped. And just where were you working this late at night?

At Wendy's, Tina told her. My shift ended at eleven-thirty P.M. and then I came home.

Why didn't you tell me? Maria said.

Zein stepped in, "You are not seventeen and don't stay home? Do you think it is right to keep your mother and I waiting for you this late?"

You're home anyway, Tina answered sarcastically.

Zein started in with the rhetorical questions one asks family members when fighting the same battle for the upteenth time: Why are you doing this to us? And Tina answered rhetorically, what am I doing? Which led Zein into complaining about her having a black boyfriend.

Maria asked, "Do you think you are going to work until midnight and the next day get up in the morning to go to school?"

"Yep," said Tina.

"No, no, no," Maria countered. The way she had been behaving lately was totally unacceptable. Tina was not going to just come home to sleep. She was not going to work at night.

Maria threatened to throw Tina out, a statement Tina pounced upon and kept repeating, "You're throwing me out? . . . Come on! Throw me out!"

The topic turned to her working, which both parents said she could not continue. "You are a she-devil," Zein screamed. "You've made up your mind? You're going to stay this way? You want to live on your own. Isn't that what you want?"

"Yes," Tina said. They fought over that.

Zein switched to Cliff. If that black guy really loved Tina, he would want to marry her, but the seventeen-year-old youth did not intend to. He just wants to sleep with you, Zein shrieked. "Are you blind? Don't you have a mother, a father, a brother, and sisters? Don't you feel shame? Don't you have a conscience? It's fornication! Go on, get out!"

In the middle of this harangue, Maria called Mona, who not only goaded her mother, she called her sister "a crock of shit." Mona went on to claim that whenever she was sent to deposit money in the bank Tina was stealing from Alliance for her boyfriend.

Maria said that was impossible—Zein handled all the daily deposits. Yet, Mona was intent upon proving Tina was guilty for the bank checks bouncing.

Meanwhile, Zein berated Tina for her lack of chastity, for causing a scandal. Maria, having finished her call with Mona, scolded Tina for ignoring her for days, for leaving a note on the TV instead of telephoning. Again, she cried at Tina, "This life of yours is unacceptable! Didn't I give you money?"

Tina's voice was not clear here on the tape: She said something about work. Her mother retaliated that if she worked, she was not living in their house. Tina taunted her with "Then throw me out!" Zein chimed in that he would not wait until past midnight every night for her to come home. He accused his daughter of stealing from him. They all argued about throwing Tina out. Maria demanded the front door key back, which Tina handed to her.

But that was not enough for Maria, who began rifling through Tina's book bag. Tina became defensive. That's the school newspaper, she said. All I want is to see it! her mother screamed. Well, here it is! Tina screamed back. Maria kept asking what Tina had in her book bag. She wanted to see!

Zein reappeared, with something in his hand. "Listen, my dear daughter. . . . Tonight, you're going to die!"

"Huh?" Tina said perplexed.

Zein repeated that she was going to die that night.

*   *   *

The large windows in the courtroom faced an inside courtyard. During lulls in the tape, everyone could hear far-off rumbles of a warm-weather thunderstorm. Like a Thomas Hardy scene of Nature reflecting Life, as the taped slaying began, so did the storm. Tina's cries were echoed by cracks of thunder and bolts of lightning striking the rods and trash cans in the connecting light wells and courtyards.

Mother and daughter continued jostling each other over what was in the book bag. Tina was emotionally guarded as well as physically protective of her books. As her mother, Maria demanded the right to go through the bag. "My books, Mom! They're not yours! They belong to the school!" Tina cried. Were her notes about going to the police if anything happened to her in Tina's book bag that night? Is that what Maria was looking for?

Zein was ignored until the attack began. Heavy thuds and cracks were heard, sounds of furniture being knocked around the room. Tina screamed, continuously. Zein ordered her to keep still.

"Mama, please help me!" Tina begged.

"What do you mean?" Maria said.

"Help! Help!"

"What help?" Maria answered.

Tina screamed loudly again.

"Are you going to listen?" Maria asked. "Are you going to listen?"

"Yes! Yes! Yes! Yes, I am!" Tina begged again. She started coughing to get air. No. Plea-a-a-a-s-s-e!" as her father stabbed her deeper.

"Shut up!" her mother said.

"No! No!" Tina cried, and tried to speak, gasping.

Her father said something, unclearly. Tina wailed louder.

"Die! Die quickly! Die quickly!" her father screamed loudly, his face close to Tina's and the knocked-over phone receiver. His wife told him to put the butcher knife under Tina's writhing body.

Tina could no longer speak. She moaned loudly. Her breathing, already heavy, became more labored. Her heart beat slower and slower, and slower.

Zein ordered his wife, "Clean her bottom! Clean her bottom!" (Upon death, murder victims often lose control of their bladder or bowels.)

Tina gave out a loud death cry, "AAAHHHHHHHHHHH!!!!!!!!"

Her father's last words: "Quiet, little one! Die, my daughter, die! Die, die, my daughter."

There was silence. Then the sounds of a barefoot man padding down a hall and urinating.

In the courtroom, Zein was nonchalant. Maria had put her hands over her face, but when she took them away, her face was dry.

Several jurors watched their reactions. One juror removed his headset and held his head in his hands. Two men unabashedly wept. Hayes frequently pressed her lips together and held them tight. Craddick focused frenetically on the equipment. Charlie Shaw wiped his eyes. Reardon kept brushing his hand to his forehead. Not wanting to bias the jury by revealing his sorrow, the judge kept his head down, his hand over his mouth, assiduously following the transcript as though if he looked up, he would see a ghost. Bailiff Ron Hill continuously dabbed at his eyes. Tim Bryant of the *Post-Dispatch* was shaking as he walked out to the press room. Hayes suggested to the judge that they give the jury a long noon recess to recuperate; several jurors had told her they could not eat.

Meanwhile, outside the courtroom on a hall bench sat Tina's three sisters and cousin. One smoked a cigarette.

CHAPTER TWENTY-FIVE

"My Best Sister"

During the recess, Reardon paced the hall floor, smoking cigarette after cigarette. When Shaw returned, he whispered, "I've tried everything to get them to show some emotion."

"I know," Shaw replied. "One tear, just one tear. They sit there so impassive. Not even a sigh."

Nor did Zein or Maria display any grief when the defense attorneys returned to the courtroom and Craddick played his last set of tapes, how Zein and Maria tried to cover up the murder of their daughter:

> Zein returned to the living room, his hands still blooded, and called the operator for the police, but fumbled. Maria took over and told him to take off his blood-stained bloodied shirt. No, he argued, she tried to kill me, her father. I had to get a knife to protect myself.
>
> The line disconnected with the police department, and Maria called back. The police dispatcher asked, "Okay, ma'am. What is going on there?"
>
> "Ah," said Maria. "Somebody is dead here!"
>
> 12:50 A.M.
> As soon as Maria finished with the police, Zein ordered her to telephone Mona. Maria told her that Tina came home and demanded their money.
>
> 12:52 A.M.
> Maria awakened Fayrouz with "Tina, may you live on" [an Arabic saying when someone dies]. Both parents referred to Tina by name again. Taking the phone, Zein told how Tina had threatened, " 'Five thousand dollars or you die.' " She would have slashed Zein had he not grabbed the knife. They stabbed her, "and she died."
>
> "Father, why?" Fayrouz asked.
>
> 12:54 A.M.
> Zein called Leilah's husband, telling him that Tina behaved so wildly, she must have been on drugs or drunk. He and his wife tried to subdue

her, but failed. The knife slipped and "went into her stomach, in her heart."

12:55 A.M.

Fayrouz, now fully awake, phoned back. Is it true about Tina? she asked. When told yes, Fayrouz repeated, "God save you! God save you!" [An expression of consolation in Arabic].

Zein picked up the phone. "I don't know what will happen to us."

Fayrouz tried to soothe him.

Zein explained how Tina had cut his hand as he grabbed the knife from her. She was on drugs. Fayrouz asked where the knife landed. In her heart between her breasts, three times, Zein answered.

"May the Lord place his wrath on you—" Fayrouz exclaimed as her father hung up on her.

The translators testified that nowhere on the tape did Tina make any demand for $5,000—nor is there any reference to her carrying a knife.

On cross-examination, Shaw turned to a transcript from a recording March 13, 1990, a conversation between Zein in the city jail and Maria's niece, Ahlam Nijmeh: Zein called Ahlam collect and said, ". . . Maria is not responsible for this affair. I am responsible for it. Maria has nothing to do with it. I am the one who is responsible."

The State rested. The prosecutors did not want to overwhelm the jurors with more evidence after listening to The Murder Tape. After that tape, everyone wondered what possible defense could there be?

Chewing gum, Sausan Nijmeh took the stand in her white *hijab*, long pink and black millefleur jumper over a long-sleeved pink blouse, and pink heels. That she would testify in behalf of her aunt and uncle, and against her dead cousin, came as no surprise. Zein had said about Sausan and Tina, "They get along like fat and fire." Unlike gutsy Tina, Sausan had meekly followed the dictates of her father. Shortly after her sixteenth birthday, she was married to her first cousin Luie Nijmeh. There was no great affection in the arrangement; they were more like intermittent roommates. Sausan was closer to her cousin Soraia, ironically as it will be shown. She began her testimony with how the father in a Muslim household dominated his family. Then, she told her story:

She had worked as a cashier, stock girl, and meat cutter at Alliance Market "for Aunt Maria and Mr. Zein." One fall afternoon, Tina threatened her parents with a butcher's meat mallet (used to push meat through a grinder). At her aunt's direction, Sausan called the police. No one was injured. (And because no one was hurt, the police did not write up the incident.)

Sausan was the warm-up act for Soraia Salem, the sister closest to Tina and the one who most wished her dead. Like Sausan, Soraia was in *Shari'a* dress—white *hijab*, a long skirt of millefleur in peach with a peach-colored long-sleeved blouse and heels to match. Soraia said she had lived with Tina until she was married at the age of "twenty-one-and-half."

Beginning in May, 1989, Soraia testified Tina became disobedient, for example, using foul language whenever Zein asked for a favor. When her parents asked her questions, Tina would answer it was none of their business. Sometimes she refused to speak to them at all. Despite such behavior, neither parent ever laid a hand on her. In fact, Tina was the aggressor, kicking Zein and Maria.

Soraia said she was a graduate of Soldan High School and had attended junior college for three semesters. While attending school, her parents allowed her to dress like other students and play sports. She was not allowed to go to proms or dates, she said, "because of our culture."

Tina was treated no differently. "We were all treated equal." Soraia sat up proudly as she said this. She spoke haltingly and slowly. One reporter whispered, how could she have made it out of Soldan when her English was slow and inadequate?

Soraia went on to explain how everyone had to obey the father of the house. His word was law. Shaw stood behind his client, lightly resting his hands on her shoulders. Didn't her mother often try to protect her and cover up her mistakes? Yes. Didn't Maria protect Tina more than she ever did her other children? Yes. Did Maria promise to take Tina to Paris? Yes.

Like Sausan, Soraia explained to Craddick that women must obey their husbands. But not to the point of killing someone? Craddick asked. Soraia had to agree.

All the girls were treated equally? Craddick asked. Yes. Weren't you jealous of the way your mother treated Tina? No. Didn't you resent the fact Tina was allowed to play sports? Soraia allowed as how she disagreed with that privilege. You didn't like Tina's other freedoms, either, did you? We did not care for it, Soraia said with pursed lips. You yourself didn't have such freedom when you were sixteen? Soraia said when she was Tina's age, she didn't live here. (Then how had she attended Soldan High?) As she answered the questions, Soraia kept looking at her mother as if for approval.

Craddick pulled out the transcript of Soraia's conversation with Zein in which he complained about controlling Tina. To wit, Zein stated a girl "like her has no more life left for her."

Soraia suddenly was unable to recall him saying that. But she primly said, "I did," when asked if she recalled recommending Zein shackle Tina with a chain and leave her in the basement; telling Zein to tie Tina up, bind her mouth, and send her back to the homeland; suggesting her father hire "a dirty black, one of those who landed in prison every day," and paying him for a hit job; and just hours before Tina was murdered, saying, ". . . [T]his coming month she will be seventeen. May God keep her from making it." Craddick repeated the question. Shaw was not the only one who used repetition for emphasis: You said you didn't want your little sister to make it to her seventeenth birthday?

I did, Soraia said almost defiantly.

That was her closest sister, the one she shared a room with?

"My best sister."

The judge announced a recess and motioned a reporter to come up to the bench. "What does Soraia's testimony remind you of?" Judge Shaw asked as he leaned over.

"Cinderella," she said. The judge nodded and chuckled. "Damn, those sisters were jealous," said Craddick, who joined them.

"The way the girls were egging their parents on, why aren't they charged with accessory murder or conspiracy?" the reporter asked. Because in a conspiracy under Missouri law, one must commit an action in furtherance of the crime, Craddick explained. For example, Zein and Soraia discuss ways to kill Tina. Accessory murder required, for example, that she buy the knife with which to stab Tina. The most common cases of conspiracy are those in which a person hires a hit man.

"What made those sisters so mean, especially Soraia?" the judge asked rhetorically.

*   *   *

When she was a little younger than Tina, Soraia fell in love with the boy next door in Beitin. They were crazy about each other, she was his true love, his first love, the love of his life.

He went off to America to make his fortune while Soraia remained in the village. He was with her always, she thought of him the first thing in the morning and the last thing at night. He wrote, telling her how he had saved money so he could come home to marry her. He faithfully wrote her every single day for a year. As they had arranged, he sent his love letters to Soraia's cousin Nasser Isa, who lived with her family; he was to deliver them to her.

Soraia rarely replied to the boy's letters. When she did, it was to admonish him for not corresponding more. He could not understand what was going on. By God, she had been so in love. They were fated for each other.

After a year, he returned home, racing to al-Dar Abu Faisal—Zein's house—to ask for her hand. But Soraia was cool. He did not know why. Because you never wrote me, she chided. They discovered that his trusted friend and her beloved cousin, Nasser, whom Zein had practically raised, had double-crossed them. Nasser had faithfully turned over all the letters to Uncle Zein "to protect the family honor." Furious, Zein would not allow him to marry Soraia.

In the course of time, the boy's father informed him—Luie Nijmeh—that a marriage had been arranged: Luie would wed his paternal first cousin, black-eyed Sausan Nijmeh, who was a maternal first cousin to Soraia. Years later, afraid of becoming an old maid, Soraia married Amjad Salem, her second cousin once removed.

CHAPTER TWENTY-SIX

Disrespect

There are several reasons why the accused may decide not to testify in his own defense: Foremost is that he can be cross-examined about prior convictions, which leaves the jury with a bitter taste when they go back to deliberate. Second, the defendant might be a lousy witness, especially under cross-examination, and hurt his own case. So when a defendant charged with a violent crime sits in the witness box, whatever he says will make news. When the media learned Zein Isa would testify on Thursday, October 24, reporters, courtroom artists, and camera crews squeezed themselves onto the hard, wooden benches.

Zein testified through a courtroom interpreter, which frequently resulted in an echo—Zein answering in English just as the interpreter did. This did not enhance his image as a poor immigrant who could not understand the vagaries of English.

He was sixty-one now, and his memory was faulty, he said. His problems began the summer of 1989 when his youngest daughter became willful and disobedient: Tina never showed him any respect. He would ask her to bring him a cup of coffee, a glass of water. Instead, she kicked him or hit his sore leg. She owed him deference: He was the father, the provider. He worked fourteen hours a day to support his family. Yes, sometimes she worked in the market, but he supported the family, he repeated. None of his daughters held real jobs, none worked outside the family stores.

Zein said he never objected to Tina's black boyfriend. But he admitted later, "This is a very shameful thing that a girl from our culture would go with boys." He claimed he sent his daughter Fayrouz as a messenger to the boy, with his offer of $5,000 plus the cost of the bridal gown if he would marry Tina. But the youth told Fayrouz he was not interested. (Cliff denied any such offer. Cliff had wanted to marry Tina, but not just then; Tina had hoped for it, too—"eventually.")

Zein agreed that those were his words on the FBI tapes, his phone calls to his children. He wanted his older daughters to "straighten Tina up."

Reardon directed Zein to November 5. Zein said he and Maria worked until about three P.M. that day, the normal closing time on Sundays. They returned home and "the woman" fixed dinner. He worried where Tina was, after all she had run away two months before. He had not penalized her for that; in fact, he never punished Tina physically. "I never hit a daughter. I used to talk to her."

The night of November 5, Zein described himself as both angry and sad, but he did not think about murder. When Tina walked in, he and his wife asked where she had been. They disagreed with her working. "I was . . . providing for them. . . . she didn't need to work."

Tina became upset when her mother went through her book bag. She ran into the kitchen for a drink of water, he thought, instead she brought back a knife. The black knife, the eleven-inch butcher knife. His lawyer asked Zein if he remembered anything mentioned on The Murder Tape about Tina having a knife.

Zein's defense was that the tapes did not record everything. In other words, he was saying that the federal government had edited the tapes, something the defense lawyers did not believe. He argued—regardless of the tapes—Tina pulled a knife on him. He testified that when he said, "You are going to die tonight," Tina already had the butcher knife in her hand. Zein showed with his hands how she held it over him. Grasping it by the blade, he bent it towards her. He pushed it, stabbing her. She fell. He stabbed again and again. He had no idea how many times, it was definitely more than once.

Where was Maria during the stabbing? He did not recall. He thought she was at home, but he had no idea where. "This was between me and my daughter."

One of his other daughters, wearing bright pink lipstick and heavy kohl eyeliner along with her *hijab*, peeled the foil back from a candy bar and daintily nibbled at it as her father described how he stabbed her little sister.

When cross-examined by Charlie Shaw, Zein said that he felt Maria was overly protective of Tina. Shaw stood behind Maria, resting his hand again on her shoulder, focusing on Maria's lack of culpability. Shaw quoted his own words back to Zein about Maria's threat to leave him and take an apartment with Tina. Shaw asked if he remembered saying that.

Zein answered, "Do I remember this?"

Shaw said again, "That's the question. Do you remember that?"

The interpreter stepped in, "He is asking you, 'Could I remember that?' "

Shaw read the long passage again from the transcript. "Now do you remember that?"

"It could be." Zein smiled.

"It could be. If we all heard it, it could be, isn't that right?"

"Yes, sir." Zein smiled, his lips curling in mirth.

"Is this funny, Mr. Isa?" Shaw's voice had an edge to it.

"No," Zein admitted.

Shaw addressed Zein's complaint that Maria hid money from him and gave it to Tina. Shaw read several passages, asking each time if Zein remembered.

"Do I remember everything?" Zein answered. "I don't remember everything."

Shaw, maybe for the first time in his nearly fifty years as a defense lawyer, was incredulous. "You don't remember ever saying that?"

Zein replied calmly, "It is possible."

"Well, 'if it is possible,' it's agreed by Mr. Reardon and myself and the prosecution that this is a transcript of a tape that everybody has heard. Does that make it more possible that you said that?"

"The tape didn't have everything, but assume that everything is in there that has been said."

All right, Shaw went on. His job was to save Maria; if Zein wanted to mock the American justice system in the middle of a death penalty trial, the jurors would see that. Shaw asked hadn't Zein complained to Soraia that his wife was hiding money from him to give to Tina?

"Problems like this I don't remember. This is—it's a family life, and you say so many things. You don't remember every detail," Zein explained.

Shaw was not buying selective memory retention, especially when he was trying to score a point for his client. How come, he asked, you could remember all those details when you told Soraia her mother was hiding the money?

Zein claimed he could not recall the exact story. Shaw pointed out that that tape had just been played in open court and Zein's interpreter had translated for him. Was that not true? Shaw asked. Zein conceded that it was. He finally saw where Shaw was going with this, so when Shaw thundered, wasn't this conversation all about *his* problems with

Tina, Zein agreed: Yes, this had nothing to do with Maria. Shaw took a deep breath and went on not knowing Zein would not follow.

"All right . . . you talked about Maria taking the money . . . [and giving] it to Tina for her extracurricular activities at school. Isn't that correct?"

"That is reasonable," Zein said.

"That is reasonable. That is *true*, isn't it, Mr. Isa?"

"As you like," Zein said.

"No," Shaw tried to contain himself. "It is not as I like. It is what is true that counts."

"They close our account in the bank," Zein smirked.

With this non sequitur, Shaw gave up and turned to the murder. "Now, I'm going to ask you about the melancholy events of November the sixth. No one can but hear that tape and not feel some emotion."

His interpreter interjected, "He says you didn't hear everything."

"I heard enough," Shaw snapped. Was it not true that Maria had tried to pull her husband and daughter apart that night? This was the most diplomatic way of phrasing what had happened.

"I didn't see her," Zein said.

"You didn't see her?" The woman weighed two-twenty-four pounds and had a back broader than any man in the courtroom and he didn't see her?

"No."

"Isn't it a fact that Maria grabbed Tina by the hair and tried to pull her away from you and that Maria fell down with Tina?" After Shaw repeated himself twice, Zein agreed.

"And then Maria slipped and fell?" Shaw continued.

"Okay. She almost faint then and she fell."

"She almost what?" Shaw stared at Zein.

"She almost fainted and she fell on the couch," Zein explained.

"Did Maria, Mr. Isa, ever hold Tina so that you could stab her, stab Tina?"

"No. The only time she grabbed her from her was to protect her, to pull her away from me while Tina was there with the knife in her hand."

Earlier, before Zein began acting as though testifying in a court of law was the same bargaining game a merchant could play in a Middle Eastern souk, he had revealed a great secret: His duty as a man. It was, Zein said, to take care of his family. "All my life I was working, and whatever I was making I was spending on my daughters. All my life."

And in return, you demand submission, Shaw said gently.

"To respect me. All my daughters respected me except for Tina." A lack of respect was a wound worse than death, Zein explained. Life was worthless without honor and respect. Not just Tina's—his, too.

"Death is better than being insulted. I would rather be dead than insulted."

Hayes and Craddick had been furiously jotting notes during Zein's bizarre rejoinders. Hayes was tired. She had been working very late every night, and was further drained by guilt when her three-year-old daughter kept asking, "Where's Mommy?" To look at her, however, one could not see the strain. She was the poised professional in public. This was the high point of the trial, and so she was quick and alert.

She coolly approached the witness stand. If Zein had been disdainful of Shaw, an older man, he treated Hayes as though she did not matter. Not only was she a woman—a much younger woman—she spoke with a soft Southern drawl to her voice, having been born and raised in Virginia. Underestimating a prosecutor was a terrible mistake to make before a jury for Hayes was far more clever than she appeared to be.

Did Zein ever strike his unruly daughter? she asked. Zein did not recall. Nor could he remember ever hitting her that day when she raised the meat mallet in the store to smite him. Matter of fact, Zein said proudly, he had never raised a hand to any of his girls.

Well, then, Hayes said, why did you tell Soraia you had given Tina a deadly beating? Zein shrugged. He could have said that, but he never really had struck Tina. Oh, responded Hayes, were you lying then to Soraia? Zein shrugged some more, he could not remember.

Hayes looked Zein in the eye and asked who Tawfiq was? Zein admitted knowing him, a man in Wisconsin, he said. But he could not recall talking with him on October 16, 1989. Hayes offered to refresh his memory—they were talking about his problems with Tina. Zein recollected, yes, he had phoned Tawfiq to ask him to talk with Tina, to straighten her out.

Well, then, how come on tape Tawfiq advised you to beat Tina?[*]

"Did I ever listen to anybody?" Zein joked. "But I never listened to Tawfiq or anybody else."

---

[*]This tape was not admitted into evidence. Hayes was allowed only to refer to certain lines.

Hayes read aloud what he had said to Tawfiq; "By God, my brother, the stick won't do. The stick was used here more than even a mule can bear. The stick was used to hit her with. It seems I have to return to the more difficult method."

Zein refused to remember. Hayes's voice deliberately rose. Was he saying he did not say that or that he could not remember saying that? Zein said he did not recall.

Well, did he remember testifying that he was trying to persuade Tina to reach a behavior that was at least 50 percent acceptable to his code?

"I might have said that."

Zein was still trying to control the court. "He's refusing to say anything, so why testify?" one reporter whispered to another.

Hayes had other questions. The night Tina died, did Zein not talk with her? Yes, he did, he said. She was still disrespectful that night, still seeing Cliff. Was she still abusive to him? Hayes wanted to know. Zein answered, but not that particular question.

"It sounds to me that she was involved in some kind of cult. It wasn't the young man. It was a cult," Zein explained.

"Was she coming even close to fifty percent cooperation with you?"

"I was accepting to live a half human way, not a full human way," Zein said.

"Was she willing, on the night she died, to live even half a human way?"

"We didn't have that long of an argument."

Zein agreed what really upset Tina the night of November 5–6 was that Maria went through her book bag. He said his wife and daughter argued bitterly over what was inside it. Hayes quoted Tina telling her mother that the books were the school's, not hers. Did he remember that? Zein said he could not.

Hayes pounced, "Is that because you had already gone to the kitchen at that point to get the knife?"

"Me?" Zein looked surprised. "No."

Wasn't Tina stabbed while Maria diverted her attention by going through her belongings?

"I didn't attack her," Zein insisted. But Hayes pointed out that the tape went directly from the discussion about the schoolbooks to Tina's screaming.

Zein had an explanation: "That's because she went so quickly as lightning, and she brought the knife from the kitchen and came back that fast."

"That fast? No wonder this girl is an athlete!" Hayes waved the two knives in Zein's face.

"I actually thought she was coming toward her mother, to attack her mother," Zein protested.

Hayes played along. "Okay. So like greased lightning, Tina sprinted into the kitchen and got this black-handled knife?"

"Yes."

"This knife, Mr. Isa?" Hayes asked, brandishing the murder weapon before him.

"Yes, ma'am."

"The one that Tina's blood is on?"

"Right."

Hayes asked if he knew where the white knife came from. Zein said he did not. It could have been in her purse, or on the table, or on the TV.

"Well, Mr. Isa, explain to me if Tina came at you with this knife, and you struggled with her over this knife"—Hayes held it up again—"and this knife is the one that you cut your hand with because of the struggle, then how did your blood end up on this knife"—Hayes raised the white-handled knife—"and not this one?" She flashed the black one again. Earlier, an expert on blood typing had testified that the blood on the white-handled knife was likely Zein's, not Maria's nor Tina's.

"Honest to God, I don't know."

"Could you explain to me how this one [the white knife] came to have your blood on it?"

"Honest to God, I don't remember. Could be that my wife brought fruits for me, and she had the knife with her, and that is how it ended up on the table. I don't know."

"Isn't it because after your daughter was dead, you picked up this knife with your hand that was bleeding and placed it beside her body?"

"I can't recall."

"And isn't it true, Mr. Isa . . . that when you were trying to stab [your daughter] through the breastbone into her heart, your hand slipped on the knife and you cut yourself?" Judge Shaw inadvertently smiled and put his hand over his mouth. As a former prosecutor, he seemed to enjoy watching this defendant impale himself.

"No, no. It was when I tried to grab the knife. And she was scream-ing before I started stabbing her."

"Tina was screaming *before* you started stabbing her?"

"The first time, yes."

"Because she saw a knife in your hand, right?"

"No. When I tried to bend the knife towards her chest, my hand was already bleeding."

Hayes asked if Maria had participated in the stabbing. No, Zein said. Maria only tried to intervene by pulling Tina away? The mother fainted, he said, or almost fainted and fell back onto the sofa.

If she had fainted, Hayes asked, angrily enunciating every word, her tone clipped and precise, but never so sharp it would alienate a jury, then how come we can hear her on the tape telling Tina to listen and to shut up her screaming? Oh, maybe she didn't faint, Zein explained. Maybe she was very exhausted. Maria was on the couch while Tina was on the floor, he insisted. But she encouraged you, didn't she?

No.

Well, then, why do we hear your wife on tape telling your daughter, who was screaming at the time, to shut up?

"Because she was upset with—with Tina." Several jurors stared at him, brows knitted. With Tina? Hayes asked. She was upset with Tina's screaming because she was being stabbed?

No, said Zein. She was upset from earlier that night.

Hayes asked how Zein could physically dominate Tina, who was slightly heavier and in better health. How did he restrain her to stab her so deeply?

The first stab made her fall to the ground, Zein answered.

How were you able to keep her still to continue wielding the knife?

"Oh, she fell on her back," Zein said.

She was no longer struggling?

Only her feet moved.

Hayes swallowed and paused. "We heard sounds of what appeared to be a struggle, an enormous struggle. Mr. Isa, what were those sounds?"

"She was still struggling."

"Did you put your hand over her mouth at any time?"

"I put my foot."

CHAPTER TWENTY-SEVEN

"Shame Is Worse than Death"

Hayes finished her closing argument with, "Mr. Shaw told you east is east and west is west, and never the twain shall meet. Well, ladies and gentlemen . . . it meets here in the United States every day, where people from all parts of the world and all cultures have come to find a better way of life . . . But . . . part of our greatness is that we can accept and deal with different people from different backgrounds and different cultures under one law. And that's the law in this courtroom today.

"We are not here to rail about [the] Islamic culture or to blame that culture. We are here to blame these people for what they did under this law in this country."

The jury of nine blacks and three whites (five men and seven women) retired to deliberate at 11:14 that morning. At 3:27 P.M. they returned with their verdicts: Zein Hassan Isa, guilty of murder in the first degree. Maria Matias Isa, guilty of murder in the first degree. "It's your case now," Hayes was overheard saying to Craddick.

During an impromptu news conference outside on the courthouse steps, Hayes said while she was pleased with the verdict, "I can't feel good about it, thinking about what happened to Tina."

A loud wailing filled the empty courtroom. It came from the inside corridor near the judge's chambers. Two sheriff's deputies looked at each other and ran back to the corridor. The keening came from Maria in her holding cell, screaming at Zein in Portuguese, "You bastard, why did you bring me to this country?"

As the well-mannered, well-dressed Arabic translators milled around during a recess, watchers contrasted them with the large group of the Isa family and friends. Most of the latter were boorish at best: One hefty man with a mustache, open shirt, and perpetual scowl on his face sneered at a group of reporters.

"Would you get on a plane with one of those guys?" Charlie Shaw said with a wink. In the main hall stood Zein's sons-in-law, who talked without once looking over at their wives—one of whom was quite pregnant—segregated from the men and sitting on a bench. A photographer from the *Post-Dispatch* pointed her camera at the Isa women. When they saw her snap the shutter, they cursed at her.

"Yeah," the photographer said under her breath, "you went along with killing your own sister because she had too many freedoms, and now you worry about a picture. Get a life."

In the drab witness room, Cliff and Helena sat quietly with a court worker. A deputy came in, "Did you hear that wailing?" They all nodded. "It's Maria. Now she's calling for one of her daughters."

When Lieutenant Hegger heard the verdicts, he said, "No murder outside of street crime is monocausational. Zein is a political assassin; he was willing to sacrifice his own child to make himself look like a big man to his cadres."

Meanwhile, the four lawyers worked on the death penalty instructions to the jury. In Missouri, death penalty cases are bifurcated (two-part) trials, each with opening statements, witnesses, evidence, and closing arguments. The first adjudicates guilt and the second—after a verdict of murder in the first degree—decides the punishment: life without parole, or death.

After heated discussions in chambers and at the bench, the lawyers were ready. It was nearly five P.M. on Friday evening. Testifying on behalf of Tina would be her friends and colleagues from school. Traditionally, a victim's parents and siblings tell these heart-rending tales of loss during the victim impact statement, as it is called.

Craddick began with Helena Mylanos who looked as though testifying again would inflict unbearable anguish. After her best friend was murdered, Helena had suffered severe depression requiring two hospitalizations. What did the loss of her best friend do to her? Craddick asked gently.

"To this day, I wish I could join her right now," she whispered.

Cliff's psyche, too, seemed withered. "I feel real sad," he said, "like a part of my life has been stripped away from me. There is no one I really can trust anymore. It hurts me a lot, because I feel like I caused it in some way."

Tina's counselor, Pamela Fournier, told how she knelt down in the dirt with several students and planted red and white tulips and a redbud tree outside the main portals of Roosevelt High School so that whenever someone walked in, he or she would remember Tina. The high school principal spoke of special memorial services and a ribbon for remembrance day. Tina's portrait, a copy of the photo Helena had taken from the apartment, hung in the high school corridor. The 1989–90 yearbook, for the year Tina would have been graduated, was dedicated to her.

Tina's three sisters were desperate to save their parents' lives. All swore that the custom of their country demanded the mother and her children obey the father. All swore their parents were loving, generous, gentle. At which point their father turned around from the witness table to smile winningly at his family and friends. Hayes wondered whether the women had been threatened if they did not perjure themselves.

Although the sisters sounded sincere, many of the jurors may have doubted their testimony. After so many media stories on child abuse, jurors nowadays are aware that domestic violence does not begin one day with a brutal murder. In every known case of familial homicide, there has been an escalating spiral of brutality long before the knife is drawn.

Zein was called to plea for his life, but he seemed oblivious, no matter how hard Reardon labored to portray him as a kind patriarch trapped in cultural crossfire. He appeared flippant, answering, "One hundred percent,"[*] and "This is true."

He became serious only when asked if he had a request of the jury. "Yes," he answered. "My punishment was losing my daughter. They can punish me any way they want, but my wife doesn't have anything to do with it. I am asking to spare her the death penalty."

---

[*] "One hundred percent" may be an idiom that Zein and Tawfiq often used instead of a direct "yes." It seemed deceitful to a courtroom filled with jurors and media old enough to remember George McGovern's "one thousand percent" support of Missouri Senator Tom Eagleton just before he dropped him from the 1972 Democratic ticket.

Then why, oh why, had he not agreed to the pretrial bargain he could have made? thought Charlie Shaw.

Zein's defiance continued during Craddick's cross-examination. The prosecutor's line of questions centered on Tina's incapacitation to fight for her life. Wasn't Tina helpless after the first stabbing? Craddick asked. Didn't she fall down?

"She was still moving, but I was the strong side."

Wasn't it true that Tina suffered immense pain from her wounds? Craddick wanted to emphasize to the jury what she had endured during her last moments was torture. Torture is one of the aggravating circumstances for which a jury can assess the death penalty in Missouri.

"Am I a physician?" Zein asked in response.

You were there during the attack, weren't you? Craddick asked.

"One hundred percent."

You continued, one hundred percent, to stab her after she fell down?

"That is correct."

You continued to stab her, one hundred percent, after she pleaded for help?

Zein snapped, "Why didn't she have mercy on us when she had the knife in her hand?"

Craddick took a deep breath. "Mr. Isa, please answer the questions I ask you. Isn't it true Tina continued to beg you and her mother to help her?"

"I heard her screaming. I didn't understand what she was saying."

You could not understand your own child saying, Help, help me, please?

"I was out of my mind," Zein said. "Could I hear anything at that point?"

Did it help you to understand her when you stuck your foot in her mouth?

"No."

Did it help you to understand her when you told her, "Die, my daughter, die?"

"Of course, not."

Isn't it true that you didn't care?

"You are agonizing [sic] me. If you want to punish me with the death penalty, do that."

Again, Judge Shaw admonished Zein to answer what Craddick asked.

You wanted Tina to die, didn't you? Craddick asked.

"I wanted her to become an engineer, but once she brought the knife, and then I had to do that."

Were you helping her to become an engineer by stabbing her over and over?

"Shouldn't I defend myself when she brought the knife?"

You don't feel anything you did that night was wrong, do you?

"The worse punishment that could be is my daughter's death."

You previously told this court that the worst punishment is to lose your honor, to be shamed, isn't it?

"Shame is worse."

Did you not testify that you would rather die than be shamed?

"Yes," Zein glared. "I just told you again."

Several jurors' heads bobbed, as if to say, okay, Zein, we'll help you with that.

While this was going on, the sheriff's deputies chided one man from the Isa group three times for talking. He seemed unconcerned. And Zein periodically turned around and laughed and smiled at him and other family and friends. Various circuit judges who had come by looked disgusted. During the frequent skirmishes between the lawyers and the judge, Soraia would giggle.

The next morning, Craddick explained to the jury that they must consider the punishment against each defendant separately. To sentence Zein Hassan Isa and Maria Matias Isa to death, the jury would have to find each of them guilty of an aggravating circumstance under the law. The aggravating circumstance in this murder was torture. Craddick wished he had another aggravating circumstance, one stronger. Years later, he would learn that one did exist.

Palestina Isa was most remarkable, Craddick said over and over in his closing argument, most remarkable: An immigrant child, not even of the Western culture, she accomplished much in only five years here. Yet her successes, ones that any parent would be proud of, were unacceptable to the Isas. They sacrificed her to save their honor. All Tina wanted from her parents was what other American teens are routinely given.

"She (Tina) needed to be protected from her own family. A family whose conspiracy of murder continues . . . in court . . . "

Craddick had little idea that there was a larger criminal conspiracy within the family.

Reardon had few choices. What possibly could inspire the jury to spare Zein's life? He argued, this man has no criminal history. Reardon did not lie; he did not know the whole truth.

Shaw argued culture clash. "But for *this thing* sitting here, this would not have happened. . . . she was under [his] dominance." She was not involved in Tina's murder as much as her sisters who, sour with envy, nagged their father on. Maria was the only one who loved her. Shaw's oration was good, thought veteran court watchers, but the wrong person gave it. Why was Maria not on the stand?

The jury retired to deliberate at 10:25 A.M. At 2:55 that afternoon, the court reassembled to hear the verdicts: Zein Hassan Isa was to be sentenced to death. Maria Matias Isa was to be sentenced to death.

When Tom Murphy picked up the jurors' headsets—the state had replayed part of The Murder Tape—he noted that six of the headsets had been turned off. The jurors could not bear to listen to it again. Several jurors later said, the tape and the medical evidence eroded the Isas' chances of anything less than murder in the first degree.

A few days later, two years to the day Zein had been locked up in jail, Hayes dropped the armed criminal action charges against Zein. He was already on death row.

Within weeks, Arabs nationwide were writing to the defense attorneys. One man in New York blamed "the boy" for seducing a minor. He, the boyfriend, had "shattered" the Isa family. They were "victims of immoral American society," which sees females as lust objects. Arab men, in contrast, "glorify" women. The American courts failed the Isas by judging them by American standards, and the judge was "prejudicious." American society killed Palestina, not her parents. Zein's "destiny" took him to America where he was "in hell."

Judge Shaw, too, received letters about the case, from as far away as Australia. All of his correspondents were appalled at such a hideous custom as honor killing. For two months after the verdicts, the judge thought about the trial. This was his first death penalty case. Under Missouri law, a judge can reduce the jury's recommendation for sentencing.

Would Judge Charles A. Shaw sentence Zein and Maria Isa to life imprisonment instead of death? Even he wondered.

* * *

As he dressed the morning of the sentencing hearing on December 19, knotting on his burgundy Armani tie, Judge Shaw thought about Charlie Shaw's arguments for sparing Maria Isa's life. "Sentencing a human being to die is the single hardest thing there is to do. I wanted to reflect over it, I agonized. My mind was made up, but I decided to leave that door open—not all the way open, just unlocked, slightly ajar. When Charlie spoke in court later that morning, he kicked it wide open with his big foot. I thought about what he said, that she was only following her lord and master. I wondered whether Zein had bought her from her parents. But when you reflect back on the tape, she was a full participant. And there's no remorse. I hadn't intended to say anything, but—"

Outside the courtroom, the German shepherd, Buster the Bomb Expert, was sniffing again while a deputy sheriff was busily frisking the huge crowd trying to squeeze inside. As if they were attending a condolence call, all four lawyers (and the judge, beneath his robes) had dressed in navy suits. In khaki trench coats were Jim Steitz, a federal prosecutor, and a cadre of FBI agents; all sat in the back of the court, unobtrusively, near Tom Murphy. Steitz, who knew Murphy from his days as an assistant circuit attorney, had taken a break from reading the logs on 12,000 hours of FBI-recorded conversations of the Isa clan.

The sentencing proceeding began with the defense attorneys filing motions for new trial, a standard procedure. Charlie Shaw told the Court that in his eighty-page motion for a new trial, the main error was that the Isas were tried jointly. Motion denied, the judge said predictably.

Shaw and Reardon wanted to address the court on punishment. Reardon protested the tapes. When the tapes were secretly obtained and then censored, what exculpatory material—as ordained by the U.S. Supreme Court under *U.S.* v. *Brady*—did the government leave out? All the jury heard were Zein's daughters goading him into murder. The selected tapes given to the jury turned them into "a lynching mob," Reardon argued.

The government's surveillance of the Isa apartment, store, and telephones reminded Reardon of Pearl Harbor: Where was the look-out guy on November 5–6? Why wasn't Tina's murder stopped by the FBI? Then Reardon argued cultural differences between the Middle East and the West, then begged for mercy.

Afterward, everyone agreed that Charlie Shaw's argument was more than vintage Charlie Shaw, more than eloquent, it was the best performance he had ever given. He was more than Maria's advocate, he was her knight in shining armor jousting for her in this legal tournament, he was everything an ideal defense lawyer is supposed to be. This was the very reason that in the days before television, courthouse drama was the daily entertainment of choice. In his deep baritone, his broad hands resting occasionally for emphasis on his client's shoulders, Shaw invoked an impassioned plea for Maria Isa, who sobbed silently into a Kleenex.

"Now, Judge, I have practiced law, I think, longer than most lawyers in this courtroom. And I think it's safe to say that never in that experience have I ever been exposed to such a traumatic event as State's Exhibit Number 1-A." His voice became choked up. His client rubbed her eyes with her tissue.

"What happened, Judge, was that the jury became audio witnesses to what took place. . . . The horror of the audio is they could not see what was going on. And as radio really has more of an impact than television, when we hear what we hear, our mind is left to roam in those regions of the imagination. If you lived in a rural area where you didn't have television as a young man [Judge Shaw had left rural Tennessee as a small boy in the 1950s], and you listened to the radio, you would imagine far more better scenes just from the sound effects than you do today in television . . . television has to get more and more violent . . . because people get used to seeing these things. But when you hear something without being able to see it, your mind goes to work and creates pictures *that may not be there.*

"Now, this is the problem in trying these two people together. After that tape, the jury was unable to discern the difference between the actions of these two defendants. And you couldn't blame the jury. . . . they were subjected to this overwhelming State's exhibit, which changed them. . . . When I turned around . . . I saw fourteen faces hardened in a blast furnace. . . . And their punishment became the voices of vengeance. And I don't blame them . . . at the time that they heard that tape.

"Now, months later . . . after cool, calm deliberations, your function as a judge takes place. You should not, as far as Maria is concerned, feel any vengeance. I'm sure you don't. I think more of you than that. But you must do what a judge must do. And you stand between the emotion of that moment back on the twenty-sixth of October and the imposition of punishment today. And if you do that, you cannot give her the death penalty."

Shaw turned to Maria, touching her head, which was bent over as she wept. "We are used to women in this country who are our equals . . . We are not used to being exposed to women such as Maria . . . she comes from a rural environment in Brazil. . . . Maria is . . . like a puppy dog, she does nothing. She takes it. She lives with him. She raises his children. . . . She knows nothing but what Zein Isa wants her to do." Shaw's voice broke.

"And if it weren't for *this thing* sitting right here, she wouldn't be here." His voice cracked again. Maria wiped her eyes and blew her nose. "You know that, Judge. She would not have done that on her own. All the evidence in the case was that she was the only one in the family that was kind to Palestina . . . but . . . because of that particular piece of evidence [the tape], they [the jury] could not discern the difference between these two folks.

"You know, Judge, I'm glad Mr. Reardon mentioned Pearl Harbor. That was an event that was so traumatic to one of the most liberal Supreme Court justices that the United States has ever had, Earl Warren, then attorney general of California, issued orders . . . he regretted the rest of his life. And that was to impound the assets of and imprison all the Japanese-Americans . . .

"And that was done, Judge, in the heat of passion and vengeance. And he [Earl Warren] was a good man . . .

"What legal grounds we have or have not is not important at this time. I feel that we cannot consign this lady here to the Almighty based on what we heard in this courtroom." Shaw choked up. "And I pray to God that you will commute her sentence"—his baritone lowered—"to that of life without parole." He choked up again.

"Thank you, Judge."

Craddick's last words centered on the Isas' lack of contrition. There had been none in this whole sorry case. And today, he reminded the court, Zein and Maria still showed no remorse. Maria's lawyer, however, had his head in his large hands, hands covering his eyes, as Craddick spoke.

The judge asked Zein to stand before him, and then asked kindly, in a soft voice, if he wished to say anything before his sentence was imposed. He opened his hands as he offered Zein his last words in court. There was much sniffling among the women wearing *hijabs*.

"I don't know what to say," Zein said. "I am raising my children. I have been in the goal of having my life with my children and my family. I don't really know what to say. All I want is—I don't even know what I am standing here really for. What sentence I'm going to get, I am not sure."

The judge raised his eyebrows at this. Softly, he asked again if Mr. Isa wanted to make any appeal, any comment.

"What do you want me to say?" Zein said through his interpreter.

That is up to you, sir, said the judge.

"That's what I say. What do you want me to say? . . . I have been in the prison . . . I hope you guys help me to continue my life."

Judge Shaw addressed his court, emphasizing that the United States was a country of laws, not of men. Culture might explain a murder, but it could not and did not sanction nor excuse it. Judge Shaw said he saw no reason to change the jury's punishment: Therefore, I sentence you—he paused, to death.

Zein asked again that his wife be spared. She had done nothing. Turning around, Maria kissed her fingers and waved to a daughter. Then she sniffled and wiped her pink eyes and red nose. Zein stared at his wife without expression.

Judge Shaw gently asked Maria to step up and speak her mind. Zein stared at her as she approached the bench.

"I am innocent," she whispered so softly that none of the reporters could hear her. "I don't understand what is happening." She was crying audibly now, her lawyer had put his arm around her. The judge wrinkled his brow, looking so torn between the concept of mercy and the law in the statutes that Hayes wondered what he would do. The judge asked Maria again if she wished to make a statement.

When Maria did, the two Charles Shaws were dumbfounded. "What I know is that I have a good husband. I was treated well and my children."

"Your husband treated you well?" Judge Shaw asked softly.

"And my children. He was a good provider."

"Anything else?"

"This is very unfair. The justice is not working if you are going to condemn a good father to death, because my daughter was very rebellious, disobedient. We shouldn't be going to prison. We shouldn't have to pay for it with our lives for what she did.

"I am glad it turned out this way and I am the one in prison. I wouldn't like to see my daughter in prison. That's what would happen if she was (sic) alive today. She would end up in prison, in this filthy prison and dirty system."

The judge leaned over and looked at her. All doubt was erased from his face. Was that all? he asked.

It had been a very emotional trial. But he and the jury had seen that Tina could not have been murdered by her father without the assistance of her mother.

Judge Shaw sentenced Maria to death, in accordance with the jury's recommended punishment. "Now you understand why I didn't want her to testify," Charlie Shaw told the judge.

In his suede cowboy hat and fleece-lined corduroy jacket, Charlie Shaw walked out behind Maria and her guards. Maria turned, kissed her fingers, and tearfully waved good-bye to her children. Shaw, who had celebrated his seventieth birthday just before the trial, kept coughing; he was hospitalized the next day with pneumonia.

Reardon turned to a reporter. "No one listened to me today, including my client," he said ruefully.

A television reporter from a local station asked the Isa sisters if he could interview them. "No," one of them answered. "We won't talk to you because your boss is Jewish and wouldn't put our stuff on the air."

Craddick and his parents walked to the dark and creepy municipal parking garages. His mother worried, for the police had warned him, in this case, to be careful in parking garages, at stoplights, on seemingly empty streets. As they waited for the one elevator, two of the Isas' male relatives walked over. The five people stood in silence waiting for the elevator to creak up and open. They all stepped inside together. The doors creaked shut. The burlier of the two men turned to Craddick and said, "Fuck you, you've taken another life."

A month after Zein's and Maria's sentencing, the then director of the FBI, William Sessions, sent the St. Louis circuit attorney a personal letter congratulating Hayes, Craddick, Murphy, and Tully for their work in "this very important case."

Having spent weeks going over and over his every word, the translator of the FBI murder tapes, Mohammed Masad, was to finally meet Zein al Abdeen Hassan Isa—in prison. The graduate student would be interpreting Isa's words for a field producer from ABC-TV's "Prime Time."

The beast who once had mauled his daughter was now a pathetic broken man, practically paralyzed by diabetes, disoriented. Later, his fellow inmates would ridicule him for his political rantings and call him "Abu Arab."

The producer kept asking Zein: Are you sorry? Do you feel any remorse? Any guilt? Zein kept insisting on camera that it had been a case of self-defense. Over and over he insisted he would not behave differently given the chance. He believes it, Masad thought. Has he internalized some kind of delusion? For forty-five minutes, Zein repeated himself. Then the old man cried.

Zein's daughters would cry on camera, too, for "Current Affair" and during other interviews in St. Louis and in Beitin (where they go back and forth to live.) Their eyes would fill up talking about their dead sister and their parents on death row. Soraia blamed Tina's boyfriend for her death. "Why didn't Cliff wait for Tina that night?" she asked.

Soraia's cousin Sausan was extremely uncomfortable talking in front of her in-laws in Beitin and said little to a visitor, whereas she talked openly and freely to her in St. Louis. There, she and the sisters laughed and told stories over treats from the homeland—Turkish coffee flavored with cardamom and a bag of fresh almonds. After coffee, the women asked about dating, contraception, and education. One sister confided her ambitions of going to college. The group compared their kohl eyeliner in a clay pot with the visitor's Clinique cake.

Near Sausan's home in Beitin is the house that Zein built, now inhabited by his son, Faisal, Faisal's Spanish wife, and his mother, Foiziya. Faisal was divided between loyalty to his father and to his sister. "What Tina wanted was appropriate behavior for an American teenager," he said. "I would disagree if she lived here, but she lived in the States."

He said he empathized with her, having spent sixteen years in Spain studying medicine. His "main psychological association" was Spanish rather than Arabic. "When I live in Spain, I live as a Spaniard. When I live here, in Beitin, I live as the village wants me to. I adapt to society, not society adapts to me. But the villagers here never adapt."

Faisal had visited his father three times since his sentencing, but Zein refused to reveal what took place. "It is a great secret what happened that night."

With Tina gone, Faisal has turned toward saving his father's life. "I understand the law in America is the law. [But] I hope the intellectuals in the U.S. look at the cultural differences to defend these poor people. It's not his fault. It's the fault of the situation. Why did they [the FBI] not protect Tina?"

Faisal and his half-sister Soraia obviously could not place the blame where it belonged: on Zein and Maria.

Judge Shaw was discussing the case over lunch, how much it still bothered him six months later. "One portion of this trial really touched me—[the testimony in] the penalty phase," he said. "It was clear how much Tina meant to her friends and teachers.

"While her family thought she was the property of her father."

The ritual of a murder trial and sentencing often provides solace to the bereaved. It is a public acknowledgment that a wrong has been done to them and the trespassers punished. Often those who lost a loved one find that after the sentencing, they can try to return to their own lives. But Tina's slaying has blighted the young lives of her best friend and first love.

"If I ever get married and have a little girl, I'd call her Palestina," Helena Mylanos says. She smiles when complimented on her striped vest, sizes too large for her wraithlike frame. "It's Tina's," she says, in present tense while smoothing the fabric.

She clings to her late friend through two carefully created leather scrapbooks of photographs and mementos. "It's depressing to have books filled with newspaper stories of her murder," Helena says, turning the pages. "It's hard to go through your high school yearbook and see how your best friend got murdered. By her own parents."

Helena blames herself for Tina's death, blames her own family. She couldn't stop thinking "what if." What if she had persuaded her father that November night to allow Tina to stay at their house? But Helena's family could not fathom that Mr. Isa literally meant to kill his own daughter.

Helena often seems drowning in the high waves of melancholia. She sees Cliff off and on as a boyfriend. Like Tina, she has no intention of marrying him.

Cliff Walker cannot stop talking about Tina. His tone is not obsessive but grief-stricken. He cannot bear to pronounce her name, as if saying "Tina" shapes his raw pain into something sharp, something piercing, something that will gnaw his heart. When Cliff talks of happy times or what he loved about her, his mouth softens and his eyes glow. When he describes how he misses her, his anguish and longing make him look haunted.

He proudly shows a small gold ring. Girls who meet him ask about the ring. It was Tina's. He gave it back but just before she died, she told him to keep it. He refuses to take it off now. Women think he is engaged; he explains what happened. "They ask me do I still love her.

"I do."

He twists the ring.

"I try to sketch her, but it never comes out right. What I draw never has her the way I want to remember her—her face always laughing. Guess I overlay her with my sorrow. She always comes out with sadness.

"I still dream about her a lot. People say I've changed a lot. That I don't trust anyone or let anyone get close. That I don't tell my problems, that talking has helped others with their problems. A lot of people try to set me down and talk about it. It's too painful. Most people don't understand. People tell me I'll get over it like it's a broken leg. They tell me it was wrong and tell me I got to keep living, keep going on.

"I think if I had gone upstairs that night in November, she wouldn't be dead."

PART THREE

GUARDING
THE SECRETS

CHAPTER TWENTY-EIGHT

A Safe Investment

FALL 1992   ST. LOUIS

"Call me Frank," Nai'el AbdelJabber, Zein's son-in-law, told the real estate agent when she could not pronounce his name. He and Mona were looking for a house as investment property, he told her.

"He was really nice," said the agent. "He told me he only wanted to deal with black agents. I went to his apartment, we had lunch, and then looked at houses—HUD and VA housing. Frank said he and his brother were into rehabbing houses in the Florissant area. But they didn't buy anything."

If the AbdelJabbers did not have enough money to pay the Isas' attorneys, why were they looking to invest? What kind of investments were such houses? HUD and VA housing is cheap, Bob Craddick explained when he heard the real estate story, often in poor condition and in poor neighborhoods. "Places no one cares about, places you could hide out in, places where you could hide the real investor. The feds just want the taxes. These houses are low maintenance, low overhead. You don't want a safe house in a ritzy neighborhood where neighbors get suspicious."

Tom Murphy heard that Zein had held meetings in a safe house in Florissant near where Mona and Nai'el lived.

"Hell, I heard Zein used to live there," Mike Tully added.

If they're terrorists, Craddick wondered, will there be more tapes released, besides the tapes referring to Tina's murder?

Lieutenant Hegger, who knew, was saying nothing.

CHAPTER TWENTY-NINE

"Happy April Fool's Day"

APRIL 1, 1993

Saif ("Steve") Nijmeh left his home in Bridgeton, a suburb of St. Louis, about 9:30 A.M. for work at S&L Liquor Market, on Lucas & Hunt Road, the store he owned with his brother Luie. Unusually chilly, Saif pulled the collar of his jacket up. As he slid into his car and turned on the ignition, a beige van pulled in front, blocking his way. Behind him police cars suddenly pulled up, one after another. Three men in navy windbreakers blazing with the large yellow letters "FBI" jumped from the van, and seven police officers ran out of their cars. They all faced Saif, pointing their guns.

Saif later complained to his lawyer that the agents threw him face-down on the snowy ground and handcuffed him. The problem with his story was that it had been 50 degrees that morning and the snow flurries had not begun until early afternoon.

As the FBI's Fugitive Unit in St. Louis arrested Saif, their counterparts in Dayton, Ohio, handcuffed his brother Luie and in Racine, Wisconsin, picked up Tawfiq Musa. Zein Isa, already on death row, was moved to "the hole," an isolation cell, for his safety when the news broke. Through faxes in a code cryptologists could not break, the FBI had carefully coordinated the simultaneous arrests so that none of the four indicted men could flee. "That was the easiest part," laughed the Special Agent in Charge James W. Nelson, in St. Louis where a federal grand jury had heard the case.

This was the first indictment of Abu Nidal terrorists in the United States, and the first public acknowledgment that the ANO had made inroads into America's heartland (although such groups had been suspected of working in New York City, Washington, and Los Angeles). The four men—Zein, Tawfiq, Saif, and Luie—were charged with six counts of running a racketeering enterprise between 1986 and the day of the indictment. The most serious offenses were their conspiracies to slaughter "any and all Jews," to blow up the Israeli Embassy in Washington, and to murder Tina Isa because she posed "a threat" to their secret enterprise.

The U.S. Attorney's Office leveled their biggest gun at the Beitin Four, the federal statute known as RICO, Racketeer Influenced and Corrupt Organizations Act, designed by Congress to thwart the Mafia and other organized crime syndicates. Congress, in its infinite infantile internecine battles, has not seen fit to legislate antiterrorism statutes, so Jim Steitz had to make do with RICO to prosecute the Abu Nidal terrorists. RICO allows prosecutors to combine lesser crime into an overall criminal pattern of behavior. RICO sentences are so Draconian that the charge often induces members of crime rings to testify against their brethren in return for lighter prison terms. If convicted on all charges, Zein and the other three men faced life in prison without parole, plus an additional twenty-year sentence and fines of $1.5 million each.

Count 1 of the indictment was racketeering. The Justice Department charged Zein and his three colleagues "and others" with working for a criminal enterprise. Their cell allegedly committed eleven different criminal acts in a pattern of interstate racketeering. The grand jury found five predicate acts of racketeering, two of which were needed to convict on RICO charges. (Predicate acts are those which must be proved as a basis for the racketeering charge.)

- Conspiracy to murder Tina so that the sixteen-year-old honor student could not expose their secret society.
- Conspiracy from November 1986 until April 1, 1993, to kill "any and all" Jews as well as those of Jewish extraction.
- Smuggling more than $10,000 overseas, in and out of America, three different times in 1988; on April 6 ($15,000), May 1 ($10,000), and May 26 ($25,000), without filing the required customs form. This was done while "smelling the air" in Lima, Athens, and the West Bank.

Count 2 cited sixteen "overt acts" of racketeering, some of which involved what were called "unindicted co-conspirators." While these people were not named in the indictment, they were referred to by name in the nine volumes of the FBI transcripts used in the indictment:

1. Zein, Luie, and Saif met in Mexico City with Mahmoud Atta in April 1987, who gave them "taskings" or jobs, for ANO. An affi-

davit detailed the primary task was to target Jewish and related American interests for terrorist acts. For example, conduct surveillance on local Jews and their institutions.

When Zein, Saif, and Luie returned from Mexico, they discussed possible targets. Zein said, "We are in a state of war . . . we've exported many massacres to silence these atrocities." Saif replied, "If they really want to hurt American and Jewish interests here and abroad . . . , they should plant a bomb."

Zein later said that ANO could mobilize "the trained youth here" and in Europe to "kill three thousand Jews. . . . Let's teach them how to hit people and slaughter." And Saif complained, "The Jews . . . they are America itself . . . the Jews in America whom we are fighting."

As a confidential informant told the FBI, the number one goal of Abu Nidal operatives is to target and kill all Jews anywhere they can find them.

The second chore was to obtain heavy and light weapons and store them in various caches. Saif had admitted on the FBI tapes that his horde included an automatic machine gun buried inside his apartment wall. He told a friend he owned a rocket-propelled grenade launcher. A coconspirator said of him that Saif had the weapons "to organize a resurrection [sic]."

Third, Atta ordered them to recruit more ANO cadres.

Fourth, they were also to collect and transfer money and secret information.

Passports were essential to the entire ANO. Atta's fifth command was the Beitin Four should steal or lie to obtain "clean" passports for clandestine travel by other ANO members around the world. All travel documents—passports, visas, immigration papers, INS stamps, and the like—are so vital to ANO that according to Patrick Seale in *Abu Nidal: A Gun for Hire*, Abu Nidal himself is concerned constantly with acquiring these papers through forgery, theft, or bribery.

The last task from Atta was for the men to track down informants cooperating with the FBI and police. An FBI informant told the agency that all ANO members are to hunt down and silence all informants. Saif and Luie had a plan to expose a Palestinian they believed was working for the Jordanians, but they had to be careful, Saif said.

The fifteen other acts of racketeering were:

2. A month after the Mexico City conference with Atta, Tawfiq ordered Zein to destroy his records of that meeting because Atta had been jailed.

3. On Halloween 1987 Saif told Hazzah Darwish they should kill another man from Beitin who, he said, was an informant. (No one was murdered. The man mentioned was a kindly PLO member who was alive and well in the West Bank in late 1992, when met by the author.)

4. Luie boasted to Muhamed Ghannam on January 11, 1988, that he would blow up the Israeli embassy in Washington. Luie promised, "Give me a gun, I'll do it!"

5. Zein told Sausan Nijmeh on January 16, 1988, his goal was to kill any American of Jewish descent.

6, 7, 8.   Zein transported money from the United States for ANO in early April, 1988; Luie did so, too—twice in May of that year.

9. Saif flew to Lima to meet with ANO leader al-Batma, a.k.a. Samir Darwish, in early July 1988.

10. After Samir was arrested, Tawfiq directed Saif to destroy any record he had of his meeting with Samir.

11. Tawfiq attended an ANO conference between late August to early October 1988 in Algeria.

12. Tawfiq himself met overseas with Thari Bek and Omar Ibrahim, alleged members of ANO, in November 1988. Upon his return to Milwaukee, Tawfiq smuggled money from the Middle East into the United States.

13, 14.   Saif and Tawfiq discussed how Tina was scandalizing the family, and they spoke of killing her on October 16 and 17, 1988. As Saif said, "She knows many things."

The next day, Saif told Tawfiq that there was nothing more to do, nothing but "the last solution. He [Zein] is the only one who can do it." Tawfiq disagreed, telling Saif he should help his uncle carry out the assassination. Saif rebutted that Tina was Zein's responsibility. Tawfiq argued that Tina was the cell's problem, for she could send them all to prison. We must stick together, Tawfiq counseled. Prophetically, Saif predicted they would all suffer for Tina's defiance of Zein.

An FBI affidavit noted that the cell suspected Tina of being or becoming an informant because she knew that all four men

belonged to ANO and "had a general knowledge of the ANO activities." The high school senior found these activities abhorrent for
they were based on a political philosophy she had rejected—much
as she had cast off her veil. Frightened that her father had lost control of her, Tawfiq, Saif, and Luie had more reason to believe she
would expose their criminal plans. Luie advocated kidnapping the
girl, flying her to the West Bank, murdering her there, then publicly
denouncing her for being a collaborator.

15. The worst overt act of racketeering was the slaying of Tina Isa by
    six fatal knife wounds to her heart and chest on November 6, 1989.

16. Saif had described his RPG (rocket-propelled grenade launcher) on
    December 14, 1989, and again on January 13, 1990, with Hazzah
    Darwish and Farid Badran.

Count 3 accused Zein, Tawfiq, Saif, and Luie of traveling to Athens
and Israel's occupied territories on April 6, 1988, to promote and carry
out ANO activities.

Count 4 alleged the men traveled to the Middle East for ANO on
May 1, 1988.

Count 5 stated on their return trip home from Israel to St. Louis,
Chicago, and Racine in late May, the four men violated interstate and
foreign commerce laws for ANO.

Count 6 explained how the four men—and others—conspired to
and violated passport laws for the ANO criminal enterprise from April
1987 until the present. When Zein, Saif, and Luie met with Atta in
Mexico in 1987, Atta told them to secure passports any way they
could. A month later, Saif lied to obtain a replacement passport so that
he could meet Samir in Lima. Saif and Tawfiq agreed to lie that Zein's
passport had been stolen so the latter would have a fresh one to meet in
the Middle East with ANO leaders.

The U.S. Attorney's Office recommended that none of the indicted
men be allowed bail. The FBI affidavit proclaimed that all posed a
severe threat to the community and were extreme flight risks. They all
had family living in the West Bank to which the American-Israeli
extradition treaty did not apply.

Tawfiq and Luie would be brought to St. Louis to stand trial with
Saif and Zein.

                    *   *   *

As soon as the three men were under arrest and Zein in his protective cell, the Justice Department in Washington sent out a news release announcing the first Abu Nidal terrorism case in America. The FBI office in St. Louis announced a news conference later that morning— in time for the noon broadcasts and in time for the tapes of the conference to make all four network evening news shows, ABC, CBS, NBC, and CNN.

Jim Nelson, the special agent in charge stood at the lectern. His deep blue eyes never blinked, nor did his measured voice rise when reporters asked about Tina's murder. Hadn't state prosecutors said that Tina was the victim of an honor killing? "There is no question her family problems were among the reasons she was killed," Nelson said. "But there was an additional motive. Evidence indicates her death was also to silence her."

If the FBI had tapes about a murder plot in advance of November 6, 1989, why didn't agents save Tina? "We did not know they would kill her," Nelson said. "Our electronic surveillance did not require an agent be monitoring at all times. It was sound-activated."

In a corner away from the media crowd, a reporter asked Tom Newman, the supervisor of the Abu Nidal case, if the Bureau tipped people off about murder threats. He looked horrified. "Of course we would. I don't want to see anyone killed."

"What about all those beatings Tina endured that led up to the murder?" the reporter whispered.

"There was plenty of information that the authorities who needed to know about the situation over the beatings could have warned her," Newman answered. "Division of Family and Children Services, the school."

Later Judge Charles Shaw, himself a former federal prosecutor, explained, "You can hear a lot about killing on a wiretap and it doesn't mean a thing. The mob, for example, is always threatening to whack someone." Nelson added privately later in his office, "We've warned people in the past. When I was in New York and heard there was a Mafia contract out on someone, I went to his house that night, sat in his kitchen, and told him I'd arrived early to intercept the killings." The deputy FBI director of investigations at the time of the murder, Buck Ravel, said, "I've never known of circumstances where we wouldn't intervene. I'm not sure how much the interpreter reported of the tapes' nuances, but my position and that of the then FBI director, Bill Sessions, was if we thought a child would be harmed, we'd intervene. Our responsibility is to prevent acts of violence irrespective of blowing cover."

Several terrorism experts agreed with Nelson and Newman. Had the FBI suspected Tina was in imminent danger, agents would have spirited her away. One refuted the rumor that the feds could not blow their cover in a national security investigation to save some kid's life. "People theorize, but in an actual situation where someone could get killed, national security comes second," said a man who had served as bureau chief for the CIA in Beirut.

Yet, some experts blamed the FBI. An alleged Mossad agent argued, "They screwed up. The ones who did the technical stuff were good. The ones that analyzed failed." And another former CIA specialist pointed to a parallel failure, "The tapes plotting the World Trade Center bombing sat around for two years. And Nossair was prosecuted not as a terrorist in the murder of Meir Kahane, but as a killer." A former FBI counterterrorism supervisor explained, "The FBI is perfect in a crisis, working thirty-six hours a day, but lousy at intelligence gathering and terrible at analysis. You want analysis, go to Rand Corporation. There are no long-distance runners in the Bureau." Added a professor, "The FBI is not proactive. Their mind-set is reactive."

Part of the problem was how FBI resources were being devoured by competing interests. When the wiretaps went in on Zein and his relatives in 1986, FBI Arabists were already preoccupied in New York with the *Achille Lauro*, the TWA hijacking in Greece, and Libyan problems. "A few guys handling multitaps in the Midwest are going to quickly be overwhelmed. New York won't spare anyone; St. Louis just isn't on the map politically."

After the indictments, though, St. Louis became a prime location for the media sharks drooling over a potential Bureau-blaster. From "Sixty Minutes" to programs no one watches but the anchors' mothers, producers were trying to pry open the FBI to explain the foul-up. Nelson refused those interviews, but he did talk with the reporter for *Wall Street Journal* and other writers.

But when the nine volumes of FBI tapes which the prosecution intended to present in trial were declassified, it is clear that the FBI could have saved Tina. All those agents and translators assigned to the case failed her as much as the child abuse worker Keith Dickens and her school officials did. The tapes were all translated in St. Louis; they were not being shipped elsewhere. The FBI was flying in two to three Arabists at a time to interpret the tapes. And the reels were not piling up unheard; the FBI was running only seven days behind.

It seems highly probable that long before November 5, 1989, any translator and any agent could have assessed Tina was in real danger: In June, Amjad had volunteered to kill her; by August when she ran away, the family discussed disposing of her; by October, Luie, Saif, Tawfiq, and Tina's sisters were deciding how to rid themselves of her; and on October 13, Zein tells Tina, "Will it satisfy you to go and accuse me, you and the black person . . . that I am with the guerrillas?" And on October 16, Dickins makes his visit on child abuse charges. Tina's counselors and teachers knew she was being beaten. The FBI knew that Tina knew too much about her family's involvement in Abu Nidal.

"If you heard *all* the tapes, you'd understand how ambiguous they were," Tom Newman pointed out. "One day Zein says I'm gonna kill her and the next day, he says he can't, he loves her too much. It was like their talk of killing all the Jews, not specific, a rambling rhetoric non-stop. The whole turmoil involving Tina was discussed by the FBI on a regular basis, so that if anything serious beyond the rhetoric was heard, we would have intervened. But we need something specific and immediate. Would Tina have come home that night if she thought they would kill her? It seems obvious now, but it was not clear in the fall of '89 that she needed drastic intervention."

The FBI was grossly overworked; the agents were putting in twelve-hour days for up to eight months at a time without a day off even on Thanksgiving. The Bureau had spent $20 to $30 million on an investigation in which no one had been blown up by terrorists.

Ironically, while Nelson and Newman were implied in the overall blame for not preventing Tina's murder, neither had been involved with the Abu Nidal case in the fall of 1989. Newman, a St. Louisan from a very old, very prominent family, did not take over the Counterterrorism Unit and this case until 1991; Nelson, also a St. Louisan, did not return home until 1991 from FBI headquarters, where he had become renowned for Mafia-busting. Nelson and Newman never defended themselves, which would have implied accusing their predecessors. All they did say, later, was that releasing Tina's murder tapes "short-circuited the FBI investigation. It showed our interest in Zein Isa," Nelson explained. "It would have gone on longer."

Although no more Abu Nidal indictments were expected from St. Louis, various federal and state officials continued their investigations. One regulatory agency was looking into allegations that the Isa clan had laundered millions of dollars in terrorist funds, possibly through BCCI. "So many pieces of this pie go to various people," commented undercover detective Sam Jackson. A colleague added how some Palestinian-Americans affiliated with Zein were snapping up small motels to use as safe houses.

Harry Hegger—Captain Hegger since his promotion in July 1993—was fully aware of all the activities of the Isa tribe from the various police departments and federal agencies. As commander of Intelligence, reporting directly to the police chief, Hegger was his "eyes and ears" into what was going on among the other agencies as well as out on the street. The Intelligence Division needed a mind like Hegger's, one that could synthesize information from disparate sources and make it into a whole story.

Hegger couldn't get enough of Intelligence—from coordinating his street gang squad to working with Internal Affairs on corrupt cops, to meeting with his chief on top secrets that only the two of them knew. Too secret even to be committed to paper. He frequently worked thirty-six hours in a row on a breaking case. Hearing that, U.S. Attorney Ed Dowd Jr.[*] pointed out, "See, Harry doesn't change. He's totally committed. He's always on duty, twenty-four hours a day. There's no job he can't handle, because he has no ego. One of his strongest points as head of Intelligence is that he can cooperate with anybody, any agency. It's 'What can we do to solve the problem?'

"Take the Isa case. Harry knew instinctively how horrible the murder was, and regardless how much it took out of him, he wanted to see justice done."

These qualities were much appreciated by other intelligence agen-

[*]Because St. Louis is basically a small town masquerading as a big city, it is worth noting that U.S. Attorney Dowd had been a year ahead of Tom Newman in high school at Chaminade Preparatory School.

cies, such as the FBI. Indeed, Jim Nelson repeated that a major joint investigation—a notorious sting that brought down three St. Louis police officers charged with coke dealing—originated with Hegger.

And when Captain Hegger worked with the feds, he would run into a former federal prosecutor who was now on the federal bench, Judge Charles A. Shaw, appointed in the fall of 1993.

During the news conference that day, Nelson explained that the Abu Nidal group came to St. Louis to set up business. During their six-year investigation of this cell, the FBI received sixty-two court orders under the Foreign Intelligence Surveillance Act approving the wiretaps and bugs (microphones) in the homes and businesses of the men indicted as well as other Palestinian suspects. From this were recorded 7,000 reels totaling 25,000 hours of conversations made in at least three cities—St. Louis, Racine, and Dayton—maybe more considering the group's contacts in Paterson, Manhattan, Miami, Chicago, Los Angeles, Albuquerque, Washington, Raleigh, Kansas City, San Juan, and elsewhere. (In addition, there are ANO cells in Brooklyn, where some alleged members were convicted in an insurance fraud scam.) FBI agents interviewed sources worldwide.

While some media speculated that Zein's, Tawfiq's, and the Nijmehs' names came from Atta's records seized during his arrest in April 1987, and/or from Samir Darwish's documents nabbed in Lima in 1988, they failed to note that the FBI had been investigating the four defendants since late 1986 and early 1987. It seems more probable that the arrests of Atta and Darwish resulted from the wiretap out of St. Louis than vice versa.

The indictments had been very long in coming. They had been predicted for spring 1992, and then by Halloween of that year. In fact, the entire case had been sent to Washington, where it sat and sat. At least three national experts in Washington quoted Justice Department sources that the indictments were connected to the World Trade Center bombing six weeks earlier. The Department wanted to "send a message" to all groups of terrorists. But Nelson said the FBI needed to review additional records and talk to a specific witness. Another FBI counterterrorist source put it bluntly: "A case like this would not have been hurried up just because of the World Trade Center. It was just that a lot of questions finally got answered."

Did this case connect to others in other cities? All the FBI would say was, "A certain amount of evidence in this investigation has been authorized by the U.S. Attorney General for use in this case."

Reading the indictment and accompanying documents produces a sense of déjà vu. The charges and the additional information in the affidavit are repetitive. Many people believe the only charge that is both solid and serious is Tina's murder. Taking too much money into and out of the country (more than $10,000 must be reported to Customs) and passport violations are not major crimes except in context of RICO. As for all of the reckless comments about blowing up the Israeli embassy and killing 3,000 Jews, nothing had been done in furtherance of these crimes. To paraphrase the famous defense lawyer "Racehorse" Haines, the Beitin Four were guilty mostly of "felony mouth."

Again, Tom Newman shook his head. "Does a man have to wear a three-piece suit and be an MIT chemist with a degree in explosives to be a terrorist?" he said in answer to skeptics who scoffed that the Beitin Four were such lowlifes, ANO wouldn't want them.

Experts agreed. "We're in a new era of terrorism. No longer are they all professionally trained. ANO has lost the resources it once had through its battles with the PLO and CIA. The professional hit men are dwindling. Now they have to use disposable comrades, the Zeins." Another said, "They may not be hard-core ANO, but they clearly had some contact with ANO."

Other authorities described them as "castaways," "wanna-bes," and "groupies." "Throughout his career, Abu Nidal has used low-IQ, poorly educated men. Which is why his operatives always get caught, killed, and cause havoc. He is the only brain." "Possibly false recruits," said a blond man who had worked as an agent for Israeli intelligence and falsely recruited men who thought they were working for German intelligence.

One man experienced in counterterrorism shook his head at all this talk: "The only people who really know what's going on are the FBI case agents and their supervisors who read the traffic reports daily, and they can't talk."

However, no one doubted that this was a cell, one of many ANO cells and safe houses throughout America. "There've been operatives in L.A. and Washington. The feds tried desperately during the Gulf war. No one was able to pin any terrorist activities on them." said Prof.

Robert Kupperman of the Center for Strategic and International Studies. Various intelligence officers say they knew in 1988 that ANO had a base in Caracas, that Samir Darwish was its leader and held a big ANO reunion there, during which time he was picked up by the authorities along with his membership list. And they confirmed that Atta was a midlevel ANO official as well as a possible CIA informant.

But the new case, especially after the World Trade Center bombing, had tremendous jury appeal. "It's like being a little bit pregnant. If you're with Abu Nidal, you're tainted," the former FBI man said. "With the girl getting killed, who wants to sit at the defense table and listen to that murder tape?" Did it matter how mundane the crimes were, if these men are ANO terrorists? One would need to read all the FBI transcripts to understand the context of the ANO crimes, a former Justice Department prosecutor observed.

"The problem with Americans is they really don't understand terrorism," Professor Kupperman pointed out. "We oscillate between complacency and paranoia. Most of the time we are apathetic." Added an FBI supervisor, "Any indication that ANO is totally disbanded would be naive." And some ANO members had turned to Hamas.

Some educated Palestinian-Americans scoffed at the indictments, saying the government was paranoid. Relatives of the Beitin Four professed surprise. Ahlam Nijmeh, who had previously talked about her husband Saif's "business," told the *Post-Dispatch*, "I don't know anything about this. He works at the liquor store." One St. Louisan looked around this store at the condoms and large posters of Cindy Crawford and another model in skimpy bathing suits and asked pretty Ahlam, "How can you allow those posters up in this store when you have to keep yourself covered up?"

"My husband can look all he wants, but he can only have me," she replied.

Saif's uncle, Youssef Nijmeh, said over dinner, "Maybe Luie and Saif merely went out of the country to make fun without their wives."

"All the way to Mexico City, Lima, and Athens?" the writer asked.

"It's much cheaper to make fun in foreign countries," Uncle Youssef said. "My nephews went to Mexico and Lima and met up with other Palestinians by coincidence. It's like when you're in a foreign country and by chance meet another American and dine together."

This was the man who said Zein was so esteemed by the Palestinian community in St. Louis, he was a virtual philosopher-king, while telling his nephews' attorneys no one listened to the gibberish of mad old Zein. Youssef also discussed with Saif two Arabic books on suicide operations and chemical equations.*

Who was the confidential informant hinted at in the indictment? Nelson was asked at the news conference. The informant who told them that the four defendants regularly received orders from ANO? The one who said ANO's number one goal is to target and kill Jews?

"The confidential informant will not be identified now," Nelson said. About six months later the man's name was released to defense attorneys as classified information.

After the news conference, FBI agents walked Saif Nijmeh for news photographers. Shuffling along in his handcuffs, jeans, and patriotic red, white, and blue shirt with its tail out, Saif looked at all the media and quipped, "Happy April Fool's Day."

---

*Youssef Nijmeh, with an M.A. in biology, claims cousin marriages produce healthier offspring and that "I can always tell by the eyes an Arab or Jew from anyone else with dark eyes, such as an Italian, Frenchman, or Englishman. Jewish and Arab eyes are different. Arab and Jewish eyes are alike."

CHAPTER THIRTY

Renz Farm

One of the most picturesque routes in America is a springtime jaunt along Highway 94 outside St. Louis to the middle of the state and Renz Farm Correctional Facility, where Maria Isa was imprisoned. Part of the Lewis and Clark Trail, Highway 94 is a back road running along the Missouri River. It winds and curves and loops sharply up and down steep hills past a panoply of achingly lovely scenes of Americana with more shades of green than the eye ever imagined, past dense forests of oak, past patchworks of farmland of wheat and corn, past Christmas tree nurseries that look like rows of giant, fluffy artichokes, past redbrick convents built by slaves, past white-pillared nineteenth-century mansions high on hills, past tiny antique shops nestled in hollows which East Coast dealers have yet to ferret out.

But the Isa family was not interested in the scenery en route to Renz Farm. They came, they saw, they left. Maria's eighteen visitors filled two of the picnic tables on the prison grounds and spilled over onto the grass. Everyone laughed and ate, not knowing that in a few days more trouble would come, on April Fool's Day. Her granddaughter hugged her so hard that Maria laughed and said, "You break my bones!" The little girl told how she had missed her and wanted to stay. The child reminded Maria and the other women of Tina—winsome, jaunty, and bright—so smart that at age eight, she'd already memorized the entire Qu'ran.

Maria was surrounded by all ten of her grandchildren, including the newest one, four months old; her three remaining daughters and their husbands; and her stepson, Faisal, and his Spanish wife. Afterwards, Amjad Salem would drive Faisal to meet with friends in Kansas City. For now, Maria could delight in her family. She and the other women inmates enjoyed relaxed visiting privileges.

Maria's daughters had brought the sewing materials she had requested. Having learned embroidery, quilting, crocheting, and knitting from her mother, Maria kept busy in prison with needlework. While awaiting trial, she had torn an old sheet and knotted it into strips and refashioned it into a woven wonder of a shawl that even the director of the state prison system marveled at. Since coming to Renz Farm, Maria had made thirteen quilts as well as appliqued pillow cases and clothes for her children, grandchildren, and other inmates, who photographed her works. These included a stuffed frog on a lily-pad quilt for an inmate's new infant and stuffed dolls.

"I can't sit and watch TV—except for "I Love Lucy," where sometimes he speaks Spanish," Maria said. "I like to keep busy." Often when visitors drove up, they would see her tending the flowers in the circle in front of the prison; she also volunteered in the greenhouse. "Everybody says my plants are beautiful. I like to see them growing from the ground. When my plants are going good, everything is good. My life here is good," she explained.

Well liked in prison by both officials, who praised her for helping everyone (even mopping floors after a toilet broke), and the other women, who threw her a birthday party and would call out "Hi, Maria," as she walked down the halls with a visitor, Maria actually seemed to prefer life on the inside. "I'm happy here. There are too many rules, though some days I think they need them. There are some bad people here, but most are good.

"This is no jail for me. I have no enemies here. The office respects me. I feel like I'm on vacation. I just tell my girls that I'm like in a foreign country where I can't come see them but they can come see me."

Like most grandmothers, she longs for her grandchildren. "I miss not caring for them when Mona goes to school." Then her face brightened, "But I baby-sit them in my heart."

As with many others in prison, religion became a comfort. Maria had remained a Roman Catholic despite her nearly thirty year marriage to a Muslim. Islam was too difficult, she said, with its daily fasting during the month of Ramadan. Yet, here in prison, Maria fasts every Sunday. "I need to make a sacrifice." She goes to chapel every day for an hour or two before supper and three times on Sunday. She prays for her family, that they continue to support her. She periodically talks long-distance to her mother in Brazil, and to her husband, whom she writes at least once a week. "A lot of people here believe in me, so I work hard with my heart. God won't give me a long time here," she said, thinking she would soon be released. "I have no idea where I go. Every day I pray for a surprise."

In late March 1993 Maria received her wish from the Missouri Supreme Court. It reversed her death penalty and remanded the sentencing for a new trial, agreeing with Charlie Shaw that Maria and Zein should not have been sentenced at the same time. The jury instruction that Maria deserved to die for acting with Zein was flawed—an individual must be punished only for his or her own crime. That meant that while her guilty verdict was upheld, Maria might be allowed to live out her natural life. The circuit attorney had the choice of retrying the punishment phase or allowing Maria to spend the rest of her life in prison. Not comprehending legal technicalities, Maria thought she might be going home soon and wrote her lawyer a lovely letter thanking him for what he accomplished.

A few months later, Dee Hayes, who had been elected in 1992 as St. Louis circuit attorney as well as the first woman to head a prosecutor's office in the seven counties of metropolitan St. Louis, decided that Maria's sentence would be retried and asked Bob Craddick to prosecute. To retry Maria's punishment would be an expensive five-day trial to put to death a fifty-year-old woman whose minimum punishment was life without parole. Hayes felt the public was so sickened by the murder that the sentencing must be retried. "We'll never know how much Maria was under her husband's thumb. And even so, why not save her daughter? I have no sympathy for her," Hayes said. But three highly placed sources said the retrial was political image correction; Hayes, who is very concerned about appearances, had been criticized for being soft on the death penalty when she ran for office.

Maria would be represented now by a public defender. Her family, not appreciating Charlie Shaw's victory, was unhappy Maria had not been fully acquitted. They not only did not pay him in full, they did not want to pay him further for a new sentencing trial.

Similarly, the family was angry with Dan Reardon, refusing to pay his entire fee; and turned to another attorney, Richard Sindel, to handle Zein's appeal. (The sisters also asked Sindel to sue Reardon for misrepresentation of counsel, an all too common tactic of criminal defendants after they are convicted. Reardon had done a fine job; such an accusation was ludicrous.) And as for the terrorist charges, the family decided not to retain an attorney but to have Zein be represented by a federal public defender. It seemed they did not want to throw away money on lost causes, they only wanted to spare their father the death penalty.

The day the Abu Nidal indictments came down, Maria isolated herself in her cell and refused to talk to anyone. Her daughters and Faisal called that afternoon, but she refused to come to the phone. A week later, the prison officials noted, "She's still scared of something. We don't know what. We do know that she calls her daughters and nieces a lot." None of the family wanted Maria to talk to out-of-town reporters,[*] even one who had flown down from New York. More importantly, maybe Maria was scared for her other children. If she had thought that her family wanted Tina killed to avenge their honor, what must she think now that her husband and nephews had been charged with plotting Tina's murder to silence her?

From a distance, as one drives toward it, Mineral Point Corrections Facility, south of St. Louis in Potosi, looks like St. Augustine's City of God shimmering on the plain. Then one comes closer and sees that what is shining is not flecks of silver but high-tech barbed wire. And the plain has been stripped of foliage so that if any inmate escapes from this state-of-the-art, maximum-security penal colony, he can be tracked down before he kills another human.

Like his wife, Zein made friends in prison. One was a convicted Lebanese-American car bomber, Paul Leisure, who himself was mutilated when his car was dynamited. Another notorious inmate Zein met through mosque services was Alvin Kirksey-Bey, of the Moorish Science Temple, a violent black group operating in prisons. Kirksey-Bey seemed to be functioning as Zein's agent, trying to shake down any reporters for money up front before they could even think of interviewing him. "Don't deal with Alvin," warned a judge. "He'll have you running contraband and bringing him money each time you want to see Zein." Zein, who could not speak English at his murder trial, has managed to converse with Kirksey-Bey and Leisure, neither of whom can speak good English, let alone Arabic. And Zein amuses his fellow inmates with dirty jokes—in English.

*Maria has granted interviews only to the author. She did not want to discuss what happened the night of November 5–6, but was forthcoming about other information. A very warm woman, after each interview she spontaneously hugged me good-bye.

CHAPTER THIRTY-ONE

Abu Yacov

His first night in jail, the other inmates asked Saif Nijmeh what he was in for. "I dunno," he answered. Then the evening news came on. "When they see me bein' walked by the FBI, they run over to the other side of room," Saif later told his lawyer. "When I asked the jailer where east was so I could pray, he wouldn't tell me—acted like I was gonna break out or somethin'!"

Meanwhile, in a Dayton jail cell, his brother Luie was yelling and making threats, alarming the U.S. marshal's service. Oh, Luie's just a hothead, relatives said.

And possibly a blabbermouth, who on April 1 spewed out—in a 102-page typed transcript—details of his businesses, his drug use, his sex life, and his terrorist politics, in English, to the FBI. Luie began with how he had a brother named Hitler. Despite the Horatio Alger story he and Saif concocted later, Luie admitted that ten years ago, their father "came and opened the store [in Racine] for us."

Luie sold his subsequent liquor store, S & L, in St. Louis, to Saif but retained legal ownership because his older brother had declared bankruptcy. "So, it's really not your store. It's in your name, it's your brother's store?" repeated the confused agent. "We all brothers, we all together," Luie declared. He mumbled something about his other brothers running Gold Star . . . "we all stick together, ya know, we all work together . . . we all have each other to, to make it, ya know." And a group of them lived together in his apartment.

Right now, Luie said, he also ran a rug business in Dayton, where he could clear $200 a day, selling Orientals from the back of a van. "I don't want to [work], ya know, twelve and fifteen hours a day, I just wanna be free . . . 'cause I'm single, ya know, I send some money to my wife" whom he had dispatched back to the West Bank.

While his family back home chastised the author for Americans' promiscuity and licentiousness, Luie was cheerfully candid about the drug bust arrest in his Mercedes, smoking joints, and other sins of the flesh. "Going back to God, to Islam . . . is the only way. Even though I never been in mosque. Every night I go out and get drunk. I take women to my house and sleep with them, but I have the idea, I know what I'm doing is wrong . . . but I'm still doing it. But I believe, ya know, that those guys like Hamas is the only solution to our problem."

One agent delicately asked Luie if he were involved in the politics of Palestine.

No. "I don't trust them. All the groups. I have no faith in them. All they need is money. . . . All them motherfuckers."

"Throw some names at me," the agent begged.

"They have the PLO, they have George Habash, they have Naif Hawatmah. They have Abu Nidal."

"Nidal?" one agent asked, the other adding, "Abu Nidal, you, you say he's living high off the hog, too?"

"All of them, they have villas," Luie sneered. "They spend a lot of money. They don't care about their people."

"You ever been asked for money to support their organizations?" the agents sniffed around.

"All over the states, they throw like a party . . . it's like people get together and everybody . . . express his feeling about the political situation over there and by the end of the party or this thing that they do, they start collecting . . . money for the organization. . . . [It's done by] people who live in the community. Ya just go to the Arab community and they sell 'em tickets to the event or party [costing] fifteen, twenty-five dollars. . . . They have entertainment, they dance, they sing, they eat, ya know. Then they throw a speech, ya know."

The two most popular groups were Arafat's Fatah and George Habash's PFLP, Luie explained. "But people start losing interest in that kind of organization because it's been fifty years and they haven't done anything."

"Who's filling the void?"

"The most popular organization now back home is Hamas, you know, that religious group, ya know, and people start going back to their senses and they say that the only way for us to be organized is by going to Islam . . . all organization do terrorist activity."

He discussed how "hard-headed" Abu Nidal was, how he "assassinated fifty of his own members in late 1989 . . . if this guy is killing his own people, ya know, what kind of organization is this? They said they'll liberate his people . . . instead of fightin' for freedom, he go around and killing these people. . . . It's sick."

"Would you have supported him before 1989?" The agent must have held his breath when Luie blurted out:

"Yes, I thought, yeah . . . sometimes you think this is the only solution is not to make peace. . . . Is either you or them, ya know. Sometimes, you think well, this is the only way, is to have peace with the other side. . . . We're not gonna keep killing each other for something because this is political. This political dispute is for the land and each side really thinks this land belongs to him, ya know. And you just, you just, sometimes you get to a point that that's it, you get sick and tired of it, ya know. You just as well live a decent life, ya know. You just want to be like somebody else. . . . I don't want to go back home. I'm gonna stay here because I'm sick and tired of it . . . all political things they're fighting for, who's gonna be on top. They're not organized. Sometimes I'll be ashamed to say I'm Palestinian because of what they do, ya know. . . . I don't interfere in their business. I don't go to any political or fund raiser."

"When did you get frustrated?"

"When somebody promise you something and they don't do it, ya know. If you believe in something, you have to fight for it, ya know. You have to do everything, ya know, to get to where you want, ya know. If you believe you have a problem, you have to fight. . . . All the organizations, all of them. They didn't let me down, they let their people down."

"But you . . . feel like supporting certain groups, that are your ideal?"

"I support certain groups, yes. I supported at one time Fatah . . . George Habash. Then one time I supported—then now I'm supporting Hamas."

"Hamas? They're pretty radical."

"They're not," Luie objected.

"They're killing a lot of people."

"Well, a lot of people killing their people and they killing a lot of their people, ya know."

"Are Hamas assassinating their own people because they think they're informing?"

"They assassin [sic] other people because of their collaborating with the enemy, ya know, the informer. . . . If I work for the CIA and I go to Russia and give them information, when I get back here, my ass is grass."

The agent said, "We have jail. We don't shoot you between the eyes."

"Because it's the law and this country's been built on justice, freedom of speech. But over there there's no law. . . . You have no government. You have no nothing. . . . All the Palestinians, all the organization, if they see an informer, they just go and shoot him."

The agent began questioning Luie again about any financial support he had given. Maybe a hundred dollars, Luie said, but not to Hamas. That was a few years back, at a fund-raiser.

"Our understanding is that you were a member of Abu Nidal," the agent stated.

"I wasn't the member. I was supporting that group" because ANO wanted to liberate all of Palestine, not merely the West Bank.

The agents eased Luie from ideology back to facts: What duties or functions did he have in ANO? Luie finally admitted, "They asked me one time [to transfer money for them]. To get all the name of all the Arab, ya know, who live in St. Louis, or . . . this country."

"Who asked you to do that? Name him."

"That was in 1987. I forgot the name."

"Well, his first name. What was his first name?"

"I think his first name is—Mahmoud. M-A-H-M-O-U-D. . . . I met him, ya know . . . when I used to be in Wisconsin. . . . I met with him twice. . . . I met him in—in Mexico . . . Mexico City. 1987."

"Did you give him the names?" the first agent asked and the second agent added, "Some names of some Arabs?"

"I gave him a few names. . . . Then after that I just got out."

But Luie admitted that Mahmoud had called him to fly down and meet him. Was the most fearsome of the feared "nice"? the agents asked.

"Of course," Luie said. "He got to be decent, ya know, he gotta be nice, ya know. He's not gonna be an asshole because if he wants to be an asshole he's not gonna get what he wants, right?

"I don't know if that was his real [name]. . . . See when you belong to an organization, you change your name, you don't tell your real name, ya know . . . you have to come up with fake name, you know, so nobody know about your real name except high, big people."

Then Luie coughed up Samir Darwish: "I met another guy in Peru."

"Another what? ANO member? What was his name?"

"There's two different, there's a lot of names, ya know."

"How did you come about meeting him in Peru? . . . Who told you to go to Peru? Mahmoud?"

"Yeah. . . . He bought the tickct."

"Have you ever taken money into Israel you tried to hide from the authorities?"

Luie avowed that the $5,000 he was caught smuggling into the West Bank in 1988 was for his brother who was going to get married, for the wedding.

"You got caught."

"For Abu Nidal Organization," Luie added. Another time, while he lived in Dayton, all the Arabs there gave him money to send to their families. "It's a lot simpler than to send it in the mail, ya know."

Going back to Atta and Darwish, the agents asked Luie if he knew the name Samir al-Batma.

"Uh huh."

"What about, do you know anything about the murder of Tina Isa in November, 1989, in St. Louis?"

"I heard about it on the news. I know the parents."

"You're going to have a hard time, your Honor," the lawyer told the federal magistrate judge the next day. Judge Catherine Perry was looking for attorneys who were licensed to practice in federal court and would be willing to be court-appointed to represent one of the Beitin Four. Most Jewish lawyers would not take the case for obvious reasons, and their partners would refuse out of respect for them. For attorneys without such reservations, taking on such a complex case with a lengthy trial might prohibit them from handling other clients.

While the attorney was theoretically correct, Zein, Tawfiq, Saif, and Luie would have little trouble finding representation. Some big-time criminal defense lawyers were vying to have one of the Beitin Four as a client. Money was no issue; this was a very high publicity case. In the end, all the alleged ANO cadres but Zein chose young attorneys whom they had consulted previously on business. One was an odd fit.

Three years earlier, Keith Liberman had been writing a legal brief when Saif Nijmeh walked in off the street with a business problem. "Settling that, we got to talking. It was around the holidays, so I asked him what nationality he was—could have been Indian, Mexican, I couldn't tell. He told me Palestinian and then asked me mine," apparently not understanding the sign on the door that read LIBERMAN, COHEN AND HOCHSTEIN. "Jewish," said Liberman, who clearly looks of Mediterranean descent. "We began talking about the Holy Land and Saif says, 'There could be peace in the Mideast. We're all just people walking down a street in Jerusalem.' "

Lieberman, unlike Shaw and Reardon, never had any problems collecting his fees. Saif and the other Palestinian-Americans he referred to Liberman always paid in person. They would make a special trip, come into the office, flirt with the secretary, and schmooze for about an hour and a half with Liberman, who had clients waiting. "It would be offensive to say, 'Where's the money?' " he said. "Although the whole procedure makes me feel like something out of *Shogun*." As Saif and Liberman became friendly "and I got to know and like them," the Palestinians bestowed an Arabic nickname on the soft-spoken, well-mannered lawyer: Abu Yacov, for Liberman's eldest was a boy named Jacob.

While Liberman's friends at Westwood Country Club were unhappy with his defending an Arab who wanted to "kill all the Jews," his family supported him. His nine-year-old daughter didn't want her father to read her bedtime stories, she wanted to know about what Daddy did that day in court. When Liberman went to court for Saif's arraignment and detention hearing, his father came along to watch.

Liberman Sr. sat in the right section of the courtroom with Saif's family, while on the left side sat the media, trying not to stare at the women in white *hijabs* and the thuggish-looking men. Afterward, as the men filed out first, and the women followed behind, a reporter approached Liberman Sr., a darkly handsome man like his son. Mistaking the lawyer's father for an Arab, the reporter asked, "How do you feel about your relatives being charged as terrorists?"

The hearing was basically a contest between the government and the defense on whether Saif—dressed in the same clothes he'd been arrested in—should be allowed bail. Liberman said Saif had come to St. Louis in 1986 with $20 in his pocket and now owned two stores. His uncle Youssef Nijmeh testified how Saif worked fourteen hours a day, not getting home until nearly midnight from his two stores, Deir Dibwan Trading Company and S&L Liquor,* both of which he co-owned with Luie. Saif won't flee, Youssef protested. His wife is here, pregnant with their fifth child.

Jim Steitz, the assistant U.S. attorney who had spent three years going through the FBI tape logs, argued that Saif was a flight risk. His main evidence was a fifteen-page affidavit written by the FBI case agent detailing how Saif and Tawfiq had tried to obstruct justice by moving Zein before he could be arrested for Tina's murder. Tawfiq's plan for the escape had been thwarted by Lieutenant Hegger.

Saif's conversation with Luie was cited by the FBI as evidence of admission that Saif belonged to ANO: Luie told Saif a month after Tina's murder that he was worried—Investigators were questioning Zein in his jail cell. "Does this mean they are asking questions . . . because of this business?" Saif said. ". . . they are tying this business to that business."

The affidavit noted that when Saif believed the police had an Arab informant helping them on Zein's case, he said, "It's time to start the cleansing." In fact, the informant was an FBI source, but was not help-ing Lieutenant Hegger with the murder investigation. Hegger knew nothing of his existence.

Liberman and Steitz continued sparring about Saif being let out on bond. "Two guns were found in his store while he was arrested last week," Steitz said. "But they were lawfully registered," Liberman argued.

"Yeh," said Steitz. "He instructed a co-conspirator to remove a rocket-propelled grenade launcher kept in his home or mobile van, and it was never found."

"Mr. Nijmeh would let the FBI tear down his walls and look for the weapons," Liberman countered. "We would like to ask the court for work release. Mr. Nijmeh would wear an electronic ankle device. We owe it to him. When he calls home at night, his son cries, 'Daddy, Daddy, when are you coming home?' He won't flee. I'll give the court Mr. Nijmeh's passport."

"That's not the only one he uses," Steitz wrinkled his nose.

*   *   *

*The stores were all named for the family. Deir Dibwan was the bus company owned by Saif and Luie's father, and S&L stood for Saif and Luie. Luie's store in Dayton was called Gold Star Market, star in Arabic being *Nijmeh*.

While Saif was being arraigned, his brother Luie faced a federal magistrate in Dayton for his detention hearing (the arraignment would follow in St. Louis). Luie's case was more complicated. An FBI agent from St. Louis testified that while Luie had denied most of the allegations, he admitted he had "been in contact" with an ANO rep in Wisconsin. When agents searched Gold Star Market during the arrest, they uncovered a handgun, two loaded clips for automatic weapons, and a booklet on how to use an AK-47. Out back, they discovered a photo of Luie brandishing a long-barreled revolver. The agent noted Luie's drug charge in St. Louis for possession of 150 grams of cocaine. And inside Gold Star the FBI found "additional evidence of drug involvement."

Luie was a terrible flight risk: His wife and child now lived in Beitin, he used more than one Social Security number, and he made "threats" just after his arrest. "My understanding is he is the most violent of the four," the U.S. marshal in St. Louis said later.

So at Luie's arraignment in St. Louis, security was tight. Five deputy marshals flanked Luie inside the courtroom and one stood outside guarding the door. For a man who was anti-American, Luie looked like an ad for Banana Republic—distressed brown leather bomber jacket with the collar up, a decorated denim shirt tucked into khakis, and hiking boots. Skinny Luie stood askance, with one hand on the lectern facing the judge and the other smoothing his thick black mustache and very thick, wavy black hair. Samir Darwish had called him "the Thin Man" and his portly brother "the Fat Man." Now, in court, he was arrogant, too.

People back in Beitin said Luie was like that. The Nijmeh brothers had thought they didn't need an education because their father was a rich man—they'd never need to work. Yet they told their lawyers they came to America to make their way, and Luie told his attorney in Dayton he faithfully sent his earnings home to his aged parents. The truth was that their father had cut them loose because of their profligate lifestyle: Luie and Saif carried on like the "two wild and crazy guys" from "Saturday Night Live." They ran around on their wives while publicly proclaiming, "We treat our wives like lee-tel jewels." Privately, they complained that American women were much better in bed—not so modest, not so inhibited. The evening his wife Sausan was miscarrying in a hospital, Luie was in bed with a lady of the night. Worse yet, it has been said that he beat her.

The Nijmehs asked Neil Bruntrager to represent Luie, telling him, "We

want you because you fight with your brains, and we want Keith because
he fights with his heart." Jesuit-trained Bruntrager had followed his
father* as well as his older brothers for a term in the circuit attorney's
office. "There've been so many Bruntragers since Neil's father, we refer
to his job as the Bruntrager Chair," joked one former colleague.

"My dad was my role model," Bruntrager says. "I always loved him
and wanted to be just like him." His four siblings agreed, working
together with their father and spouses in one big happy family law
firm. It operates during crises in ways the Isa clan would have envied:
When one of Neil's twins was burned, he went to the hospital night
and day for three weeks. "It never occurred to me to go into the office.
I called in, knowing what needed to be done with my cases would be
done. Similarly, when one of us makes a lot of money, we split it. With
less time spent on office politics, you can get more work done."

When law school seniors apply for jobs at Bruntrager, Bruntrager
and Bruntrager, they receive a polite form letter: "We will hire anyone
related by blood or marriage. . . . In closing, we have available a single
brother who's quite marriageable." The firm received an award from
Washington University Law School for the best rejection letter.

Unlike the Beitin Four, who made a fetish out of family, Neil
Bruntrager was devoted to his wife and children, leaving work by 6:30
every night and not going in on weekends. All free time was spent with
his growing family—five tots under the age of six, including a set of
twins. (There were six sets of twins among the attorneys, agents, and
Palestinians in this case.) His wife's woody station wagon "looks like a
van pool for a nursery school."

The Abu Nidal case intrigued Bruntrager—the constitutional issues,
the intrigue, and the nine volumes of declassified FBI transcripts that the
government might present as evidence in the trial. "It reads like a spy
novel," he said. But Bruntrager refused to discuss this or any part of the
case with "60 Minutes," "Prime Time Live," "48 Hours," The *Wall
Street Journal*. "I don't talk to reporters.† I want a low-profile practice, and
my clients don't want to end up on TV."

---

*Bruntragger's father worked under Ed Dowd Sr., father of the current U.S. attorney.
In the 1950s Dowd Sr. hired the first black (who went on to become a federal appellate
judge.) In 1979 Dowd Jr. yelled down a bigot in an Ozarks bar filled with more racists
because the man had insulted Dowd's black colleagues—including Judge Charles A. Shaw.

†Obviously, he spoke with the author.

Despite their sexist attitudes, the clan went to a woman attorney to represent Tawfiq Musa. They believed she would fight for the principle that every defendant is entitled to a good defense—and they were right. Linda Murphy was a superb choice, having won several surprise victories in what had seemed loser cases. "A defendant believes that if the attorney doesn't think he or she is innocent, the lawyer won't work on the case. But to a lawyer, guilt or innocence is irrelevant. In fact, when your client *is* innocent, it can be paralyzing," Murphy explained.

After winning a murder second for a black youth facing the death penalty for murdering four people in a supermarket robbery, Murphy received a lot of referrals. One was an ACLU discrimination case with no fee provided. Murphy got the charges dismissed.

"So if you take a really big case like the supermarket murders and do well, it leads to other business—even bigger and better nonpaying cases," she laughed. "One day we'll be talking—as I sit under a bare lightbulb. And you'll say, "Linda, Linda, you had such a thriving business. What went wrong?' " She laughed again. Even under the most extreme pressure, both in the courtroom and in her personal life, Murphy maintained an enviable easygoing sense of humor.

Murphy stood with her client, Tawfiq Musa, before the judge at his arraignment and detention hearing. A short, fat, brutish-looking man, Tawfiq only came up to Murphy's eyes. A few dirty strands of black hair were combed over the back of his balding skull. The right collar of his short-sleeved khaki shirt was flipped up as though at half-mast. Like the others, he wore a mustache. And like the others, security was tight—a handful of deputy marshals watched inside and outside the courtroom.

After the deputies took Tawfiq away, Murphy spoke with reporters. "You can go to any Irish pub in St. Louis any night of the week and hear Irish-American singers play songs about blowing up the British, and no one is charged with conspiracy. But these men just *talk* about killing and blowing up an embassy and they get indicted. What Americans were killed? What building dynamited? If you apply the same standards as in the indictment, why are there no sweeps of the Irish pubs?" Of course, the IRA has not yet plotted to kill Americans on American soil.

Of the four defense lawyers, Murphy would ultimately face a special legal issue.

                    *   *   *

As Zein was being escorted from his holdover cell to his arraignment, four deputies came running into the courtroom, checking under chairs for hidden weapons, running their hands under tabletops for contraband. Other deputies shut down the entire eighth floor hall as Zein was brought up. "We're using the highest-level security in this case, and more on Zein," explained one guard, "because Zein's on death row." Soon there were five deputies inside the courtroom—two behind Zein, two in front of the locked double doors, one in the jury box, and three more in the hall. This was the first time a courtroom had been locked for a hearing.

Although he was shackled in leg and arm irons, Zein walked in without a cane or crutches. His beard was now white and his dark, wavy hair was now mostly gray. Wearing a short-sleeved shirt, brown pants with no belt, white tennis shoes, and with papers stuck in his back pocket, Zein appeared quite casual. Indeed, he seemed nonchalant. In thick glasses, he peered around the room and smirked. "He feels evil," one reporter whispered to another who shuddered.

A few weeks later, Liberman filed motions asking the prosecutors to reveal the names of the coconspirators and confidential informants and the number of each. He now represented nine Palestinian clients and did not want a conflict of interest.

Steitz replied that he would reveal those identities as soon as he could. He was getting orders from Washington, he added.

So who was this confidential informant? The defense attorneys tried to guess.

CHAPTER THIRTY-TWO

Party in the Bat Cave

EARLY 1994

Saif's wife, Ahlam, and her sister Sausan had prepared a feast of meat pies, pita bread, olives, and goat cheese. For dessert, they had arranged a veritable orchard of fragrantly perfumed fruit from the Holy Land—apricots, star fruit, and the small apples like those in the Song of Solomon. As Neil Bruntrager carried in their platters of food, Linda Murphy bought cans of soda from vending machines nearby on the seventh floor of the federal courthouse. Even the federal marshal's deputies chuckled as they opened the doors to let in a procession of defense attorneys toting the goodies and Ahlam's two Palestinian flags, followed by the orange-jumpsuited Tawfiq, Luie, and Saif—all shackled in leg irons and manacled.

The group had something to celebrate. The government was giving the four defendants and their attorneys a special room that only they could enter, where they could come and go twenty-four hours a day to listen to tapes as they prepared the defense. The room was called a SCIF room—Secured Classified Information Facility—which the lawyers quickly took to calling the Bat Cave. It was a leftover jury room of twenty feet by twenty feet, redone in wretched yellow vinyl grasscloth. Against the walls were file cabinets packed with tapes in Arabic and logs in English that the government intended to use in its case. Better yet were the other logs filling three file drawers. These logs were for tapes that the government still deemed classified but had released as exculpatory information that the defense might want to use. As for these tapes themselves, there were rows and rows of them in boxes—about 150. The logs were notations FBI agents had made over the years when they came in to check the voice-activated tapes. The agents would jot down date, time, names of the speakers, and a synopsis of each conversation. By culling the logs, the lawyers and the defen-

dants could narrow the field as to what they wanted as evidence to use
in their defense.

There would be no time to hear all of the tapes, for as Bruntrager
said, "If we had someone listening five hours a day, it would take 19.2
years to hear all 25,000 hours of tapes." That is, if the government ever
allowed them access to all of it.

After the lawyers made their selections from the logs, they could hire
translators to interpret what was being said on tape. (Defendants are not
allowed to translate materials in their own cases, for obvious reasons.)

The Beitin Four laughed in some instances at the government's inter-
pretations: On January 22, 1988, Saif and his friend, nicknamed Abu
Zibdeh ("Father of Fat" or "Butterball"), were discussing the police and
FBI agents. Zibdeh called the agents Abu Asa al Kabira or Abu Abbas,
"Father of the Big Stick" (even though there is a real terrorist by that
name), and the police were Umm Abbas, "Mother of the Big Stick." In
what must have been the worst translation in the annals of law enforcement, these Palestinians whose everyday vocabulary included *nigger
slave*, *shithead*, and *whore* suddenly became genteel speakers.

> ZIBDEH: Abbas has a long penis.
>   SAIF: Yes.
> ZIBDEH: He's looking for someone needing to have sex badly.

What Abu Zibdeh really said was, according to Saif, "This agent is a
dickhead and he's going to fuck us over."

While the government could hire translators to rectify their selections—as the state did before the Isas' murder trial—as it stood, the
nine volumes of FBI transcripts were replete with ridiculous misinter-
pretations. For example, referring to the town of Beit Hanina as "the
house of Hanna," as though it were someone's home, shows the interpreter had never been to that area just outside East Jerusalem, where
the street signs are in English as well as in Arabic. (The Holy Land
was under the British Mandate from World War I until 1948.) As anyone knows who has done it, translating is subtle work, especially when
dealing with foreign idioms; what would an inadequate English translator make of "wearing your heart on your sleeve"? One former FBI
man commented, "They must have used a guy fresh from Arabic
school armed with a dictionary."

The U.S. Attorney's office directed a verbatim translation to avoid arguments over interpretation since the defense alleged the interpretation may have been wrong in places.

While the translations were important, the biggest issue in this case was discovery. "The government cries national security, so we have to carefully craft discovery requests," Bruntrager explained. For example, the feds would not release tapes disclosing that a trusted relative is really a foreign spy for the French (who have long tracked ANO since it bombed a synagogue school there, killing some children). Discovery is difficult under FISA, the Foreign Intelligence Surveillance Act of 1978.

FISA cases are usually initiated by FBI supervisors from the Counterterrorism or Counterintelligence* Divisions at headquarters. Only a supervisor at the headquarters of the various agencies can apply for FISA status (agents in the field cannot). The supervisor writes the application based on highly classified information from a compendium of sources—the CIA, FBI (the lead agency in counterterrorism), State Department, or military intelligence. The supervisor might note, "In 1983 London police learned that Saddam Salameh worked for ANO when he lived in the Sudan. Salameh now lives in Miami and travels frequently to Lebanon."†

If the suspect is an alien, the affidavit doesn't have to be as specific as it would be in the case of an American citizen. The affidavit then undergoes an interminable review at the Office of Intelligence Policy and Review. It is signed by the attorney general of the United States, and armed with the affidavit and supporting documentation, the requesting supervisor goes to special court.

FISA cases are heard in a secret court on the sixth floor of the Justice Department, a court without windows, a court inside the double doors of a vault—like the vaults in bank safe-deposit rooms. Inside the hidden chamber is a large conference table headed by a federal judge, one of twelve selected around the country to serve on the FISA court. Around the table are seated officers from the intelligence agencies.

Never in the history of FISA has any of the 7,500 applications been

---

*Counterterrorism fights foreign terrorist organizations who use violence or force for political ends. Counterintelligence undermines schemes by foreign governments trying to acquire American military technology (e.g., the Walker and Pollard cases). The terms are not synonymous.

†This example is fictitious.

rejected, and probably none will be as the process is so demanding and harrowing. "The judge reviews the FISA applications, and asks questions that may cut your guts out," says a former FBI counterterrorism supervisor who made trips to the vault.

The secret court wants it that way, so that the statute stands firm against attacks that FISA infringes on the Fourth Amendment right to privacy. All FISA orders are sealed. FISA is limited solely to matters of national security,* because there are fewer safeguards for defendants. Each FISA order to install a wiretap and/or microphone lasts for one year, and the procedure must be repeated for extensions.

Only the case agent and his or her supervisor sees the tape logs in translation. The agent sends teletypes to Washington, where they are disseminated to the White House, State Department, CIA, NASA, Secret Service, and Department of Justice. Then, for example, an official in the FBI in Washington or the Justice Department calls the St. Louis FBI office with, "There's something you might want to take a look at."

But sometimes the local FBI office calls headquarters with some shocking news: "Dave Binney [then in charge of the St. Louis office] called me that day [November 6, 1989] as soon as he knew the Isa murder tape existed. My position was we had to release the tape," recalled Buck Ravell, now retired, who was head of investigations in the FBI headquarters at the time, as well as the FBI's specialist on counterterrorism to the National Security Council. "But under FISA, we had to initiate the procedure from St. Louis through headquarters to Justice to the FISA Court to get the authority to release the tapes."

FISA is vital to national security; without it, our intelligence apparatus could not operate, said one expert.

It had been difficult for the defense counsel in the Abu Nidal case to obtain the FISA tapes. First, Washington threw in CIPA, the Classified Information Protection Act, as a roadblock. CIPA put FISA matters under protective order; which in everyday terms, meant if a lawyer leaks the information, he can be prosecuted for espionage. So, think of FISA as the information, SCIF where one gets the information, and CIPA the special clearance necessary to obtain it. (There is also a CSO, or court security officer, who oversees dangerous cases—"the com-

---

*While evidence from a FISA tap also can be used in a regular criminal case, one cannot apply for FISA status to gain evidence in a routine criminal case.

mando of the marshals of the Eighth Circuit," as one lawyer called her, the keeper of the classified documents and the prisoners. The CSO in this case had been the CSO in the Iran-contra trials.)

With all of these alphabet laws, defendants still have some Sixth Amendment rights with their accusers. The courts have been known to throw out cases in which the government refuses to disclose the source that led to the FISA tap—for example, the source is a foreign agent and the U.S. government does not want to jeopardize relations with that country. The big clue in the case of the Beitin Four was whose information about Zein led to the original FISA tap? And who aided the FBI?

It didn't appear to be Samir Darwish. The four defense attorneys asked for information about him after his 1988 arrest and subsequent release in Peru, but the U.S. government refused, saying the information was from the CIA. "The FBI wants to keep Samir under wraps," Bruntrager said. "And he's part of the predicate acts for RICO."

What is known is that by the late 1980s, the FBI was desperate for a live source of their own into Palestinian terrorism—one not brokered by Israeli or any other foreign intelligence. Not a NSA satellite, but a person reporting directly to them.

The defendants seemingly were unconcerned with these issues. Nor did any of the men note the connection between the wiretapped conversations about meetings with Mahmoud Atta and Samir Darwish and their subsequent arrests. All the Beitin Four knew was that Samir had vanished into some secret place.

After they finished eating Ahlam's and Sausan's specialties, the defendants turned to their work, listening to the FISA tapes through headsets and making notes. They were shackled to the table the entire time, until the clock neared three P.M., time for one of the five daily prayers. Tawfiq removed his headset and announced it was time to pray. Saif, Luie, and Zein, who called Tawfiq "Mr. Musa," obeyed. By a signal through the one-way mirror in the door, the deputies came in and unshackled the men, who went into a corner, bowed facing east, and prayed (Another oddity considering that Luie used to sleep through the mu'zerrain's call to morning prayers in Beitin). When the prayers were complete, the guards who watched through the mirror came in and reshackled the men.

The guards had been somewhat surprised by the appearance of the Beitiners who looked like hoodlums—long shaggy hair, monobrows, and beards. "Real scary-looking," commented a man close to the case. Alarmed, Ahlam called Liberman and asked why her husband wasn't allowed a razor. None of them was. Zein looked the worst—when he was able to come at all, since he was intermittently in a wheelchair.

The first time the attorneys met him, Zein walked into the SCIF room without the aid of crutches or a cane. Liberman, Murphy, and Bruntrager all trotted over to be introduced by Zein's public defender, Tom Day.

They all said, "Pleasure to meet you, Mr. Isa," and shook hands with Zein.

In the hall afterward, they were aghast.

Wildly optimistic, the defense lawyers pondered what would happen to their clients after the three-month trial if they were acquitted or sentenced to only a few years. "They can't go home." Liberman said. "The Israelis don't want them in, the Palestinians shun them—they won't donate money for their defense, they don't want to be associated with them, they don't want the FBI knocking on their doors."

Acquittal didn't seem likely except in the minds of the four lawyers. But then there is the old adage that trial lawyers believe their own B.S. The feds were still interviewing possible witnesses three months before the trial, including some as far away as immigration officials in Israel, and finding more evidence. Discovery of evidence to the defense was agonizingly slow—everything was coming out of Washington, where it seemed to be chronically delayed. The photos of Atta and Zein that Ramsey Clark had told Bruntrager about still had yet to be released. "Time is not our friend," Bruntrager commented dryly to Murphy.

Discovery was not the only problem. There was the issue of Zein Isa. He was like an albatross for the other defendants. Who'd want him sitting at the defense table as the FBI played The Murder Tape? How would that taint the three other men? Zein was now even more bitter, no longer joking around, quipping his puns. His fellow conspirators avoided him. His own lawyer was having problems communicating with him. It wasn't just the language barrier, but a far deeper rift. Indeed, in late fall 1993, Tawfiq, Luie, and Saif reported that Day wanted Zein to testify against the other three. To protect her client,

Murphy suggested all the lawyers sign a joint defense agreement so that if one defendant turned government's witness, his lawyer would have to promise not to reveal the trial strategy of the other three men.

For a while it seemed Zein would be too ill to stand trial. Physicians for each side argued in court, one citing the time Zein's heart had failed and his blood pressure once dropped fifty points so that doctors had to jump-start his heart again. Three times he was hospitalized, all lengthy stays in a special facility, for congestive heart failure and kidney failure, both conditions resulting from his diabetes. Three months before the trial he was wheelchair-bound yet apparently bound for trial regardless, as Day spent more time than Zein in the SCIF room going over the logs.

Tom Newman remarked, "This could be a lot like Mafiosi who get heart attacks when served with subpoenas, but outside range of TV cameras and FBI agents, manage to get well."

The trial was set for September 19, 1994. As the date grew closer, the men seemed more disgusted with Zein, whom they ridiculed as "Abu Arab," than with the men who had betrayed them. Some said the other three secretly hoped he would die soon: It was his fault about the murder of Tina.

There was no doubt as to the identity of the one known betrayer of the cause of Abu Nidal, and it was no hearsay made up by some FBI agent. Jim Steitz turned over to the defense the canceled receipts signed by the informant. Paid receipts, the man had ratted on his relatives for money. The defendants were surprised at first, then seemed indifferent. They felt it would not hurt their case. An odd reaction, remarked someone close to the case.

An odd reaction indeed. The informant was the leader of their cell, Tawfiq Musa.

CHAPTER THIRTY-THREE

"Persons Known and Unknown"

JULY 26, 1994   ST. LOUIS

Resting her chin in her left hand, Ahlam Nijmeh sat listening thoughtfully. Her husband Saif stood at the courtroom podium as U.S. District Judge Donald Stohr apologized for "mispronouncing everyone's names." When the judge asked him if he had something to say, Saif admitted that he and "persons known and unknown" had joined an international network of terrorists, Abu Nidal.

Saif, Luie, and Tawfiq pleaded guilty to one count of RICO (racketeering) through foreign travel on behalf of ANO. The men admitted that they worked as clandestine couriers of money and information for Abu Nidal from 1986 until 1993, all for the criminal enterprise known as Abu Nidal.

The government cited many overt acts in 1987 and 1988 to the one count: the group's trip to Mexico City to meet Atta; Tawfiq's directive to Zein to destroy records of that trip; Zein's taking $20,000 into Israel; Luie's journey to Athens to meet with Samir Darwish who gave him $20,000; Saif's meeting in Lima with Samir; Tawfiq's order to Saif to destroy documents of that encounter; a co-conspirator's meeting in Algeria with Abu Nidal, ordered by Tawfiq; and Tawfiq's two trips overseas to see Thari Bek and Omar Ibrahim after which he brought letters and large amounts of cash for ANO back into the U.S.

There was no public mention of Tawfig's couriering three letters for Abu Nidal into America, an act which had led to his becoming a paid FBI informant. Tawfiq was called "The Lemon Snitch" for never providing any useful information to the FBI. He had been stopped by a U.S. Customs agent upon his return from Algiers in 1989 where ANO leaders had given him three letters to deliver in the United States.

(Zein also had met with upper echelon ANO leaders in Algiers.) Less than a year later, FBI agents speaking Arabic made a little visit to Tawfiq in Racine, saying they had copies of those three letters.

Tawfiq, who was "on a fishing expedition within the Palestinian community during the Gulf War," had not wanted to cooperate with the Bureau. The Feds had bestowed upon him the code name of Drummer because Tawfiq was to be their salesman drumming up business. Instead, Tawfiq let them pay his overdue bills to turn his phone back on and took their money, some $5,000 to $7,000, for two years. In return, he gave minimal, if any, information, which is why he was indicted along with his cellmates. "The Bureau has many Islamic snitches, most of whom lie," one Justice official commented dryly.

The trio had decided to avoid a lengthy and expensive trial by accepting the good deal their attorneys had worked out for them. Upper-upper echelon Justice officials had approved the plea agreement the night before the pleas. Negotiations for the plea bargain had begun after a tragic mishap a year earlier. A few months after she finished writing the original grand jury indictment, Mary Lawton, of the Office of Intelligence and Policy Review that oversees FISA cases in the Department of Justice, had undergone surgery. While she was home recuperating, a blood clot formed and flowed to her brain, causing an aneurysm and killing the attorney in her late fifties. After her death, DOJ basically abandoned the case; only one attorney helped the St. Louis Attorney's office on what was essentially a four-prosecutor team case. Lawton, a brilliant attorney, was one of the four people who could cow the CIA.

For three years, the CIA had made the Abu Nidal case almost unprosecutable: They did not want to allow any of their documents or informants or sources to be presented in court, such as the ten photographs shot by an Agency contract person in Mexico City. There would have been "serious evidentiary problems in presenting in open court documents seized from Samir Darwish involving the four men from Beitin." (One Middle East and CIA specialist, Mark Perry, had hypothesized that the original April Fool's indictment was CIA contaminated.) "They didn't want it out what they do to get information," one official said. "All they care about is intelligence. They don't give a hoot about prosecution," the source added. "And they hate the FBI, who had tipped them off by telex how to get Atta and Darwish arrested."

The Israelis and Venezuelans, on the other hand, helped as much as they could on the case. The latter offered up their photographs of Atta's room and the items, such as his little black book, seized during his arrest.

By spring of 1993, doctors were debating whether his diabetic strokes had incapacitated Zein Isa so much he was unable to stand trial. Zein had been in and out of a special prison hospital where his heart had stopped a time or two. Whether Zein was unfit by illness or by his own hand remained a secret. Some said he refused insulin and ate candy bars from the prison canteen to exacerbate his diabetes. Worried he might have to stop a trial mid-way, Judge Stohr told counsel he did not want to try the case several times. Defense attorneys for the other three men would be elated if Zein could not stand trial.

A few months before the trial was to begin September 19, the lead prosecutor, Assistant U.S. Attorney Jim Steitz withdrew from the case, to go on the bench as an administrative law judge. The defense counsel then made their pitch to the prosecution team, now consisting of Mark Eggert, Kenneth Tihen, and former U.S. Attorney Tom Dittmeier who had returned to the fold. The three federal prosecutors agreed to file a superseding Criminal Information that would override the original indictment. And the three defense lawyers agreed their clients would plead guilty to the charges in the Information. The maximum the men could be sentenced to would be twenty years. Zein might plea at some undetermined future date, if at all. Some attorneys predicted he would never plea when he had nothing to lose by a long trial.

But the U.S. Attorney, the FBI, and the CIA would. Why reveal top clearance documents and special informants to convict a dying man on death row? Why reveal their sources? "The pleas kept the government from making hard choices," said one highly placed official. "You have to balance national security versus the convictions, especially that of a sick old man."

All that the U.S. Attorney's office announced was that these were the first convictions in America of Abu Nidal terrorists. And that these were hard won, the joint effort of the U.S. Attorney of Eastern Missouri, the FBI, the State Department, the CIA, the Terrorism and Violent Crime Section of the Justice Department, and the intelligence agencies of "several foreign countries."

*   *   *

At four minutes past ten, the morning of July 26, Tawfiq, Saif, and Luie walked into the courtroom smiling broadly, waving, and greeting their family with, "Sa-lem [Peace]." Their family—Saif and Luie's father Hassan, their mother, two sisters and Ahlam (Sausan, Luie's wife was back in Beitin), and a sister's husband—smiled back. The eight deputy marshals carefully noted this exchange of pleasantries while court watchers stared at the terrorists.

They looked like prosperous businessmen attending a civic luncheon. All three dressed in dark suits, white shirts, and tasteful ties. Their hair was cut short and simply, although the back of Luie's curled over his shirt collar. Tawfiq had shaven his mustache. Saif sported eyeglasses in traditional black frames. In a word, they were clean-cut. With prison pallor, they were now lighter-complected than the suntanned and freckled Irish-American FBI agents in court, something Tom Newman noticed.

What one prosecutor noticed was how much eye make-up the Nijmeh women wore and how, despite their white hijabs, the four women were fashionably dressed Western style. Ahlam, thin, in a smart straight ankle-length navy skirt with a kick-pleat walked out with her sister-in-law/cousin who was chic in pleated pants.

While the family was jubilant—Saif, Luie, and Tawfiq would be released before Ramadan—their attorneys were less than ebullient. For fifteen months, they had been revving up into high gear for the trial which would have begun in seven weeks.

"I was so primed for trial," Keith Liberman told Neil Bruntrager. "I'd been so worried with performance anxiety about the trial. Now I feel deflated."

Bruntrager shook his head. "It feels like coitus interruptus."

As the deputy marshals manacled them to take back to jail, the three defendants discussed what kinds of women they wanted the night they were freed:

"I like Italian," Saif said.

"Me, I want a Mexican girl," Tawfiq announced.

"What about you?" a deputy asked Luie. "You look like a real lady-killer."

"No," Luie quipped. "You're thinking of Zein Isa."

                        *   *   *

Less than a month later, the U.S. Government dropped its terrorist case against Zein Hassan Isa on August 16. One of the prosecutors told Tim Bryant at the *Post-Dispatch* that an official in the Justice Department weighed the additional factor that Zein's death penalty was unlikely to be reversed on appeal and his health was poor. Why waste an exorbitant amount of money and reveal secret sources?

The day Tawfiq, Luie, and Saif were sentenced, October 21, 1994, the Jewish community nationwide was outraged. "These people don't want peace [in the Middle East]; they've targeted Jewish communities across the world—London, Beunos Aires," said Stephanie Seleman of the Anti Defamation League and B'nai Brith of St. Louis, and Avi Goldfarb, an Israeli now with the Jewish Federation of St. Louis, said on the courthouse steps. "We'd hoped this case would shed light how terrorism has reached North America." Indeed, the national ADL, the ADL Leon and Marilyn Klinghoffer Foundation, in a letter urged U.S. Attorney General Janet Reno to appeal the incredibly light sentences imposed by U.S. District Judge Donald Stohr. "This is precisely the wrong signal to send concerning . . . terrorism."

Facing a maximum of twenty years, Tawfiq, Saif, and Luie had been sentenced to twenty-one months, with the clock starting with their April Fool's arrest. Three days later, on October 24, the men were quietly released from prison. They had spent less time in a cell than Steitz had preparing their case for indictment and trial.

These were the men deemed so dangerous—they allegedly had conspired to kill Tina and "any and all Jews"—that after their indictments, the U.S. Marshal in St. Louis had ordered a security threat analysis. Then, deputy U.S. Marshals had videotaped the homes of the federal prosecutors, agents, and judge in case of "hostage situations." These homes also were installed with very high-level security systems. The prosecutors and judge were allowed to carry guns, if they wished. Their families were "terrified" by these measures.

Actually, there was another Abu Nidal member now freed from prison who was more threatening than Tawfiq, Saif, or Luie.

"You gotta be kidding me!" said one of the federal prosecutors when he learned the news. Neither the U.S. Attorney's office nor the FBI office in St. Louis knew until called by the defense and a reporter who had heard it from Ramsey Clark's office: Mahmoud Atta had been released. The Israeli Supreme Court had overturned Atta's 1990 conviction on September 29, 1994, ruling that there was "insufficient evidence," according to a terse paragraph in the *Jerusalem Post*. The Supreme Court ruled one of the witnesses was unreliable. Details were unavailable; an Israeli official, asking to remain anonymous, said even he had been unable to find out anything.

"He's an American citizen, he has an American passport, he can come back here," Tom Newman said, shaking his head. "He has been here before, three times," a source said. The first time was around 1986 when the surveillance began. "Here's a real terrorist," Steitz remarked. "Zein described the bus attack to Soraia and Amjad, saying Atta had done it. What insufficient evidence?"

"There's an abundance of evidence against Atta," said Atta's former prosecutor Jacques Semmelman. "His two cousins signed affadavits. One made a videotaped confession in which he reenacted the crime. Which our trial judge noted negated the premise the cousin had been beaten into confession. I hear they now have recanted." Semmelman was trying to obtain a full transcript of the court decision. Semmelman added, "I think the mentality in Israel is the court wants to bend over backwards to show how equitable it is toward Arabs."

Even if Atta was somehow cleared of the Dir Abu Mishal incident, what about all those documents seized in Caracas?

Israeli terrorism expert Dr. Ariel Merari of Tel Aviv University said there had been no outcry in Israel over Atta's release. "Atta was an ANO member, a recruiter, whether or not he participated in this attack," Dr. Merari explained. "ANO is still in business, although weakened since 1988," he said. Followers continue to work in Lebanon where they train their militia, Libya, Iran, and Latin America and Europe, although several members had been expelled from Germany in early October. "They are still capable of carrying out attacks," Dr. Merari said. "The internal infrastructure is still there."

The secret photographs of Zein, Luie, Saif, and Mahmoud Atta happily "smelling the air" in Mexico City would be hidden away forever in packing boxes of classified documents. Sealed with it, too, would be the nationality of the spies who had pursued Atta across oceans and seas to take this picture. Had Zein and his cohorts been truly covert and less garrulous in discussing this meeting as well as the one with Samir Darwish, perhaps Abu Nidal would have taken deeper root in the New World.

ANO was largely stopped here by the FBI. How that happened will partially remain shrouded in classified files. One theory is that as men signed up to become comrades of al-Banna, informants turned their names over to the FBI, who put every one of them under strict surveillance. This was a wonderfully successful operation, one the Bureau can never publicly take credit for while they are blamed for Tina's murder. Had Jim Nelson and Tom Newman been in the St. Louis office, she might have been saved.

The case per se in St. Louis is not closed. "We'e increased our interest in terrorism," Jim Nelson said the day of the Abu Nidal sentencing. "There is not a terrorist group in the world that does not receive funding from the U.S. Hamas obtains substantial funding in America. Often, they collect money [as Zein used to do] saying it's for widows and orphans, and that's just a front."

The 1994 Crime Bill bans giving money to a terrorist group; the penalty is a ten-year prison sentence. "But that's going to be hard to prove—did someone knowingly donate money to such a group? What if there's a new group, not on the list?" Nelson said. Steitz added, "We need a separate anti-terrorist law.

"Terrorists move from one organization as it dies out to another. The premise is the same—anti-Israel, anti-Jewish, and anti-American."

The Final Secret

Lurid murder cases are "relived" on tabloid television, the modern equivalent of the old-fashioned circus sideshow. "Ladies and gentlemen, here inside this tent you'll see real deformities of nature," only instead of the bearded lady, we are offered an intimate glimpse of a murderer: A tender-hearted, doting father who slew his beloved daughter one midnight.

There is no nobility in Zein Isa, nothing to transcend his loss, no ancient themes from the Sacrifice of Isaac nor the Sacrifice of Iphigenia nor from *King Lear*.

Tina's murder was rooted in her father's failings as a man. He was weak. He was nihilistic. To him, if one was a Jewish schoolchild or a defiant daughter, one was an object that did not deserve to live. There were no innocents in the war against Israel, no innocence in a girl who threatened his honor. He refused to see that the world is not one of absolutes, black and white. Tina, who lived in the postmodern world of grays, challenged Zein, and being stronger-willed, would have won. The family secrets were a prologue to her death. He killed her to redeem himself.

And by doing so, damned his wife.

In Israel and in the West Bank, a group of Israeli Arab women are working to make certain that no more Tina Isas—or any women for that matter—will be murdered in an honor killing in their country.

It began with a group of Muslim Arab men eating desserts in a Haifa restaurant called Al Fanar—"The Lighthouse"—in 1989. One of the men wanted to kill his sister to avenge his family honor. After his friends agreed to help, they attacked the woman with knives.

Her murder caused a group of women to band together to found an organization that fights against honor killings, forced marriages, wife beating, control of women's behavior by gossip and slander, taking girls

out of school to become house slaves, and a lack of educational opportunities for women. The group calls itself Al Fanar, in memory of that
honor killing.

One of its founders, Tamam Fahiliya, received death threats, and
her apartment was broken into. She was admonished that women are
supposed to be subject to the will of men. The Fundamentalist Islamic
movement has been most vitriolic in its attacks against Al Fanar.

Yet one former mayor in the West Bank publicly expressed support
and men have begun joining their marches. And the Arab press has
written stories against domestic violence and runs the group's ads.

But the charges against Al Fanar and other women's groups continue: that they are traitors to the Palestinian cause, that they are playing into the hands of the Israelis revealing the sins of the Arab world.
Tamam Fahiliya told the *Jerusalem Post*, "Until now, not one has stood
up and publicly condemned [honor killings]. Anyone who stays silent
is a collaborator."

A Palestinian man who works for UNWRA (United Nations Work
and Relief Agency) believes that Palestinian women are making the
same mistake Algerian women made during their fight for independence from the Colonial French. Those women acquired tremendous
freedoms during the Algerian war, when they were needed. But they
failed to press for their rights afterward, and instead appeased the men.

Shaking his head, the UNWRA official said, "Today, they're behind
the veil again."

For the sisters so afraid Tina's shame would stain their honor for generations so that no one would seek their daughters' hands in marriage,
life has become very hard indeed. They are now pariahs, more isolated
than even before. Friendly and eager to please before the Abu Nidal
indictments, they have since practically cloistered themselves, reluctant to talk to outsiders. No one knows what they are thinking, or suffering.

Do they wonder what would have happened to their dead sister?
Would Tina, who would have graduated college in 1994, be a pilot now
flying to Paris as she longed to do?

Their mother Maria seems safer and happier in prison than she did
living with Zein for three decades. Life is more secure. Whether after
her re-sentencing she is allowed to live the rest of her life in prison, or

whether after about seven years of appeals she is executed, Maria may be living with the harshest sentence of all:

Laying her head down each night and wondering if she will hear Tina cry out again, "Mama, save me! Help me, Mama, help me!"

And as Zein Isa slumbers, what images arise unbidden from the secret places in his soul?

Acknowledgments

There are a few people who were essential to this manuscript. Foremost is my editor, Lisa Drew, who foresaw this project as a complex one that worked on several levels within one narrative story. When I couldn't see the trees for the leaves—thinking I'd brilliantly whittled down to five pages my twenty pages on Palestinian embroidery—Lisa gently pointed out the tree branches. I have yet to meet anyone who can juggle so many different projects and yet, when I'd call after months of silence with an obscure problem, could immediately resolve it with no preamble. Lisa was always there with encouragement and enthusiasm, even for late-breaking chapters that threw off the production schedule. And in an age when people get back to you days later, Lisa calls back to say when she'll be able to really talk.

Katherine Boyle, the assistant editor, helped cut and paste as well as ferrying me through the shoals of publishing details that felt like they would swamp the project.

Since 1989, Harry Hegger has said the Isa case is a good story. He never said no whenever I needed some police report or doublechecked some fact, and suggested I meet with Sam Jackson before I began research in the West Bank.

In 1991, there were three journalists and two academics who led the way with Middle Eastern connections. Repps Hudson of the *Post-Disptach* editorial page plied me with books and names—such as Howard Goller in the Reuter's bureau in Jerusalem, who suggested I talk with Majorie Olster who was working on an honor killing piece, and Sami Aboudi who sent me to Bethleham University. There Professors Bernard Sabella and Adnan Musalem kindly arranged for me to meet with other faculty—Suda Hindiyeh, Vivian Khamis, Khader Musleh—as well as students.

Hudson also sent me to Radwan Abu Ayyash, who made certain I never went into the villages alone. He recommended my photographer-cum-field producer Rula Halawani who in turn set up interviews with Palestinian leaders, journalists, and women Tina's age who all wish to remain nameless.

The second journalist was Orayb Najjar, an academic at DeKalb Univeristy, who recommended Kamal as well as Islah Jad and Lisa Taraki, professors at Bir Zeit Univeristy. In turn, Taraki suggested interviews at the Friends School.

A chance meeting with film director Elia Sides led to Israeli Arab professional women for interviews as well as the Israeli authors Yurim Binur and David Grossman and the famed Professor Joseph Ginat at Haifa. Sides also generously acted as a big brother. Ginat's interview and works were critical to this book.

Journalist and author Mark Perry generously helped with contacts as well as pointing out that this case was "CIA contaminated."

The two academics who offered the basic background with which to begin research were Prof. Victor LeVine, Political Science, Washington University, and Prof. Robert Kupperman of the Center for Strategic and International Studies. Prof. LeVine gave a reading list, loaned books, and read this manuscript and all with good humor.

313

Lou Stephens offered leads and direction on FISA and terrorism. Poor ol' kindly Judge Kinder, as he calls himself, read every draft and daily discussed The Book. Bob Craddick, Neil Bruntrager, Jacques Semmelman, Linda Murphy, Keith Liberman, Ramsey Clark, Jim Steitz, and Judge Charles Shaw helped with the trials; Meg Crane and John McGuire provided advanced hand-holding and suggestions; Sue Hubbell and John Lutz made some more; Judge Theodore McMillian explained legal issues; and David Rosen, others; Sharon Tettenhorst has essential contacts for whatever book I'm writing; Sam Jackson and his cousin Al Christian, who revealed the other stories; Tom Murphy and Mike Tully, who helped every which way they could; Jim Steitz, Mark Eggert, Bill Francis, and Jim Nelson answered as many questions as they could; David Capes gave expertise in criminal law; Bob Mohme took on a slumlord; Helena Mylonas, who must have suffered painful recollections in our many conversations; Tina's mother, Maria Isa, and her sisters, Mona and Leilah, were very generous in providing background as well as enjoyable to spend many afternoons with. Mike Wolfe, the legal counsel to Governor Carnahan, helped also.

I also would like to thank: Buck Ravell; Candy Green, Charles Poole, Christine Nelson, Mike Guzy, Billy Qualls, Jim Scego, Steve Sorocko with the St. Louis Police; Mohammed Mosad, Michael Bobroff, Al Schweitzer, Cliff Walker, Dan Reardon, Charlie Shaw, Batya Abramson-Goldstein, Paul Schoomer, Judge Paul Simon, Judge Terry Adelman, Christy Marshall, Tom Dittmeier, Jane Kochman, Tracy Baum, Loretta Flynn at St. Louis Public Library, Helen Simpson, Steve Higgins, Michael Newmark, Lenny Frankel, Don Wolff, Ruth Yaron, and Susan Weis of the Israeli Embassy, Heim Koren of the Israeli consulate, Brian Goeke, Vincent Cannistraro, Ed Dowd, Georgia Clark, Jack Gabryelski, Jane Johansen, Herb Humphries, Bob Tseuscher, Sue Fadem, Rita Wells, Deborah Parks, Connie Gibstine, Carlos Martinez, Prof. Keshavaraz, P. Katrinka Wall, and Circe Wall.

Felice Javit made the vetting process less tortuous.

Friends who literally put me up for extended stays—Ellen and Byron Kinder in Jefferson City, Barbara and Nelson Rosenbaum in Washington, and Andy Drexler in New York.

Judge Kinder always says, "Make a list of your friends. Your enemies, you'll remember. But it's a terrible thing to forget a friend." If I've forgotten anyone, I apologize.

NOTES

NOTES ON SOURCES

The following Isa relatives provided extensive information: Maria, Faisal, Mona, Leilah, Fayrouz, Soraia Salem, Sausan Nijmeh, Youssef Nijmeh, and five other (anonymous) relatives. Tina's closest friends, Cliff Walker and Helena Mylanos, and soccer mate Jeannie Chapman helped on details.

Two young women from Beitin, interviewed in Beit Hanina, who wished to remain anonymous as did four other young professionals who were Palestinian and Israeli Arab women.

Faculty and students at the Friends School, Ramallah, West Bank, gave interviews also.

In East Jerusalem: Zahira Kamal, Hanan Bakr, Sami Ashasha, Rula Halawani, Natalie Albina, Ahmed Saif, and Ollie Kadan.

At Bethlehem University: Professors Suda Hindiyeh, Vivian Khamis, Adnan Musalem, Khader Musleh, and Bernard Sabella, who is the chairman of the sociology department there.

At Bir Zeit University: Professors Lisa Taraki and Islah Jad.

For those interested in the criminalization of honor killings, visit Al Haq, Law in the Service of Man Library, in Ramallah.

Defense Attorneys: Ramsey Clark, Charles M. Shaw, Daniel Reardon, Linda Murphy, Neil Bruntrager, Keith Liberman, and Donald Wolff.

St. Louis Police: Capt. Harry Hegger, Sgt. Michael Guzy, Sgt. Billy Qualls, Sgt. Steve Sorocko, and Det. Sam Jackson.

St. Louis County Police: Lt. Ron Varner and Sgt. Gary Berra.

FBI: Special Agent in Charge James Nelson, St. Louis; Supr., Counter-Terrorism, Tom Newman, St. Louis; then Special Agent in Charge Oliver "Buck" Ravell, Dallas, and former FBI executive asst. director of investigations. Louis F. Stephens, former FBI supervisor, now, L.F. Stephens & Assoc.

St. Louis Circuit Atty. Dee Joyce-Hayes and Asst. Circ. Atty. Bob Craddick.

Judge Theodore McMillian, Eighth District U.S. Court of Appeals, and Judge Charles A. Shaw, Eastern District of Missouri.

U.S. Administrative Law Judge Jim Steitz, former asst. U.S. Attorney, prosecuted the Abu Nidal case.

U.S. Attorney Edward L. Dowd, Jr. and former U.S. Atty. Steve Higgins, Asst. U.S. Atty. Mark Eggert and David Capes, former assistant U.S. Attorney and lawyer in the Justice Dept. in Washington.

Jacques Semmelman, the former asst. U.S. Attorney in New York who prosecuted Mahmoud Atta, and now in private practice.

Asst. Prof. Orayb Najjar, DeKalb University.

Prof. Victor LeVine and Prof. Peter Heath, both of Washington University, as well as Mohammed Mosad, at Washington University.

Dr. Ariel Merari, Dir. of Political Violence Research Unit, Tel Aviv University.

Elia Sides of Set Productions in Jerusalem.

Prof. Joseph Ginat of Haifa University.

Dr. Robert Kupperman, Sr. Advisor, Center for Strategic and International Studies.

CIA: Vincent Cannistraro, former director of the Counter Terrorism Center, former director of Intelligence at the National Security Council. Charles Waterman, former CIA bureau chief in Beirut, now of Charles Waterman & Assoc.

Noel Koch, chief of counterterrorism for the Department of Defense under Reagan.

L. Paul Bremmer, former Ambassador-at-Large on Counter-Terrorism under Reagan.

Sources not named in the manuscript had requested that their identities remain anonymous. Similarly, relatives and friends of Tina Isa asked that their names be changed.

EPIGRAPH

The quotation from the Qur'an is Sura (Chapter) 4, verse 38, in Arberry's translation and interpretation, although Mernissi in *The Veil and the Male Elite* says it is verse 34 in Arabic.

PROLOGUE

20   The spies were fascinated . . .

From various anonymous intelligence sources. Because this incident has not been declassified, the exact date and place are not known; nor is the investigating agency. However, it should be noted that the ANO headquarters in 1986 were in Tripoli. Vincent Cannistraro believes the meeting was under technical surveillance, probably through the NSA or CIA. One highly placed person says, "Zein Isa was the linchpin to the entire Abu Nidal investigation. The CIA picked him up and in a matter of days, or the next day, the FBI found him in St. Louis."

CHAPTER TWO

Material pieced together from three anonymous sources.

CHAPTER THREE

31   The forebears of Zein Isa . . .

Some Palestinians are quite proud of their ethnically diverse blood—Canaanites, Philistines, Phoenicians, German Jews, French Crusaders, Slavic slaves, Egyptian Mamelukes, Turks, Kurds, Sau'dis, and with the Isa sisters—Italian and German. Says scholar Mohammed Musad, "Purity of race does not exist. Who wants it? My family runs all the gamut of coloring from blue-eyed blondes to swarthy brunettes." A woman told me that she had siblings who were blue-eyed blondes "from our German Jewish grandmother." While the name "Palestinian" is derived from the tribe of Philistines that lived on the coast, no one tribe is believed native to the area in the Judean Hills. Zein's son and daughters say the Isas moved to Beitin from a nearby village, Borqa, within the last few hundred years. The Isas belonged to a clan called Yemeni, with the sub-clan of Jeraba, a large extended family, all related through the father's side. There had been a feud in Borqa between the Yemeni and the Kayses with the Yemeni losing and forced to flee. The sheikh of nearby el-Bireh gave the wanderers some land.

Jacob's tale may have had additional meaning for Zein Isa. According to local custom, Jacob dreamt of his ladder rising to Heaven on the site of Zein's village, Beitin. The Israelis disagree; they have a village nearby called Beth El, meaning "house of God" and they say Jacob slept here. Archeology in Israel and the Occupied Territories is less academic than a recorder of deeds contest over whom orginially owned the land. Regardless of where Jacob really rested that night thousands of years ago, there are a number of alleged Biblical sites in Beitin. For example, a crumbling watch tower associated with Jacob. Beneath its pile of stones dating back thousands of years, villagers say there is a cow of gold. Within walking distance is an ancient tree marking a well where Jacob's grandfather Abraham is said to have sipped the waters.

32 South of Jacob's Shechem . . . lies the West Bank village of Beitin . . .

The stretch from Jerusalem south to Bethlehem and north to Ramallah has many Christian Arabs. Two prominent ones are PLO spokeswoman Hanan Ashrawi, who also is a literature professor at Bir Zeit University, and is from Ramallah, and Edward Said, distinguished author and professor at Columbia University, who was born in Jerusalem. In this century, many Christians around Ramallah emigrated to Europe and America. In Bethlehem, the Christian Brothers order established a university there. The Christians and Jews integrated and intermarried, to some degree. Israeli Arabs are often Christian, too. Both Christians and Muslims use Arabic versions of Biblical Hebrew names, eg. "Musa" from Moses, "Daoud" from David, "Sulieman" from Solomon, "Mariam" for Miriam or Mary, "Sausan" for Susanna (and also the flower, black-eyed susan.)

33 . . . a Mediterranean farmhouse . . .

Which I visited and found quite impressive. The interior has fourteen-foot ceilings with one tile floor patterned like an oriental rug. The huge double iron doors are pressed into rosette patterns.

33 Neither woman learned to read and write . . .

The often religious, illiterate villagers may pray five times a day to Allah, but, commented one Palestinian, they cannot understand their prayers: Written Arabic is Classical Arabic. Spoken Arabic is vernacular. And there is a difference between what is called town Arabic and village Arabic.

34 Youssef Nijmeh . . . "This is your land."

For futher understanding of this perspective, read Rubenstein's *The People of Nowhere*, especially, chap. 1–4.

35 Maria's paternal grandmother was "half Indian but not black, no black in our family." Her father's parents grew bananas, pineapples, oranges, and onions in a mountain valley in southern Brazil. Maria's mother's family owned a larger farm

with six families working for them. For one wedding, Maria's grandmother cooked a cow, three pigs, thirty-six chickens and baked a huge sack of cookies.
36 They honeymooned for a month . . .
      That was in San Luis, then they moved to Rondapolis where lots of Palestinians from the West Bank lived, working hard at menial jobs and as itinerant salesmen. The Isas socialized with his friends from the homeland.

CHAPTER FOUR

37 . . . Zein's first wife, Foiziya, wept.
      Faisal Isa, as well as other villagers in Beitin.
41 Most of his countrymen . . . driving them.
      Carlos Martinez.
42 . . . notorious black market . . . shut it down.
      Carlos Martinez, Mark Perry, Louis F. Stephens. Kupperman cites the "sloppy" INS that allowed a couple dozen Iranian terrorists to enter the U.S. as students in 1989, p. 46.
42 . . . many government papers . . .
      Buck Ravell, 6/25/93 interview. To qualify for an American passport required that you be breathing, says one U.S. Senate aide. "INS itself to date, in 1993, has been woefully behind. This was the agency that brought you Sheik Abdul Rahmann despite a State Department warning. If you liked Dickens, then you'll love INS. They still handcarry files around. And there are no duplicates." While Vietnamese boat people could not land, the Statue of Liberty was waiting with open arms for fanatical bombers.
      According to government papers, when Atta applied for U.S. citizenship, he lied on one form, not mentioning the trips he had taken outside the U.S: Valentine's Day, 1974, Atta left Israel for Puerto Rico; April 17, 1974, he registered as an immigrant there; May 11, 1975, he left Puerto Rico. May 28, 1975, he returned on Iberia Airlines; July 10, 1976, he flew to the West Bank; Sept. 10, 1976, he returned to Puerto Rico, saying the purpose of his trip was to renew his Israeli I.D. card and bring his wife with him; August 25, 1980, he left Puerto Rico for a proposed three-month visit to his family in Dir Abu Mishal; June 19, 1981, Atta asked for extension to stay in the West Bank which was permitted; 1981, no date, Atta returned to Puerto Rico; January 27, 1982, he applied for naturalization; March 30, 1982, he was sworn in as a United States citizen; 1982, no date, Atta returned to the West Bank.
      No return date to U.S., yet in 1984, he went back to Israel. Semmelman said Atta had four passports that he knew of.

CHAPTER FIVE

For further explanation of treatment of women, read Najjar's interview with Zahira Kamal.
45 At al-Dar Abu Faisal, Zein's co-wives . . .
      Actually, this was not the first time they had all lived together, but the other two times had been visits.

45 My heart was black . . .

    Warnock, p. 34. This woman told Warnock she'd decided to get along with the
    co-wife because, "It's no good throwing stones into the well you have to drink out
    of."

45 When a Muslim couple. . .

    Men are automatically awarded custody of their children. Warnock, p. 43–44;
    personal status laws in the West Bank then were governed by Jordanian interpre-
    tation of Islamic law by which a mother only received custody at the judge's dis-
    cretion. And she lost custody upon remarriage.

46 While the Qur'an . . . antiquated custom.

    "My father's uncle had three wives," one woman told me in al-Bireh. "And
    they were like eight-hour shifts." A recent case involved a doctor in Ramallah
    whose first wife was barren after twenty years. He did not want to divorce her as
    he was fond of her and she had nowhere to go, no family to support her. So, he
    built a two-level house, one floor for his old wife and one for his new bride. He
    alternated living with the two women. The second wife understood. As for the
    first woman, she took two of the four children born of the latter union and raised
    them as her own. They called her mother. When their husband died, instead of
    spliting up his home, his two widows continued to live together.

47 . . . there was system to protect her . . . never told her

    Interview with Orayb Najjar.

49 . . . the average woman is worse off . . . earlier age.

    Attorney Hanan Rayan.

49 One Palestinian study . . .

    Najjar, p. 60, quoting Najah Manasrah's 1989 survey.

50 . . . rise in second wives . . .

    Rayan.

50 The incidence of battered. . .

    Re increase in physical abuse and rape, anonymous Arabic social worker and
    anonymous attorneys.

51 . . . in Nablus, a father walled up his daughter.

    This story was told to me by several sources, including Ginat, and in his book,
    p. 140, case XLV; also told to author by Zahara Kamal, exec. dir. of Palestinian
    Federation of Women's Action Committees and former member of the delegation
    to the Madrid peace setttlement.

55 . . . $30,000 in taxes.

    Conversation #18 of the FBI tapes used in preparing the state murder trial, p.
    65. This tape was not presented in court and therefore is not dated. Nor was it
    cited in the nine-volume FBI tapes that the government declassified to use in the
    terrorist trial.

56 ". . . when tracing membership . . . over ideology."

    Charles Waterman.

CHAPTER SIX

For additional reading, see Warnock's interviews with Palestinian women on marriage
customs, and Najjar's introduction.

60 "I won't let my daughter date . . ."
     Anonymous academic.
61 While courtship varies . . . which Daoud's family pays.
     Anonymous source.
63 . . . the bridegroom is as virginal . . . match only burns once.
     Interview with same man. Warnock, pp. 29–32, describes marriage customs
including, p. 31, a relatively public defloration.

CHAPTER SEVEN

Much of the background material on Sabri al-Banna comes from Patrick Seale's *Abu
Nidal: A Gun for Hire*. His childhood and early adulthood, descriptions of his tortures
and terrorist attacks are all from Seale. For an insightful explanation of how ANO
arose from the tradition of tribal feuds and lack of democratic process within the PLO,
read Schiller's essay in *Inside Terrorist Organizations*. Also peruse Kupperman and
Kamen in *Final Warning*.
66 . . . purged through 1988.
     Seale p. 289
66 Abu Nidal's level of torture . . . skillet.
     Seale p. 286
66 . . . death toll . . .
     FBI, Seale, and U.S. State Dept. Kupperman puts the death count at 300,650
wounded in 20 countries, p. 43. He also notes that ANO has hit or threatened
every moderate Arab nation, from Egypt to the Gulf emirates, p. 43.
67 "Abu Nidal is an honored member . . . between him and you."
     FBI Tapes, 1/25/89.
68 ANO was extorting $15 million dollars . . . freelance killing.
     Interview with Kupperman.
68 . . . President Assad . . . near Beirut.
     New York Times, 5/1/94 p. 4A
68 . . . fall of Soviet Union . . .
     Oliver Ravell.
68 Some CIA consultants . . .
     Charles Waterman.
68 . . . run by Samir Darwish . . . the Revolutionary Council.
     Seale, pp. 212, 326.
69 . . . have numerous names and aliases.
     To wit in the FBI transcripts: Luie Nijmeh whose real name is Louqai: Al
Atassi and Lulu. Tawfiq Musa: Sabu Shanab (the one with the mustache), Tony,
Abu Mazin (his son Mazin is also Matthew), Abul Huda which is Zein's little joke
as Tawfiq Abul Huda was prime minister of Jordan. Zein said, "I give them an old
system" for names. Samir Darwish was called Al Samra and El Weher. Another
man was Abu Zibdeh (butterball, literally, father of fat).
69 After the *Achille Lauro* . . . breaking up Abu Nidal.
     Interview with Mark Perry, August, 1993.
69 They had been exchanging information since the 1970s.
     Interview with Radwan Abu Ayyash in East Jerusalem, October, 1992.

69 While terrorist devoteés . . . Athens and Madrid . . .
    Athens, for example, has been especially notorious, see Kupperman, p. 60.
69 . . . counter-terrorist specialists . . . Brazil and Peru.
    Perry.
69 With the arrest of Samir . . . before he was arrested.
    FBI Tapes, 8/5/88.
69 "I have a hundred names . . . father of daughters."
    FBI Tapes, 8/19/88.
70 "If a man's family is starving . . ."
    FBI Tapes, 1/25/89.
70 "The comrades who were with us in Iraq . . . he will rise up."
    FBI Tapes, 1/25/89.
71 "It's categorically forbidden . . . Everyone is being watched."
    FBI Tapes, 7/8/87.
71 Tawfiq yelled at Luie . . . sent a fax about Luie to Israel.
    FBI Tapes, 5/26/88.
71 As a security precaution . . . random calls.
    Interview with Kupperman, August, 1993.
71 Saif Nijmeh fretted about . . . Jordanian intelligence.
    FBI Tapes, 10/31/87.
71 What governments often do . . . not compromised per se.
    Interview with Kupperman, August, 1993.
71 . . . if he knew . . . we would kill him.
    FBI Tapes, 10/31/87.
71 Another friend was so sadistic . . . "let the rats eat him!"
    FBI Tapes, 1/23/89.
72 . . . the youth can select . . . college.
    FBI Tapes, 5/9/88.
72 Kennedy's Inaugural Address . . . cause the PLO to investigate.
    FBI Tapes, 1/23/89.
73 Three cousins waited . . . track down Atta.
    Israeli documents presented by the U.S. Attorneys' office, in the Atta extradi-
    tion case, courtesy of Ramsey Clark.

CHAPTER EIGHT

78 St. Louis of all places . . .
    Actually, St. Louis has a sizeable Arabic population, according to the U.S. Census
    Bureau, about five thousand in the five Missouri counties in and around St. Louis. But
    the numbers are not broken down by country and that would not help considering
    many Palestinians would list themselves as Jordanians. There were worlds of dif-
    ference between a sixth-generation Lebanese-American—a Maronite Christian
    whose family fled Lebanon in the 1850s to avoid religious persecution from the
    Muslims and whose father is a well-liked appellate judge—and the Isa sisters.
    Within the medical schools at Washington University and St. Louis University, there
    is a coterie of Middle Eastern doctors in the St. Louis area, but some of them are only
    thought to be Arab. Many physicians are Iranian and as Iranians are acid-quick to

point out, they are not Arabs but Persians; they do not speak Arabic, their native tongue is Pharsi. They are not the same religion, they are Shi'ite Muslim whereas the Moslem denomination in the Levant is Sunni. Confusing Shi'ite with Sunni is akin to saying Catholics are the same as Presbyterians because they are all Christian.

If democratic principles had been sancrosanct, Zein probably would have joined the PLO for the Palestinians along with the Israelis are the most democratic societies in the Middle East. Which is why the rest of the Arab world—dictatorships mostly—hate them, according to Sami Mishasha of United Nations Relief and Works Agency.

78 Zein's English . . . Flowers.
       Police report.
79 Neighbors claimed . . . one customer said.
       Anonymous interviews by author, John McGuire, Tom Murphy, and Mike Tully.
79 For Zein . . . "the Jews."
       FBI Tapes, 2/15/87.
79 . . . he rarely attended services . . . mosque.
       Anonymous sources.
79 Before the Intifada . . . disaster.
       Anonymous Palestinian journalist.
81 "You know when . . . prayers."
       Helena Mylanos.
83 About this time . . . the deal.
       Helena Mylanos.
83 Zein quickly . . . in return.
       Lisa Taraki.
83 Zein said, . . ." . . . American stores."
       FBI Tapes, 2/6/87.
83 "He's not allowed back . . . did something."
       Anonymous interview.
83 Maria was driving . . . hung out with terrorists.
       Two anonymous interviews.
84 Seated around . . . "to make fun."
       FBI Tapes, 2/15/87.
84 One night . . . "know anything!"
       FBI Tapes, 1/29/87.
84 "One time he left . . . jail?"
       FBI Tapes, 5/22/87.

CHAPTER NINE

85 Zein was arrested . . . "my ass."
       FBI Tapes, 2/6/87.
85 Zein loved traveling . . . Atta.
       FBI Tapes, 2/6/87.
86 The man about town . . . with his son's in-laws.
       FBI Tapes, 2/6/87.

86   ... who later sent Zein ... the West Bank.
         FBI Tapes, 2/14/88.
86   ... his in-laws warned ... always looking.
         FBI Tapes, 2/6/87.
86   Abu Nidal Organization ran ... really did need the money.
         Cannistraro.
86   Especially if it wanted ... shops and schools.
         FBI Tapes, 5/9/88.
86   Zein willingly underwent ... starving in West Bank towns.
         FBI Tapes, 12/26/86.
86   "My position is one of great secrecy ... my phones ... are dirty."
         FBI Tapes, 4/11/87.
86   Zein quipped, "We are honored."
         FBI Tapes, 4/11/87.
         Yet, Zein and his relatives frequently discussed Abu Nidal terrorist attacks in
     Europe, and one in a West Bank restaurant, ANO conferences in Algeria and
     details of the ANO hierarchy. A comrade reported to him how an ANO faction
     from Zein's town machine gunned the American ambassador and his staff in
     Cairo; none were killed.
87   "So, we didn't have the honor," ... Zein.
         FBI Tapes, 5/28/87.
87   "We have exported numerous massacres ... Let the world burn."
         FBI Tapes, 12/26/86.
87   He said he had been a member ... joined up about 1983.
         FBI Tapes, 5/30/87.
87   Mona argued with him ... "shit over the store and the house."
         FBI Tapes, 4/22/87 and 6/1/87.
88   Zein hung up ... if she could not.
         FBI Tapes, 4/3/87.
88   Zein discussed ... mature enough.
         FBI Tapes, 4/6/87.
88   But his business trip "to open a store" in Mexico City did not coincide with her
     spring break.
         FBI Tapes, 4/5/87.
88   Zein left alone to meet Atta at the Hotel Marine in Antonio Caso, near the Mexico
     City airport.
         FBI Tapes, 4/23/87.
89   Tina ... "all that stuff."
         FBI Tapes, 4/22/87.
89   This meeting ... vulnerable to attack.
         Federal grand jury indictment, signed, 4/1/93 and anonymous sources.
         The photographs were taken by the CIA, according to sources, and remain classified.
89   Zein called his wife ... April 26.
         FBI Tapes, 4/25/87.
90   Unable to perform ... "This life is bullshit."
         Tina Woodall.
91   ... she was marching off ... "I want to die."
         Anonymous source.

CHAPTER TEN

93 Mahmoud Atta picked . . . in Manhattan.
    Israeli documents and other court papers in Atta's extradition case, courtesy of
    Ramsey Clark.
94 The Venezuelan newspaper clips are missing the masthead which would identify
    them. They were translated by Al Schweitzer.
94 "Remember the bridegroom . . . and pitch them."
    FBI Tapes, 5/8/87.
94 Zein had a copy of Atta's little black book . . . signed "by true names."
    FBI Tapes, 11/26/87.
94 Zein was open and indiscriminate . . . Dir Abu Mishal.
    FBI Tapes, 6/22/87 and 7/8/87.
94 Tawfiq cursed . . . just proud.
    FBI Tapes, 9/19/87.
94 Tawfiq had reason to be anxious . . . sue the FBI.
    FBI Tapes, 10/13/87, 10/31/87 and intermittently during the fall, 1987.
95 Saif fretted . . . "I'll insult his mother."
    FBI Tapes, 10/13/87. Amongst Arabs, the ultimate insult is to sexually impugn
    one's mother in crude, graphic terms.
95 A comrade remarked . . . wipe out the . . . Police Station.
    FBI Tapes, 8/27/87 and 8/29/87.
95 References to Sinbad Travel.
    FBI Tapes, 5/17/88 and 6/27/88.
95 Hussein Karitti . . . in the homeland.
    FBI Tapes, 1/27/88.
96 He (Luie) bragged in late 1987 . . .to sell "juice."
    FBI Tapes, 12/13. Luie said, he might come by way of Chicago, to sell "juice"
    (said in English) there. Tawfiq replied that was a good idea.
    The cocaine connection is noted in Bodansky, p. 322, who quotes an ex-ANO offi-
    cer as saying, "In 1989 . . . Abu Nidal made more than $4 million in Peru. Cocaine
    money to be sure." Bodansky also says not only was ANO operative in Peru, its men
    trained Shining Path soldiers. He also notes, pp.322-323, that three additional ANO
    officers were arrested in Lima, summer of 1988, (when Darwish was also arrested)
    following an attempted attack on the U.S. Embassy there, and there was an assassi-
    nation attempt by ANO on a high-ranking Jewish leader in Lima in 1990.
96 "Blow up the Israeli Embassy . . . ," Luie promised.
    FBI Tapes, 1/11/88.
986 Luie was as vainglorious . . .
    FBI Tapes, 4/28/88, 5/1/88, 6/13/88.
96 "Let's teach them how we hit people and slaughter! . . . with machine guns."
    FBI Tapes, 1/16/88.
97 "We have our men here in America . . . kill 200 Jews here . . . another Palestinian."
    FBI Tapes, 5/12/89.
97 "The mosque will be ruined if no one cares about it . . . This man . . . I am ready to
    kneel until I'm bankrupt." And, "I am committed to the preacher's instructions
    until death."
    FBI Tapes, 2/20/88 and 6/16/88.

97 "There are many problems . . . abandoning Atta." And "There's a complacency I can't understand . . . nothing to do with him." Zein blamed Hussein Karriti . . .
   FBI Tapes, 6/16/88.
97 Hussein said Zein was . . . responsibility.
   FBI Tapes, 3/25/88.
97 How did Hussein know this? . . . set a trap for him.
   FBI Tapes, 8/16/88.
98 Zein lacked faith in another overboss, Samir Darwish.
   FBI Tapes, 1/27/88.
98 Problems with money cited.
   FBI Tapes, 4/22/88 and 4/25/88.
98 Samir wanted Zein to fly . . . but the girls refused, saying they were busy.
   FBI Tapes, 4/8/88.
98 Samir would await Zein . . .
   FBI Tapes, 4/8/88.
98 . . . he displayed no feeling
   FBI Tapes, 4/13/88.
98 Zein could not give Atta's wife . . . trailing him all the way to Athens . . .
   FBI Tapes, 5/15/88 and 5/17/88.
98 Damn you, Tawfiq rebuked Zein . . . to yourself.
   FBI Tapes, 5/8/88.
98 Zein confided details . . . money country," she said.
   FBI Tapes, 8/14/88.

CHAPTER ELEVEN

99 Zein fumbled . . . Samir tried again.
   FBI Tapes, 6/4/88.
991 Before Christmas . . . leg in a cast.
   FBI Tapes, 12/10/87.
99 "I may go" . . . in his mind.
   FBI Tapes, 6/16/88.
99 Samir was busy . . . phone number.
   FBI Tapes, 6/4/88.
99 The next day . . . Lima.
   FBI Tapes, 6/5/88.
99 Tawfiq warned Samir . . . Tawfiq warned.
   FBI Tapes, 6/16/88.
99 . . . Zein as describing . . . in Raleigh.
   FBI Tapes, 6/5/88, 6/17/88.
99 Four days later through Sinbad Travel . . . listening in.
   FBI Tapes, 6/17/88.
100 And just in case . . . none of them did.
   FBI Tapes, 7/8-17/88.
100 Two days later . . . food-stamp application.
   FBI Tapes, 7/17/88.
101 . . . "take the first plane . . ."
   FBI Tapes, 7/18/88.

101 "The business of ... "... be cursed."
     FBI Tapes, 7/21-22/88.
102 Again Hussein ... when he arrived.
     FBI Tapes, 8/5/88, 1/23/89.
102 Tawfiq was holding ... "for activities to exist."
     FBI Tapes, 1/14/89 and 1/23/89.
103 On his 1988 tax return ...
     Copy of Zein Isa's tax return, anonymous source.
104 Tawfiq lectured ... Tawfiq softened.
     FBI Tapes, 8/17, 8/19, 9/10, 9/12, 9/15, and 10/13/88.
104 A relative of Mona's ... probably tapped.
     FBI Tapes, 10/10/88.
104 Tawfiq seems ... other members.
     FBI Tapes, 2/8/89, 2/10/89.
104 Thari Bek ... with Zein.
     FBI Tapes, 10/11/89.
104 Osama ... stepped in ... Middle East.
     FBI Tapes, 12/12/88.
105 Tawfiq was reluctant ... "Contain your emotions."
     FBI Tapes, 7/13/89, 9/12/89.
105 ... Hussein was bragging how he had manipulated Tawfiq.
     FBI Tapes, 10/11/89.
105 A comrade told ..." ... Abu Nidal!"
     FBI Tapes, 11/16/88.
105 Atta had a great piece of luck ... Occupied Territories.
     Ramsey Clark and Jacques Semmelman.

CHAPTER TWELVE

The reader should investigate Ginat, especially Chapter 5: "Honor and Shame." He notes, "Accusation and murder cannot be explained as normative behavior alone. Usually there is personal motivation and often it is of a political character." P. 115.
109 Palestina won't go ... at home.
     FBI Tapes, 12/7/88, 12/12/88.
110 ... (Soraia) smooching with a Chinese whom she had told she was a terrorist ...
     FBI Tapes, 6/18/87, and anonymous sources.
110 ... Amjad Salem ... "tell me, honey."
     FBI Tapes, 6/6/89.
112 Romantic love ... in a collective society.
     This is not to say that there is no romance in Palestine, but that the individual is not as important in the village culture. As Mernissi points out in *The Veil*, p. 22, the individual is "abhorred as a disturber of collective harmony." The very idea of individualistic behavior is not well regarded for "Islam" means "submission," (*The Veil*, p. 55.) With more freedoms, there is more romantic love-based marriages, says Warnock, p. 56, but a girl in love might shame a family and become a risk. Many parents still claim the right to choose their sons-in-law. Ginat, p. 38, adds that free choice and illicit sex illustrate that the father has not only lost control

over his daughter but that he has lost the chance to make "a politically advanta-
geous match."

115 The next day " . . . dead meat."
   Police Report; Helena Mylanos and Cliff Walker.

118 "Nigger lover" . . . "black customers."
   Cliff Walker and Tina Woodall.

120 Customers at Alliance . . . stocked the shelves.
   Police Report and interviews by John McGuire.

120 Her mother was so distraught . . . tennis shoes.
   Police Report.

121 Two days later . . . "into the sea."
   Murder Tapes, 8/16/89.

121 Confiding in Amjad . . . she would be safe.
   FBI Tapes, 8/17/89, 8/18/89, 8/21/89.

122 Amjad Salem . . . "shoot her."

123 Footnote
   FBI Tapes, 8/18/89, 8/21/89.
   The study cited was conducted by Suha Arraf, an Arab feminist who researched
   it for B'Tselem. She wrote that 81 of 107 women and girls murdered as "suspected
   collaborators" by Palestinians from 1988 to 1993 in the Gaza Strip were actually
   victims of honor killings. B'Tselem is the Israeli human rights group. Olster,
   Reuter's, "Arab Women Killed for Sake of Family Honor," Feb. 1, 1994.

123 What Amjad didn't know . . . around St. Louis.
   FBI Tapes, 11/21/87, 2/9/89.

123 Zein . . . envision . . . "sick of this life."
   FBI Tapes, 8/20/89.

124 Zein tried to console . . . " . . . about him?"
   FBI Tapes, 8/22/89.

125 . . . Hispanic female doctor . . . note of verification.
   Xeroxed copy of physician's letter.

125 Tina told . . . "chase another one?"
   FBI Tapes, 10/21/89.

125 Zein and Maria . . . knife to her throat.
   Police Report and Cliff Walker and Helena Mylanos.

CHAPTER THIRTEEN

128 Her father warned her . . . " . . . you get buried?"
   Murder Tapes, 7/27/89.

128 Her parents might . . . up in the morning.
   Anonymous sources.

128 Tina ran into Bruce . . . until afterward.
   Police report.

129 "Whore" was Soraia's pronouncement . . . " . . . because I had to!"
   Murder Tapes, 10/14/89.

129 Honor killings are against the law in . . . the Occupied Territories.
   Ginat reports that often those convicted of crimes of honor serve short sen-

tences, p. 23. They are respected by other inmates, p. 23, and society as a whole considers murdering a woman who shames her family as an established norm, p. 38. The concept of crimes of honor are rooted in Bedouin tradition which is strongest in the rural West Bank and the Gaza Strip, especially the latter where Islamic fundamentalism is predominant.

130 "Man, I got to . . . can't do nothing."
      FBI Tapes, 10/14/89.
131 Sausan told Luie . . . killing Tina.
      FBI Tapes, 10/15/89.
131 "I plead to God, . . . the guerillas?"
      FBI Tapes, 10/15/89.
131 An hour later . . . " . . . we will bear responsibility."
      FBI Tapes, 10/16/89.
132 Mona grumbled . . . "to her protection."
      Murder Tapes, 10/16/89.
133 Tina called Missouri's Child Abuse Hotline . . . "I do not think it would be abuse now."
      FBI Tapes, 10/16/89. Begin Time: 18:09:54 End: 18:21:12. This conversation was entirely in English. Dickens told police one of his visits lasted two hours. If Dickens did so, there is no FBI transcript for this other conversation. It is believed the FBI also called the Abuse Hotline.
135 Zein called Tawfiq . . . Zein said.
      FBI Tapes, 10/16/89.
135 Soraia phoned her father . . . criminals wear.
      FBI Tapes, 10/18/89.
136 To a cousin in Raleigh . . . any day now.
      FBI Tapes, 10/19/89.
136 Meanwhile, Tawfiq was so alarmed . . . " . . . he can do it."
      FBI Tapes, 10/20/89.
137 Mona and Zein were convinced . . . " . . . for two years."
      FBI Tapes, 10/20/89.
138 Zein had yelled . . . long warned.
      FBI Tapes, 4/20/87. The information about his relative is from an anonymous source.
138 Fayrouz called . . . with a knife.
      FBI Tapes, 10/21/89.
138 But Tina refused . . . " . . . cannot be repaired."
      FBI Tapes, 10/23/89.
138 Tina tapped a girl . . . consoled Tina.
      Police Report.
139 . . . Zein suggested . . . " . . . go there again!"
      Faisal Isa and Helena Mylanos.
140 Fayrouz saw . . . jail her.
      FBI Tapes, 11/2/89.
140 . . . Fayrouz reported in . . . until she was eighteen.
      FBI Tapes, 11/3/89.

CHAPTER FOURTEEN

143 Tina walked through the front door . . ."you're going to die!"
   FBI Tapes, 11/6/89. According to several Palestinian sources—Hanan Rayan as
   well as Mohammed Musad—and Prof. Ginat, women who shame their families
   are not necessarily killed, Ginat, p. 151; and as Ginat and Musad point out, mediation is the rule not murder.

CHAPTER FIFTEEN

150 At two-thirty A.M . . . Tawfiq said.
   FBI Tapes, 11/6/89.
150 Tawfiq called Rabih . . . " . . . hell was waiting."
   FBI Tapes, 11/6/89.
150 Nai'el told Jamal . . . he said.
   FBI Tapes, 11/6/89.
150 Before she left . . . she added.
   FBI Tapes, 11/6/89.
150 At four-thirty . . . was dead.
   FBI Tapes, 11/6/89.
150 At ten A.M . . . he added.
   FBI Tapes, 11/6/89.

CHAPTER SIXTEEN

158 Meanwhile, at nine forty-four, Farid Badran . . . able to later.
   FBI Tapes, 11/7/89 (The tapes are time coded.)
158 Ah, said Saif . . . nine forty-nine.
   FBI Tapes, 11/7/89.
160 Tawfiq took charge . . . no criticism.
   FBI Tapes, 11/7/89.
162 That Tina's boyfriend . . . FBI . . . Abu Nidal Organization.
   Says a well regarded Palestinian journalist (who wished to remain anonymous), "Hell, there was no way to save Zein, so his daughters in the village cry
   and make it political. Abu Nidal. Abu Nidal. Everytime there's a car accident in
   the West Bank, some Palestinian lunatic claims responsibility for ANO."
167 He called Luie . . . talk now.
   FBI Tapes, 12/5/89.
167 Saif called . . . Police Station.
   FBI Tapes, 12/14/89.
167 The members of the Beitin Association . . . the man snapped.
   FBI Tapes, 11/17/89.
168 A few minutes later, Saif's . . . Luie said.
   FBI Tapes, 11/17/89.
168 The feds gotta be tapping . . . they all trusted.
   FBI Tapes, 11/18/90.

CHAPTER SEVENTEEN

170 . . . her cousins Saif and Tawfiq . . . "Each sings his own song."
 FBI Tapes, 12/3/89.
173 The extended family . . . " . . . charging him with murder."
 FBI Tapes, 12/16/89.
174 Saif and a friend discussed . . . Saif laughed.
 FBI Tapes, 12/14/89, 1/13/90.
174 But Saif was worried . . . "There's nothing against us."
 FBI Tapes, 12/16/89.
176 Just after this, Saif . . . listening in.
 FBI Tapes, 1/16/90.
176 By Valentine's Day, Luie . . . his grocery store.
 FBI Tapes, 11/21/89.
176 "All our work . . ." . . . "phony leadership."
 FBI Tapes, 2/14/90.

CHAPTER EIGHTEEN

Information taken from police reports from various jurisdictions, as well as anonymous official sources.

CHAPTER NINETEEN

Information from Det. Sam Jackson, Sgt. Steve Sorocko, and Lt. James Scego, St. Louis Police, and Det. Gary Berra of St. Louis County Police Crimes Against Persons.

CHAPTER TWENTY

199 There was a possible scenario . . . Maria could avoid the death penalty.
 Under Missouri law, Maria met almost all the criteria for mitigating circumstances *not* to be sentenced to death:
 1. Defendant has no prior criminal record.
 2. Defendant was under mental stress at the time.
 3. Defendant played a minor role in the murder.
 4. Defendant was under the duress of another person (her husband.)
 5. Defendant lacked the capacity to understand (did she know Zein intended to kill Tina? Or, did she think this was a showdown that rapidly fell out of control?)

CHAPTER TWENTY-ONE

204 Yet, when Tawfiq Musa . . . Luie surmised.
 FBI Tapes, 11/18/89.

208 For all their work . . . " . . . stiff the lawyers."
   FBI Tapes, classified information reported by an anonymous source. (Defense attorneys usually ask for the bulk of their fee up front, before the trial. "If you acquit them," Reardon and Shaw said, "they think they don't owe you anything, that they always were innocent; and if they go to jail, why should they pay anything?")

CHAPTER TWENTY-TWO

210 Maria . . . afraid of him.
   Barbara Horlick.

CHAPTER TWENTY-THREE

While Americans demand that something be done about crime, apparently somebody else is suppposed to do it. "We can't get juries for murder cases," St. Louis Circuit Judge Charles Shaw said in his chambers. "The excuses people come up with during jury selection," he shook his head. "Watch, why, we'll have a volume of transcript on this [jury selection] before we even open the trial." It took one week, a long time by St. Louis standards.
   Number 133, for example, did not think it fair to leave her husband to do housework for a week. "That's a real woman," lawyer Shaw joked in an aside. "No point in having male harrassment, is there?" Judge Shaw quipped. Dee Joyce-Hayes tried to point out that a man doing housework for a week was not an unsurmountable problem.
   "Well, I'll have to ask my husband," said the juror.

CHAPTER TWENTY-FOUR

Exhibit 1-A has been edited and written in narrative form.
229 Were those notes . . . what Maria was looking for?
   Suggested by Bob Craddick.

CHAPTER TWENTY-FIVE

235 . . . Soraia fell in love . . . once removed.
   Anonymous interviews in Beitin.

CHAPTER TWENTY-EIGHT

261 "Call me Frank . . . didn't buy anything."
   Anonymous real estate agent.

CHAPTER TWENTY-NINE

Much of the background on the FBI information from James Nelson, Special Agent in Charge, St. Louis FBI office, and Counter-Terrorism Supervisor Tom Newman, Louis Stephens and Robert Kupperman.

263 Zein . . . was moved . . . when the news broke.
    Paul Delo, Director, Potosi Correctional Center.

265 All travel documents . . . by forgery, theft, or bribery.
    Seale, pp. 206–7.

269 "People theorize but in an actual situation where someone could get killed, national security comes second," said a man who had been there, as bureau chief for the CIA in Beirut.
    Charles Waterman.

269 And another former CIA specialist pointed to a parallel failure, "The tapes plotting the World Trade Center . . . as a killer."
    Vincent Cannistraro.

269 A former FBI . . . react against regular criminals."
    Stephens.

271 One regulatory agency . . . safe houses.
    Det. Sam Jackson

272 . . . ANO cells in Brooklyn . . . insurance fraud scam.
    Anonymous. FBI sources.

272 FBI agents had to interview sources worldwide.
    Anonymous.

272 They had been predicted . . . sat and sat.
    Five anonymous sources.

272 At least three . . . experts . . . connected to the World Trade Center bombing . . . Justice . . . wanted to "send a message" . . .
    Anonymous.

273 Experts agreed . . .
    Waterman, Kupperman, and anonymous sources.

273 "The only people who really know . . ."
    Stephens.

273 "There've been operatives in L.A. and Washington . . . on them."
    Kupperman. In addition, Grosscup p. 310, quotes a security consultant who says during the Gulf war, experts warned of a possible ANO attack in Washington, Chicago, New York, Detroit, or Southern California. Considering Abu Nidal was a thug of Saddam Hussein, there was reason for concern. On p. 313, he cites an FBI official as saying 50 Abu Nidal supporters were under surveillance in the U.S. Various intelligence officers say they knew in 1988 that ANO had a base in Caracas, that Samir Darwish was its leader and held a big ANO reunion there, during which time he was picked up by the authorities along with his membership list. And they confirmed that Atta was a mid-level ANO official as well as a possible CIA informant.

274 "It's like being a little bit pregnant . . . "
    Stephens.

274 One would need . . . prosecutor said.
    David Capes.

274 "Any indication that ANO is totally disbanded . . .
   Stephens and Ravell. Kupperman says ANO could attack American businesses abroad as well as general targets in the Far East and Australia, p. 192.

CHAPTER THIRTY

Material from three long interviews with Maria Isa.
279 But highly placed sources . . . soft on the death penalty.
   Three anonymous sources.
280 The day the Abu Nidal . . . "calls her daughters and nieces a lot."
   Bryan Golke, Supt., Renz Farm.

CHAPTER THIRTY-ONE

281 . . . in a Dayton jail cell . . . Luie was . . . alarming the U.S. Marshal . . .
   U.S. Marshal's office, St. Louis, April, 1993.
287 Saif's conversation with Luie . . . the informant was an FBI one . . .
   FBI Affadavit.
288 An FBI agent . . . after his arrest.
   FBI Affadavit.
288 People back in Beitin . . . so inhibited.
   Several anonymous sources.
290 . . . Murphy spoke . . . "Irish pubs?"
   Her point is valid, but there are no known IRA cases of Irish-Americans in St. Louis threatening to "kill all the English Protestants," which would be analogous to this Abu Nidal case.

CHAPTER THIRTY-TWO

295 FISA cases are heard . . . "take a look at."
   Stephens.
295 "David Binney . . . release the tapes."
   Ravell.
295 FISA is vital . . . expert.
   Stephens.
297 . . . the FBI was desperate . . . to them.
   Cannistraro.
297 . . . considering that Luie . . . in Beitin.
   Source in Beitin.
298 . . . in late fall, 1993, Tawfiq, Luie, and Saif reported . . .
   The three men may have believed this but it was unlikely that Zein would plea guilty. What would a dying man on death row have to lose in a trial? Day did not return phone calls about this.
299 Steitz turned over . . . the betrayer . . . Musa.
   Anonymous sources.

CHAPTER THIRTY-THREE

301 "The purpose of this conspiracy . . ."
   Taken from the Information filed by the U.S. Attorney.
   All other information not cited in this chapter is from sources who asked to remain anonymous.
305 Indeed, the national ADL . . . "terrorism."
   St. Louis Jewish Light, Nov. 2, 1994, p. 11.

EPILOGUE

309 It began with a group . . . "is a collaborator."
   Joel Greenberg, *The Jerusalem Post Magazine,* "Honor Thy Sister," Jan. 3, 1991, pp. 12–13. Article courtesy of Marjorie Olster of Reuter's, who in preparing her own material, allowed me to copy this piece. Rula Halawani and I tried to reach Tamam Fahiliya, in October, 1992, but her phone numbers had been changed and no one would release the new one.
310 A Palestinian man . . . "veil again."
   Sami Mishasha.
   Mernissi amplifies this issue in *The Veil,* p. 23. and in *Islam and Democracy,* pp. 149–71, among others. She warns that Islamic fundamentalism has never ceased to exist parallel to feminism, p.160. And in poor areas with high unemployment, the easiest thing for politicians to do is to reduce unemployment by sending women back home and in a veil, pp. 164–65.

Bibliography

(Books starred are especially relevant to the Isa and Abu Nidal cases.)

Abdul-Rauf, Muhammad, *The Islamic View of Women and the Family*, Robert Speller & Sons, New York, 1977. The then director of the Islamic Center of Washington, D.C., cites Qu'ranic references *against* forced marriages.

*Abu-Lughod, Lila, *Writing Women's Worlds: Bedouin Stories*, University of California Press, Berkeley, 1993. An Arab anthropologist quotes tales with universal themes.

Abu Omar, Abed al-Samih, *Traditional Palestinian Embroidery and Jewelry*, al-Shark Arab Press, Jerusalem, 1987. Extensive color plates.

Ahmed, Leila, *Women and Gender in Islam*, Yale University Press, New Haven, 1992. Prof. Ahmed traces the historical roots of misogyny and feminism from before Mohammed—who advanced the rights of women—until today with anti-Western sentiments rooted in colonialism and Zionism. (Some scholars say anti-Westernism goes back to the Crusaders, then onward to Napoleon's conquests and the fall of the Ottoman Empire.) Ahmed debates whether veiling is regressive.

*Amiry, Suad, and Vera Tamari, *The Palestinian Village Home*, The British Museum, London, 1989. Illustrations and text of how villages near Beitin looked and functioned.

Ajami, Fouad, *The Arab Predicament: Arab Political Thought and Practice Since 1967*, Cambridge University Press, New York, 1992. A pivotal work by the famous Johns Hopkins University scholar .

Arberry, A. J., *The Koran Interpreted*, Collier Books, New York, 1955.

Badran, Margot and Miriam Cooke, editors, *Opening the Gates: A Century of Arab Feminist Writing*, Virago Press, London, 1990.

Bodansky, Yossef, *Target America: Terrorism in the U.S. Today*, S.P.I. Books, New York, 1993.

*Bushman, Inea, trans. and editor, *Arab Folktales*, Pantheon Books, New York, 1986. Wonderful stories that provide cultural insights. I.e.: "The dictates of custom rather than religion . . . the honor of the family rests on the moral conduct of its women . . ." (p. 312); "Where so little is certain, the personal virtues of a man and his name, not his possessions, give him fame" (p. 5); and "Yet the rules are clear if [she] should bring dishonor on her tribe. There is no mercy. If she does not kill herself, her kin will do so, and kill her seducer as well. . . . The code: only blood will wash away the stain . . ."

Carta's Historical Atlas of Israel, Jerusalem, 1983.

Devine, Elizabeth, and Nancy L. Braganti, *The Traveler's Guide to Middle Eastern and North African Customs and Manners*, St. Martin's Press, New York, 1991.

Friedman, Thomas, *From Beirut to Jerusalem*, Anchor Books, New York, 1990. A work that for many Americans is their Bible to understanding the Middle East. To

335

understand the tribal nature of politics and culture, read "Hama Rules." Friedman notes some Arabs play the victim because the victim never needs to take the hard look at himself.

**Ginat, Joseph, *Blood Disputes among Bedouin and Rural Arabs in Israel: Revenge, Mediation, Outcasting and Family Honor*, University of Pittsburgh Press, Pittsburgh, 1987. *The* major work on honor and shame. An internationally respected Israeli anthropologist, Prof. Ginat delineates honor related customs as well as providing detailed case histories, including that of a Yemenite rabbi with two wives who slew his daughter in an honor killing.

Goodwin, Jan, *The Price of Honor: Muslim Women Lift the Veil of Silence on the Islamic World*, Little, Brown, Boston, 1994.

Grosscup, Beau, *The New Explosion of Terrorism*, Far Horizon Press, Far Hills, 1991.

*Grossman, David, translated by Haim Watzman, *The Yellow Wind*, Farrar, Straus, and Giroux, New York, 1988. A critically acclaimed Israeli novelist and journalist's exposé of the horrors of occupation for Palestinians in the West Bank. Written in 1987, Grossman predicted how the suffering would erupt in rage, which it did with the Intifada.

Hijab, Nadia, *Womanpower: The Arab Debate on Women at Work*, Cambridge University Press, Cambridge, 1989. This Palestinian scholar/writer/journalist explains why some Muslims fear feminism will undermine all of Islamic society and why Westerners and Zionists are abhorred. She notes that Arabs resent other Arabs "who wash their dirty linen in public."

The Intifada: A Message from Three Generations of Palestinians, Knight Financial Services Corp., UK, 1988. Color photographs shot in the West Bank and Gaza Strip by Agence France Presse, Sipa-Press, and Gamma.

Khaliefh, Sahar, *Wild Thorns*, trans. by Trevor LeGassick and Elizabeth Fernea, Olive Branch Press, New York, 1991. A popular Palestinian novel about West Bank life.

King James version, *The Holy Bible*, Gordonsville, TN, 1985.

Khalidi, Walid, *Before Their Diaspora: A Photographic History of the Palestinians, 1876–1948*, Institute for Palestinian Studies, Washington, D.C., 1984.

**Kupperman, Robert and Jeff Kamen, *Final Warning: Averting Disaster in the New Age of Terrorism*, Doubleday, New York, 1989. Kupperman predicted four years before the World Trade Center bombing that there would soon be a major terrorist attack on American soil. He also noted, on page 45, that the FBI had discovered an ANO infrastructure capable of attacks within the continental United States. Kupperman argues also that poor antiterrorism programs in the United States and Western Europe—especially their airports—have made an enticing enviroment for terrorists.

Lawrence, T. E., *Seven Pillars of Wisdom*, Doubleday, Doran & Co., New York, 1935.

Livingstone, Neil C. and David Halevy, *Inside the PLO*, Quill, William Morrow, New York, 1990.

MacDonald, Eileen, *Shoot the Women First*, Random House, New York, 1991. Includes interviews with women fighters in the Intifada and an acknowledged woman terrorist.

*Mansfield, Peter, *A History of the Middle East*, Viking, 1991. Good for general background, especially when Mansfield explains the lack of secular states in Muslim countries—because the Qur'an is the literal word of God and the Hadith, those traditions of Mohammed, govern every facet of daily behavior, are the foundation of the Shar'ia. Shar'ia law is translated as Islamic law "but it is much more than this. It is neither canonical law (Islam has no priesthood) nor secular law, because no such concept exists in Islam; it is rather a whole system of social morality, prescribing [how] man should live . . . according to God's will. If he contravenes the shar'ia, his offense is against God and not the state" (p. 13).

Mattar, Philip, *The Mufti of Jerusalem: Al-Hajj Amin Al-Husayni and the Palestinian National Movement*, Columbia University Press, New York, 1988.

*Mernissi, Fatima, *Islam and Democracy: Fear of the Modern World*, trans. by Mary Jo Lakeland, Addison-Wesley Publishing Company, Reading, Massachusetts, 1992. This renowned Moroccan sociologist and author delineates the sacred text ordering women to obey the patriarchy—it means obeying God. "The modesty of the Arab woman is the linchpin of the whole political system" (p. 153).

**Mernissi, Fatima, *The Veil and The Male Elite: A Feminist Interpretation of Women's Rights in Islam*, trans. by Mary Jo Lakeland. Addison-Wesley Publishing Company, Reading, Massachusetts, 1991. Mernissi shows that misogyny in the West is based on alleged biological inferiority, while in the Middle East it is founded on fear of women's sexual power, hence the veil and the crimes of honor. She is a wonderfully fluid writer, and fun to read.

Morgan, Robin, *The Demon Lover: On the Sexuality of Terrorism*, W. W. Norton & Co., New York, 1989. When men are powerless, they must keep "women in their place." Morgan labels this "patriarchal terrorism."

*Moyers, Bill, moderator, "The Arab World: Conversations on Arab History, Religion and Culture," Mystic Fire Video Inc., 1991. Arab-American academics, including Edward Said, in group interviews. A few are quite defensive, i.e., if Saudi women really wanted to drive cars, they would. This series should be mandatory in American schools to eradicate stereotyping.

*Muhawi, Ibrahim and Sharif Kanaana, *Speak, Bird, Speak Again: Palestinian Arab Folktales*, University of California Press, Berkeley, 1989. A collection with tales of cousin marriages, a girl put to death for pregnancy out of wedlock, co-wives, courtship and weddings, along with other stories, all cross-indexed by topic.

**Najjar, Orayb Aref, *Portraits of Palestinian Women*, with Kitty Warnock, University of Utah Press, Salt Lake City, 1992. A series of good interviews with a cross-section of women, along with studies and research citations.

Ostrovsky, Victor and Claire Hoy, *By Way of Deception*, St. Martin's Paperbacks, New York, 1991. A former Mossad agent's exposé of that organization.

*Patai, Raphael, *The Arab Mind*, Charles Scribner's Sons, New York, 1983. A general overview explaining such cultural basics as shame, honor, saving face, sexuality, and the obsession with female chastity. He wrote a companion work entitled *The Jewish Mind*.

*Perry, Mark, *Eclipse: The Last Days of the CIA*, William Morrow & Company, New York, 1992. Perry tells a compelling tale, on pages 190–94, of how ANO in the Middle East and North Africa was weakened by a joint CIA-PLO operation.

Radford, Jill and Diane E. Russell, ed., *Femicide: The Politics of Woman Killing*, Twayne, New York, 1992.

*Rapoport, David C., ed., *Inside Terrorist Organizations*, Columbia University Press, New York, 1988. David Schiller's essay on the Palestinian Fedayeen describes rise of the paramilitary groups willing to martyr themselves within the context of Arab patrons who use them to avoid unrest in their own lands. ANO is a symptom of

Palestinian failure and dissension within the PLO. Palestinians lack cohesion because of a history of tribal feuds; their nationalism is a reaction to Zionism. Lacking a democratic process, they rule by consensus.

*Rubenstein, Danny, trans. by Ina Friedman, *The People of Nowhere: The Palestinian Vision of Home*, Times Books, New York, 1991. An interpretation of what is home. To the Arab, it is tribal and site-specific. One of the worst curses is "may your house be destroyed." This is why refugees refuse to settle elsewhere. Rubenstein, an Israeli journalist, also notes that "the overwhelming majority of Arabs living in Palestine in 1948 remained in their homeland."

Said, Edward W., *The Question of Palestine*, Vintage Books, New York, 1992. One of the most distinguished cultural critics, Prof. Said of Columbia University serves on the Palestinian National Council, discusses Zionism and Palestinian self-determination.

**Seale, Patrick, *Abu Nidal: A Gun for Hire*, Random House, New York, 1992. The standard text—most current, most detailed, most regarded—about ANO and Sabri al-Banna, although some would refute Seale's thesis that the Israelis have penetrated ANO and are running it.

Shaaban, Bouthaina, *Both Right and Left Handed: Arab Women Talk About Their Lives*, Indiana University Press, Bloomington, 1991.

Al-Shaykh, Hanan, *Women of Sand and Myrrh*, trans. by Catherine Cobham, Anchor Books, New York, 1989. A novel of four wealthy women in a desert kingdom who have lovers and luxury, everything but freedom.

Tuchman, Barbara, *Bible and Sword: England and Palestine from the Bronze Age to Balfour*, Ballatine Books, New York, 1984.

Wallach, John and Janet, *The New Palestinians: The Emerging Generation of Leaders*, Prima Publishing, Rocklin, California, 1992. A series of profiles, from Hanan Ashrawi to Faisal al-Husseini as well as those less known to the general American public such as Radwan Abu Ayyash and Zahira Kamal.

**Warnock, Kitty, *Land Before Honour: Palestinian Women in the Occupied Territories*, Monthly Review Press, New York, 1990. Warnock shows how Palestinian women have worked in the nationalistic movement and this has fueled social changes. Women reveal how they feel on marriage, the mahr, and second wives.

ARTICLES:

Carley, William M., "Lifting the Lid: Their Secrets Revealed, Abu Nidal Terrorists Are Becoming Targets," *The Wall Street Journal*, Oct. 15, 1987, 1A.

Carley, William M., "A Trail of Terror: Teen's Murder Reveals U.S. Group Suspected of Ties to Abu Nidal," *The Wall Street Journal*, June 16, 1993, 1A.

Crime Control Digest, Vol. 25, No. 5, Feb. 4, 1991, pp. 1–2.

Edington, Mark D. W., "Terror Made Easy," *The New York Times*, Op-Ed, Mar. 4, 1994.

Emerson, Steven, "A Terrorist Network in America?" *The New York Times*, Op-Ed, Apr. 7, 1993.

Friends Schools Newsletter, Ramallah, West Bank, Feb. 1992, vol. 5, no. 2.

Gordon, Evelyn, "Supreme Court frees Man falsely Accused of Murder," *The Jerusalem Post*, Sept. 30, 1994, 2A.

Joel Greenberg, "Honor Thy Sister," *The Jerusalem Post Magazine*, Jan. 3, 1991, pp. 12–13.

Grossman, David, "Guests Can Be Shown the Door," *The New York Times Magazine*, Dec. 13, 1992.

Hedges, Chris, "Arab vs. Arab," *The New York Times*, Mar. 8, 1994.

The Jerusalem Post: "Honor behind year-old murder of Taibe mother," Aug. 28. 1991; "Brother admits to 'honor' killing," Oct. 25, 1991; "Family honor killing," Dec. 22, 1991; "Two sentenced for murdering their sister," Sept. 10, 1992.

Kaplan, Robert D., "Tales from the Bazaar," *The Atlantic*, Aug., 1992.

Kupperman, Robert H. and David A. Andelman, "TerrorDollars," *The Washington Post*, Mar, 6, 1994.

Lambrecht, Bill, "Officials Link Drug Trade, Terrorism," *St Louis Post-Dispatch*, Apr. 8, 1993.

Miller, Judith, "The Islamic Wave," *The New York Times Magazine*, May 31, 1992.

Marjorie Olster, "Arab Women Killed for Sake of Family Honor," Reuter's Wire Service, Jerusalem, Feb. 1, 1994.

McGuire, John, "Masters of the Courtroom," *St. Louis Post-Dispatch Magazine*, Mar. 30, 1980.

Ozick, Cynthia, "Mutual Sorrow, Mutual Gain," *The New York Times*, Op-Ed, Mar. 2, 1994.

St. Louis Jewish Light, "ADL Decries Abu Nidal Sentences," Nov. 2, 1994, p.11.

Said, Edward W., "The Phony Islamic Threat," *The New York Times Magazine*, Nov. 21, 1993.

Shammas, Anton, "The Art of Forgetting," *The New York Times Magazine*, Dec. 26, 1993.

Schleicher, Lisa M., and Derek M. Stoldt, "Eighth Survey of White Collar Crime," *American Criminal Law Review*, vol. 30, no. 3, Spring, 1993.

Wood, Michael, "Lost Paradise," review of Edward W. Said's *Culture and Imperialism*, *The New York Review of Books*, vol. XLI, no. 5, Mar. 3, 1994.

DOCUMENTS:

Federal Bureau of Investigation, transcripts, *Missouri v. Zein Hasan Isa*, Case No. 891-03465, and *Missouri v. Maria Isa*, Case No. 891-03724.

Trial transcript, Vol. I–VI, 2,005 pages, *Missouri v. Zein Hasan Isa*, Case No. 891-03465, and *Missouri v. Maria Isa*, Case No. 891-03724.

Federal Bureau of Investigation, transcribed interrogation of Luie Hasan Nijmeh, Apr. 1, 1993, 102 pages, FD-302a, 265B-SL-175746.

Federal Bureau of Investigation, transcripts, Vol. I–IX, 1,738 pages. *U.S. v. Zein Isa, Tawfiq Musa, Saif Nijmeh, Luie Nijmeh*. Case No. SI-930089 DJS.

Indictment, Affidavit, and Waiver of Indictment, *U.S. v. Zein Isa, Tawfiq Musa, Saif Nijmeh, Luie Nijmeh*. Case No. SI-930089 DJS.

U.S. Department of State, *Patterns of Global Terrorism 1988*, March, 1989.

GLOSSARY

ARABIC:

abu (ah'boo)   Father, literally and as an honorific. An Arab man is so named after the birth of his eldest son, e.g., Abu plus the name of his son. Similarly, a woman is renamed Umm, mother, plus her son's name. Should the couple have daughters only, then they become Abu and Umm plus the name of their eldest daughter. In parts of the Arab world, a man is not deemed "whole" until he has sired a male heir. Palestinian political leaders often adapt the allegorical honorific, such as Abu Nidal.

Abu Nidal (ah'boo knee-dahl)   Literally, the Father of Struggle, the *nom de guerre* of Sabri al-Banna, who founded Abu Nidal Organization when Yasir Arafat proposed seeking a peace settlement. Abu Nidal has been called a thug for hire, an extortionist of patron states, and the most vicious and violent terrorist group.

al- and *el-*   Those articles meaning "the," *al* is formal and used in writing classical Arabic, and *el* is conversational.

fedayeen (fed-ah-yeen)   Freedom fighters, guerillas, paramilitary groups. Singular is fedai.

fellahin (fell-ah-heen)   Peasants. Singular is fellah.

Hadith (hah-deeth)   The teachings of Mohammed as recorded by his faithful. The Hadith collectively are the Sunna. (Hence the name Sunni Muslims, as compared to Shi'ite Muslims.) The Hadith regulate literally every facet of daily life, including cleansing with water, or if none is available, sand; why one must change clothes if a dog touches them while one is praying.

haram (hah-rahm)   Forbidden or improper. Harem—women's quarters—is derivative of this.

hijab   Literally, the "curtain." It is the veil, be it a black swath across the face and over the head or the white headscarf covering the hair and neck like a nun's wimple. For the philosophical connotations, read Fatima Mernissi, *The Veil and the Male Elite*, in which she points out that the veil demarks the public life from the private life. She points out the hijab is the key concept in Islam as sin is in Christianity. The veil not only protects women from men but from the West.

341

imam (ee-mahm)   He who stands before. The imam leads the faithful in prayer in a mosque. There is only one per mosque. Usually, he is theologically trained and holds a diploma from a Middle Eastern university. He is appointed by the ministry, not chosen by the worshippers.

Intifada (in-tee-fah-dah)   Literally, shaking off or rising up. The name of the revolution for independence in the occupied territories which began in December 1987.

Islam (iz-lahm)   Literally, to submit to the will of Allah. From the verb aslama, which means to surrender with total commitment. A person who surrenders or submits to the will of Allah is a Muslimum or Muslim. (Patai, *The Arab Mind*, p. 147.)

kaffiyeh (caf-ee-yeah)   The checkered headscarf worn by men and held in place by a coil. Yasir Arafat has made it a symbol of Palestinian nationalism, although Arabs in other countries wear the kaffiyeh as well.

mahr (mar)   The dowry or bride-price paid by the bridegroom and his family to the bride's family. In cousin marriages, the mahr is often half of what it would be if the woman married outside the clan. Another incentive for endogamy, marrying within the tribe.

mukhtar (moohk-tar)   The administrator in a village who represents the village families and their interests to the government. An appointee, he registers all births, deaths, and land deeds and can collect taxes and act as a police power. With only one mukhtar per village, this is a prestigious position, and one of wealth.

Qur'an (quo-ran)   The Word of God as given to His Prophet Mohammed. Sometimes still spelled Koran, although Qur'an is what many Muslims now prefer.

Shari'a (shah-re-ah)   Social law of divine origin (Mernissi). Shari'a courts hear cases of marriage, inheritance, divorce, and custody. This law is theological, not civil, and more extensive than Catholic canon law. There is no alternative. Yet, marriage is a civil contract, not sacramental, and divorce is easy. The nuptial ceremony is performed by the ma'zun (mah-zoon) from shari'a court. Women who wear the hijab and long, dark overdress are said to be in shari'a dress.

sharaf (shah-rahf)   Honor. The root of a man's honor is his ability to protect his female relatives from sexual indiscretions or the appearance of impropriety. A woman's transgression may be punishable by death, a crime of honor, as Arabs call it, and honor killing, as we call it. This ritual murder is to repair the woman's damage to her clan's honor. Her male relatives must kill her to show their reestablishment of control. 'ird is the woman's chastity, not literally, but ethically speaking. Once lost, it cannot be resurrected.

sheikh (shake)   A political figure of which there can be many in a Palestinian village or city. Often, it denotes a wise old man of moral and religious stature and high character and learning. Some are wealthy.

U.S. FEDERAL COURT TERMINOLOGY:

Brady v. Maryland   The landmark U.S. Supreme Court case ruling that in electronic surveillance cases under Title 3, a defendant is entitled to all of the government's tapes to check for exculpatory information. In FISA cases, under Title 50, Justice Department attorneys make what they call a Brady sweep of the tapes for exculpatory conversations.

CIPA (The Classified Information Protection Act)   CIPA put FISA matters under protective order, which in everyday terms meant that if a lawyer leaks the information, he or she can be prosecuted for espionage. Think of FISA as the information, SCIF where one reads the information, and CIPA as the special clearance one needs to obtain the information.

counterterrorism   Counteracting groups making political statements through violent crimes designed to terrify the general civilian population. (The Mafia makes a statement sticking a horse's head in the bed of a capo but this doesn't scare the average person the way the World Trade Center bombing did.) The various agencies involved in counterterrorism are the Federal Bureau of Investigation, the Central Intelligence Agency, the National Security Agency, the Secret Service, the Justice Department, the State Department, military intelligence, and the intelligence divisions of big-city police deparments. The FBI is the lead agency in counter-terrorism. This term is not interchangeable with counterintelligence—counteracting foreign governments trying to acquire sophisticated techology from the United States, as in the Walker and Pollard spy cases.

FISA (Foreign Intelligence Surveillance Act of 1978)   A secret court held inside a vault must authorize FISA cases. FISA permits electronic surveillance of people loosely suspected of terrorism and espionage. FISA is limited solely to matters of national security.

RICO (Racketeer Influenced and Corrupt Organizations)   RICO was designed by Congress to thwart the Mafia and other organized crime syndicates. RICO convictions carry very harsh sentences.

SCIF (Secured Classified Information Facility)   The room where defense attorneys and their clients charged under FISA can read the logs and listen to the government's tapes.

INDEX